The Battle of Jutland:
The Sowing & the Reaping

The Battle of Jutland:
The Sowing & the Reaping

The Great Naval Engagement of the
First World War, 1916

ILLUSTRATED

Carlyon Wilfroy Bellairs

LEONAUR

The Battle of Jutland: The Sowing & the Reaping
The Great Naval Engagement of the First World War, 1916
by Carlyon Wilfroy Bellairs

ILLUSTRATED

First published under the title
The Battle of Jutland: The Sowing & the Reaping

Leonaur is an imprint of Oakpast Ltd

Copyright in this form © 2021 Oakpast Ltd

ISBN: 978-1-78282-918-8 (hardcover)
ISBN: 978-1-78282-919-5 (softcover)

http://www.leonaur.com

Publisher's Notes

The views expressed in this book are not necessarily
those of the publisher.

Contents

We made many mistakes, and it is our business today to see that the lessons have been taken to heart, and that we shall not again be found in such a state that we have to face the greatest crisis in history with improvised methods, working from hand to mouth. It may be said that the result was good enough with such methods; but was it? We have surely no right to continue to rely on improvisation. We in the navy know well our defects and it is our business to face them, to leave no stone unturned to avoid a repetition of the mistakes from which we have suffered in the past. The work of reconstruction has to be taken in hand with a full knowledge of our requirements, learnt by bitter experience in the past 4½ years. It must be our endeavour to profit by that experience.

The navy is today what it has been for the past 200 years, the same sure shield of Britain and the British Empire. The mere repetition of this very true and well-known phrase will not ensure that we remain so. The sure shield must be kept sure. Clear thinking and concentrated effort on scientific lines in the necessary struggle for retrenchment and such economies as certainly will be required must be applied with wisdom and a proper understanding of the problems before us in the light of the knowledge gained during the war. Only so shall we avoid impairing the essential efficiency of the navy.

Admiral Sir David Beatty
at Liverpool, March 29th, 1919.

DEDICATED WITHOUT PERMISSION
TO
THE MAN
WHO WILL GIVE THE ROYAL NAVY
A REAL WAR STAFF

Preface

Though there was much criticism of our War Staff organisation before and during the war, it may be asked why were not the direct criticisms of Lord Jellicoe's handling of the Grand Fleet at Jutland forthcoming at the time? The answer is that there is a real distinction between criticism of a system of administration, or even of the Board of Admiralty, and an admiral or general in charge of fighting forces.

There is nothing so detrimental as criticism of a command, if it does not achieve its object at once. It undermines the prestige and authority of the leader both with the country and his comrades, and it heartens the enemy. We had a bitter experience of this danger in the Crimean War when the commander-in-chief remained at his post. There can be only one method while that course is pursued, and that is, for the man who is convinced that a mistaken line of action is being pursued to remain silent or even to go so far as to strengthen the position of the war leader rather than to weaken it.

Mr. Balfour having decided to retain Lord Jellicoe in the command of the Grand Fleet, it was the duty of all patriotic writers to endeavour to strengthen Lord Jellicoe's authority with those serving under him and his prestige with the public. Nor was it wise to deal critically with the Battle of Jutland while he directed the navy as First Sea Lord. The war is over, and Lord Jellicoe has written a book dealing mainly with the Battle of Jutland. The views there put forward may influence naval thought in years to come, and establish good or bad traditions.

If vitally false principles of war are held by the navy, nothing can prevent its defeat by a materially inferior foe animated by a true doctrine of war. Our object now must be to place the traditions and methods of the navy on right lines. This course becomes the more necessary as we economise. It has been one of the chief sources of trouble in dealing with the Admiralty that they have been unable to indicate when their expenditure was vital and when it was merely useful. It is the doctrine of war which, when shaped on sound lines and put into practice by an efficient War Staff, enables us to bring about the only real combination of economy with efficiency.

The Jutland despatches withheld the truth about the battle; and Mr. Balfour, who is said to have set aside responsible advice from within the Admiralty itself, refused to assemble a court-martial to inquire into all the circumstances. Retaining Lord Jellicoe in command, he knew, and indeed asked the Press, that criticism should be silenced.

The ban on discussion, which was felt by many as applying right up to the time of the surrender of the German Fleet, no longer exists. Nothing that can be done now can remedy the past; but much that can be said may safeguard the future. Hence this book, which must stand or fall in proportion to its influence on future thought and action. It is not intended to be any more than a critical survey. It is not a full history of the Battle of Jutland, for the policy of secrecy pursued by the Admiralty, and the failure to hold an investigation, have made an accurate history impossible for the time being.

As Herodotus was born during the short period which saw Marathon, Salamis and Thermopylae fought, it may well be that the historian of Jutland has only been born during the war. The broad outlines of the battle and the events which led up to it are, however, well known, and the writer has had access to much new information which enables him with some confidence to believe that the main lines of his account and criticisms will not be upset. A navigating officer, Captain Harper, with assistants, is now working at the Admiralty, on a description of the battle.

It is necessary to remember that Captain Harper has never been a staff officer. He was navigating officer of the Royal Yacht from June 6, 1911, to Feb. 10, 1914, and then assistant Harbour Master at Portsmouth. The performance of these honourable services does not demand any knowledge of war. They are not a training for tactical investigation and give no criterion of ability such as the great war staffs of different armies bring to bear on the descriptions of battles.

Captain Harper and his assistants will present to the board a "narrative" and charts describing the Battle of Jutland which the board may or may not publish in whole, or in part, or in a revised form. These junior officers are examining all the data available such as reports, logs and signals, and wireless records. They will produce a narrative, but they will not give us either a critical survey or a considered judgment such as would have been achieved by the old procedure of court-martial. It is simply a method of persuading the public that something is being done in the way of inquiry.

Captain John E. T. Harper, M.V.O., has been attached to the War Staff for the purpose of collecting from official records the narrative of the Battle of Jutland. He has a number of officers under him rendering, assistance in the compilation. I am advised that no point has arisen yet on which oral evidence is required, and as stated by the First Lord last Wednesday the question of publication of the narrative will be considered when it is completed. If it is published, any extracts from logs and signal logs and diagrams forming a necessary part of the narrative will be published also. (Answer of the First Lord of the Admiralty, House of Commons, March 26, 1919.)

The Battle of Jutland has been one of the war's great mysteries. Mr. Balfour issued an explanation. We all issued explanations; but, as Mr. Balfour somewhere remarked in his "Foundations of Belief," it is not explanations which survive, but the thing itself. Certainly, the thing has outlived the explanations, and the consequences are with the world today. Since the British Government refused to adopt Chatham's policy in regard to the American Colonies there has been no lost opportunity to equal in its consequences our failure in leadership at the Battle of Jutland. We fought the War of American Independence and at least drew conclusions from it in regard to the government of colonies, so that we never again repeated our mistake. Though we cannot help the consequences of the Battle of Jutland, we can at least draw conclusions which may fructify in thought and action in future years.

Introduction

In his lectures to the Mediterranean Fleet in 1902, from which he subsequently printed extracts for private circulation, Lord Fisher prophesied that Armageddon would be fought in the Mediterranean and affirmed that he had high authorities on his side. It is worth mention as showing the persistence of ideas in regarding France and Russia as our great rivals. In the *Times* edition of the *Encyclopedia Britannica* I had myself at that time traced the growth of the German Navy. Even so recently as 1897 we had five times as many battleships and six times as many cruisers. It suffices to say now that this great naval power was created out of the Prussia of 1848, then the despair of Moltke, who contemplated emigration to Australia.

If he had gone, he would have crossed seas where, as a naval power, Prussia possessed an old corvette and a couple of gunboats which seldom left her harbours. The diabolical acts which disgraced the German Navy, and the ignominious surrender of the German submarines and internment of the fleet at Scapa, which followed as a natural consequence of Foch's victorious campaign, should not blind us to the fact that that navy maintained its existence for four and a half years, was in unchallenged command of the Baltic, and stood behind the submarine campaign which so nearly lost us the war.

On the occasion of the Battle of Jutland, that navy, with its weaker force, fought and inflicted a much greater relative loss on our Grand Fleet. It did all these things, while five, and ultimately when the United States entered the war, the whole six of the other great naval powers were arrayed against her. It does not detract in any way from the remarkable character of the achievement that it owed so much to the fact that ships are unable to fight modern fortifications. All the advantages lie with the concealed gun, on the absolutely stable land, with greater facilities for range finding and whose protective armour is not limited by any provision for buoyancy. If, again, the gun can be mounted at a height, as in Heligoland, the advantages are multiplied. These things could all have been foreseen, as they were by the German Naval War Staff. It should have been the business of a War Staff, had a real one existed, to prepare and devise methods during peace for attacking the German fleet in spite of fortifications, or to force the German fleet by other means to come out and fight.

Mr. Churchill's unhappy phrase about *"digging them out like rats,"* led to the erroneous idea that the German Fleet could only be got at by direct attack in its home ports. I had pointed out that if a relentless hunt were kept up elsewhere, or if a real blockade were enforced, it would probably bring out the fleet to release the pressure. Lord Jellicoe confirms this view when he says:

> Many surmises have been made as to the object with which the High Sea Fleet put to sea on this occasion. The view which I have always held is that the frequent light cruisers sweeps, which had taken place down the Norwegian coast and in the vicinity of the Skagerrack during the spring of 1916, may have induced the German commander-in-chief to send out a force with the object of cutting off the light cruisers engaged in these operations, and that he took the battle fleet to sea in support of this force.

A GUN CREW IN ACTION

An alternative bait was the Norwegian trade, which was very extensive, as it was an important supply route for Russia.

It should be remembered that no war had ever been so plainly seen from afar. This arose from the necessity of the German Military Party educating their people by propaganda. Von der Goltz had himself written that the war was inevitable. The date was conditioned by the fact that German naval and military preparations matured in the summer of 1914, while any delay would add to the strength. of France and Russia, and the building up of a Russian naval threat in the Baltic. The cards were so plainly on the table that on several occasions I publicly gave the year of the war; and in speeches and interviews in Canada, in 1910, I stated that it would break out in the summer of 1914. As reported in the Press, I added that it would probably be brought about by Germany engineering some trivial outbreak in the Balkans.

There can be no doubt that when the time came the German Government was persuaded that we were in no condition to interfere. They believed that they were justified in relying on what was probably an accurate estimate of the temperament of the Asquith Cabinet, and they made an all-important count of the state of Ireland showing here as elsewhere a constitutional inability to understand the forces which sway democracies. Hence the highly dangerous positions in which they had placed their fleet in the Norwegian *fiords*. Hence also the fact that the *Goeben* and the *Breslau* in the Mediterranean were sent bombarding west of Malta. German ships were exposed elsewhere, even in British harbours, at the time we sent our forty-eight hours' ultimatum to Berlin.

The second mistake which the German staff made was in not drawing the correct inference that the ease with which they escaped from those positions argued unpreparedness on our part, and advantage should have been taken to strike hard and to strike quickly. The audacious cruise of the *Goeben* and *Breslau*, in face of an overwhelming British force, proved in the first days of war to what lengths success can be pushed in face of a navy which is not prepared by a true doctrine of war. Conversely, if the British Navy had been prepared for a rapid blow, the German Fleet might have been defeated in the first week of the European war, for it was unprepared for the entrance of Great Britain. (*The Goeben & the Breslau: the Imperial German Navy in the Mediterranean, 1914—The Flight of the Goeben and Breslau*, by A. Berkeley Milne, Julian S. Corbett, W. L. Wyllie and Others is also published by Leonaur.

Before even the Heligoland Bight was defensively, mined we could have offensively mined it ourselves. We could have blocked the Elbe Channel, which extends beyond the effective range of shore guns, with concrete ships. All this, however, pre-supposes a non-existent condition of affairs in which policy in regard to mines, etc., had made preparations for definite acts, and the Foreign Office worked in the closest harmony with the Admiralty. The crossing of the Belgian frontier for instance was a definite act of war and did not need the notice in answer of a forty-eight hours' ultimatum.

It was well known in Germany that from the moment the British Empire entered the war, her fleet would become the main support of all the Allied operations. The titular god of German strategy, Jomini, in his *History of the Wars of the French Revolution*, had laid it down that it should be the object of any power seeking to dominate Europe to limit the naval armaments of a nation which cannot be reached by land. The reference could only have been to England. It is a demand which is only disguised under the propaganda for the freedom of the seas. While maintaining our naval supremacy, it is to our interest if we enter upon a war to do so with Allies so that Europe is divided. We have not forgotten the War of American Independence, when Europe united against us.

Equally, if Germany had obtained the coal, iron and shipbuilding resources of Europe by military domination, our own efforts to maintain our naval supremacy would have been strained to the utmost. Apart, then, from all treaty obligations or understandings, our intervention against Germany was an overwhelming necessity. Whether an intransigent attitude on the part of Great Britain in the earlier stages of the Austro-Serbian crisis might have postponed the war is a matter of speculation. The action of the Asquith Government in seeking a *via media* while refusing to mobilise the army, completely deceived the enemy by its obvious genuineness; Germany's naval preparations were directed towards a French war and she lost many of the advantages that might have been derived from her original policy of a sudden onslaught.

There are three main causes of Anglo-Saxon supremacy. The first is the geographical one, which constrains an island nation to seek its destiny on and across the seas, and to build up the various elements which constitute Sea Power. These elements are not purely naval, they comprise all that belongs to seafaring work with its adventurous spirit and amphibious ability, in peace and war, to penetrate and occupy transmarine territory naval power is, however, a primary condition of the existence of all the other elements, and therefore needs to be the first charge on the minds and the pockets of the people.

The second cause is moral, and consists in liberty being held in high esteem. This love of liberty is an attribute of seafaring nations, and it is exceedingly repugnant to what is known as Prussianism. The third cause of ascendency is the one to which we have already referred, namely, the military rivalries of Europe preventing any concentration of naval strength, and absorbing the energies of rival nations against each other. All three causes were ebbing on the one occasion when England was nearly crushed, and Pitt declared that the sun of England had set for ever.

In the War of American Independence, our naval strength had been diminished by a reactionary government; the United States was fighting for liberty; and for once the continent of Europe composed its differences and united against us. Such naval power as we possessed barely kept us from overwhelming disaster, and we were saved to some extent by the failure of our enemies to co-operate. In 1914, all three causes compelled us into war. Our sea-power had been Steadily challenged, for Germany aimed at a navy in 1920 in every respect much stronger than the one we possessed when we entered the war.

At the beginning of February, 1915, a former commander-in-chief of the High Seas Fleet, Grand Admiral von Koester, who was also president of the Navy League, lectured at Kiel, and said that to accept battle was to stake all on death or victory. It is worthwhile to make a very full quotation from the *Times*, February 11, 1915, of these remarks:—

> Our confidence in our navy is as firm as a rock. But we know that the naval battle means death or victory, and that, once a fleet has been destroyed, it can never be renewed during the course of the same war, even if the campaign goes on for years. We must therefore in all circumstances be cautious in our actions, and not allow ourselves to be tempted into taking any action in the performance of which we might be defeated. For what would be the result if a naval battle took place tomorrow in which each of our ships was accompanied to the bottom by one of the enemy's ships and perhaps by even a few more? Then we should be without a fleet, while England would be able to proceed step by step with her attacks upon our coast. That, then, no town would be spared; of that you may be certain, in view of what England has done in our colonies.

Our coast from Emden to Memel would be most seriously menaced. Attempts to land might succeed, if they were adequately prepared beforehand, and they might be made at points which would be in the highest degree inconvenient for us. Our fleet must in all circumstances protect us, and must accept battle only when it can count on success. We must emerge unvanquished both on sea and on land, in order that we may win for ourselves an honourable peace which shall shake England's world-dominion to its foundations. May God grant us the victory!

In considering the battle which was fought nearly sixteen months later, there is no need for the reader to enmesh himself in a web of refinements and expedients. He can safely hold to the bed-rock facts. For what did he and his countrymen build the Grand Fleet? The answer is given in every page of naval history for the ten years before the war. We concentrated and built the British Fleet to fight and beat the German High Seas Fleet. As to the object of Germany, Admiral von Koester merely repeated the famous preamble of the Navy Bill of 1900:—

In existing circumstances, in order to protect Germany's trade and colonies, there is only one means, namely, Germany should possess a fleet of such strength that even for the mightiest naval power a war with her would involve such risk as to jeopardise its own supremacy. For this purpose, it is not absolutely necessary that the German fleet should be as strong as that of the greatest sea-power, because, generally, a great sea-power would not be in a position to concentrate all its forces against us. But even if it should succeed in confronting us in superior force, the enemy would be so considerably weakened in overcoming the resistance of a strong German fleet that, notwithstanding a victory gained, the enemy's supremacy would not at first be secured any longer by a sufficient fleet.

The object of the German Navy was, then, to keep this risk, so that it governed British action. As von Tirpitz said on the second reading of the 1911 Navy Estimates:

This risk is, in fact, the *ceterum censes* of our naval policy.

It is unfortunately the case that the Germans at Jutland inflicted on us the greater loss and returned safely from a naval battle in which, through the masterly manoeuvres of the battle cruisers, the British Fleet had been placed between the High Seas Fleet and its mined and fortified havens of refuge. The enemy's total loss had been only one battle-cruiser, a pre-Dreadnought battleship, and a few small units. In other words, we failed to attain our objects and the Germans did more than they had ever expected. They achieved this too with a fleet partly consisting of old vessels, or pre-Dreadnoughts, which the British public had been officially assured, as far back as 1906, were rendered utterly obsolete by the *Dreadnought*.

How this came about is a matter worthy of full investigation, even to its remote causes, and is the chief object of this book. No account would be worth anything which neglected first to survey the state of affairs which, controlling naval thought, dominated our actions when the crucial test came. Professor Holland Rose has pointed out that Guibert was Napoleon's favourite author, and in his marked copy Napoleon had heavily lined the paragraph concerning the governments of Europe in 1770:—

They direct affairs at haphazard and in accordance with established routine.

If we met the great opportunity which came to us at Jutland Bank with a navy directed at haphazard and in accordance with established routine, we need not wonder why the most was not made of an opportunity which had it been brought to fruition in the way we had the right to expect, would have saved the world from years of "death, damnation and disaster."

The proud record of the British Navy is a wonderful one of magnificent fighting, and this war is no exception; it is that of a bad starter, though a good stayer and a sure winner. But is it necessary for us to start badly to gain our knowledge by experiencing the hard knocks of war, and to go through the agony of its prolongation if it can be shown that there is a better way by which we can train ourselves into a condition to strike hard and to strike quickly? In July, 1914, we had lost even the idea of shadowing, or, as Drake called it, "dogging," by which in 1885, we followed Russian ships over thousands of miles while war seemed imminent.

That may be one reason why war did not then break out, for we were so obviously ready. Good judges recognised the possibilities of the Serbian ultimatum as early as July 24, 1914. It is, therefore, a matter for inquiry why in the ensuing eleven days we had not provided for shadowing a single prospective enemy ship. We had elaborated a centralised system of wireless control from Whitehall, which deprived admirals of initiative, and which ordered the movements of all fleets or ships from the Admiralty. The argument advanced in the Press was that Tokio did it in the Russo-Japanese War. That is true, as also that it worked badly and had to be modified.

When Kamimura was chasing the *Rurik* and her two consorts, Tokio issued orders conflicting with those given by Togo, and the former was wrong both in issuing orders and in the orders themselves. Kamimura should have had a free hand in carrying out a definite plan. The danger in the necessary power which the Admiralty exercises of regulating the distribution of forces is that there is a constant temptation for men who have not studied war to meddle in other directions. The orders issued by the Admiralty at the outset of this war are known in the case of the Mediterranean Fleet, and are believed in other cases to have been calculated to preserve the British forces, but they were not orders devoted to the main purpose of destroying the enemy.

If we find that similar ideas prevailed at Jutland, we can only conclude that the British Navy had, so far as the high command was concerned, entered upon the struggle with a perverted doctrine of war. If that is the case, we cannot too soon take steps to prevent it ever happening again.

CHAPTER 1

Policy and Preparation

The preparation of a navy for war is the outcome of years of study, organisation and training. History shows how its past successes were due to a more correct appreciation of the qualifications for high command and their interrelations with each other and with the government; to a better insight into the strategy and tactics of war; and to deriving from this knowledge the most suitable organisation and training for the navy as a whole. Our victories in the past are no criterion as to the future, though a renowned navy has the advantage of handing down high standards and traditions.

Success is apt, however, to blind men to the need of adaptation to changed conditions, and to cause the command at the Admiralty, and in the fleets, to rely on experience rather than on well-directed studies. The latter are generally more important for, as Frederick the Great pointed out, he had a couple of mules which had been through twenty campaigns and were mules still. In the British Navy the experience was peace experience prior to the war, and, since there was only the one great Battle of Jutland, experience *qua* experience could contribute little to replace well-directed studies.

Success, again, is seldom followed by inquiry, though the latter is both useful and necessary. There is reason for great anxiety in this respect, for we have never had less inquiry than in the present war. Take the court-martial system, which from time to time has saved the navy from disaster. So sure, were our ancestors of its value that for all the centuries of the navy's existence, up to the break in the case of the destroyer *Ariel* in 1907, whenever a ship was lost there was a court-martial to inquire into the circumstances. A naval court of inquiry is not on oath. Its findings and evidence are never made public.

It is therefore no substitute for a court-martial. In this war, courts-martial were discarded except for mere disciplinary offences and for the junior ranks. The exceptional one held on Rear-Admiral Troubridge, in connection with the escape of the *Goeben*, was due to the wise insistence of that officer in refusing to accept the report of a court of inquiry which had not all the essential facts before it. With this exception, Mr. Churchill never held a single court-martial for any losses of ships or miscarriage of operations during the eight months of war in which he was First Lord of the Admiralty.

He broke the custom of the navy in ordering the one on Rear-Admiral Troubridge to take place in secret and to issue a secret finding, and no other reason can be ascribed for his action but that the Admiralty were protecting their own reputation, though naturally they plead that the course was taken in "the public interest." Thus, it was revealed over four years afterwards in the House of Commons that the finding showed that the rear-admiral acted in accordance with orders from the Admiralty and Sir Berkeley Milne. To take another case, the court of inquiry for the *Cressy*, *Aboukir* and *Hogue* was legally secret, as courts of inquiry are intended only to be informal affairs to guide the commander-in-chief or the Admiralty as to whether a full inquiry on oath is necessary.

The practice is liable to gross abuse as in this case, for, apart from the unbroken practice of the navy up to 1907, a court-martial was obviously necessary in the case of such a terrible loss of life in order to obtain evidence on oath, as well as a finding from a court bound by oaths, and with a view to the publication of the proceedings so that Parliament could judge. In spite, however, of the limited and informal character of the inquiry into the loss of these three ships, it is known to the navy that the finding blamed the Admiralty, and the President of the court is credited with having refused to revise the report when the suggestion reached him from the Admiralty.

These few, among many examples, suffice to show that the operations and conduct of the war should be investigated as well as the preparations made during peace. The object is not to expose the men responsible, but to reform a system which is known to be faulty. That is the only sure way to make progress, to give confidence, and to ensure peace. It might be said why inquire, for instance, into the successful passage of the Expeditionary Force across the Channel? Lord Jellicoe has stated that the Germans could have made an attack on this cross-Channel traffic and returned to their base before the Grand Fleet could intervene. In that case they "would only have had to deal with the comparatively light forces based in southern waters." This is clearly a matter for inquiry and subsequent report to Parliament. There should be investigation into the question whether there was anything in the war orders to the Grand Fleet about protecting the Expeditionary Force.

One fails to see how it could have done so from Scapa Flow, for as Lord Jellicoe has pointed out our "destroyers were constantly returning to the base to fuel," and "if our fleet arrived on the scene without destroyers the Germans would have possessed no mean advantage." The vessels on the spot referred to by Lord Jellicoe as "comparatively light forces based on southern waters" were without a protecting screen of destroyers, and were exposed to both submarine attack and a concentrated surface attack. Just as Lord Jellicoe casually reveals that the arrangements, which were thought to be so good, were as a matter of fact most imperfect, so Mr. Balfour was stung by a speech of Mr. Churchill into saying that there was no defence of the trade routes, and no defended bases for the Grand Fleet on the East Coast.

Later on, Sir Edward Carson in the House of Commons, and Lord Curzon in the House of Lords, revealed that the navy had fought over two years of war without blockade or sea mines. The position taken up by the German delegates to the Hague Conference and the open German advocacy of minefields on the high seas, left no doubt as to their intentions. It was our business not merely to get in the first blow, but to foil the enemy. As a matter of fact, the German minefields were laid with the loss of only one minelayer, for the simple reason that the problem had not been considered by us nor the necessary provision made to meet it.

Obviously, our patrol flotillas would have to be scattered, and must therefore be additional to any concentrated force which would deal with an attempt to raid or invade our coasts. We know from Lord Jellicoe's book that the number of destroyers was inadequate for any one of the four purposes of screening the Grand Fleet when operating from the selected base at Scapa Flow; for attacking invading or raiding forces; for patrol work against submarines; and for the prevention of mine-laying. In regard to the last, Lord Jellicoe says:—

> The policy of attrition of our battle fleet might thus be carried out with such success as to produce equality, or even inferiority, on the part of the British fleet as compared with the German in a comparatively short space of time. . . . The first effect, therefore, of the submarine menace, combined with possible German action in regard to mine-laying, was to cause the battlefleet to confine its movements under ordinary conditions to the more northern waters of the North Sea, where the risk might be taken of cruising without the presence of a screen of destroyers, and where it was improbable, owing to the depth of water and the distance from enemy bases, that the Germans would be able to lay mines without discovery.

It is obvious that provision was not made against these things because they were not thought out and only discovered after war had revealed them. Lord Jellicoe's explanation is that the "people" were to blame! As reported in the *Morning Post*, February 21, 1918, he said?—

> Our shortage of destroyers was due partly to the fact that before the war the nation thought in 'Dreadnoughts.' 'Dreadnoughts' had caught on, and if you wanted money, you were pretty sure, with a certain amount of pressure, to get it for 'Dreadnoughts.' But in the shout for 'Dreadnoughts' people forgot that there were other classes of craft that were quite as necessary for other purposes. If money was asked for for those craft there was not quite the same response. The result was that at the commencement of the war we were short of destroyers.

It is impossible not to feel contempt for such a plea. Even if we toy with the idea for a moment, who but the Admiralty taught the public to think in 'Dreadnoughts'? Investigation will, however, show that the lack of material preparation was due to ignorance of the principles of war.

This lack of preparedness on the material side involved a corresponding lack on the training side. It affected the Battle of Jutland, though, happily, the fight took place after the material defects had been remedied by the heroic means of making every requirement of the army give place to the supreme needs of the navy.

We had to remedy a lack of training prior to war due to misplaced economy. Thus Lord Jellicoe tells us:—

In the German Navy a great increase had been made in the allowance of ammunition for practice. Before the war this was much higher than our own, and there was no doubt in my mind that the German allowance would be well expended. Indeed, we had obtained information which placed this beyond question . . . The Germans possessed an excellent practice ground in Kiel Bay with every appliance for carrying out gunnery exercises. . . . We were not in so fortunate a position. There had been no recent opportunity for carrying out gunnery and torpedo exercises and practices: Scapa Flow had not been used as a base for such work in peace time, except for destroyers, and consequently no facilities existed there, although the proximity of Cromarty, which had been a fleet practice base, neutralised this disadvantage to a certain extent at a later period.

But there was no protected area outside the harbour where practices could be carried out in safety, and the harbour itself was not at first secure against submarine attack. Much use, however, was made of the Moray Firth outside Cromarty later when submarine obstructions had been provided, and the Germans had obligingly laid a minefield which protected the practice area from seaward. . . . The practices themselves were carried out under conditions which laid the ships open to submarine attack. This was most unsatisfactory, and the work suffered considerably as the result.

It is only right, however, that we should point out that the real *training* of a navy for war takes place during peace. Lord Jellicoe naturally does not mention that it was his influence with Sir George Warrender's Committee that caused the retention of the stereotyped Gunlayer's Tests, and the system of competitive target practice, against the advice of those who urged a more realistic system of training.

So far from the heroism and endurance of the officers and men blinding us to the direction in which preparations for war had failed, it is a duty that we owe to them that we should inquire as to why we failed to give them our best support. Lord Jellicoe sometimes blames the politicians and sometimes the public, and certainly in his successive posts as Director of Naval Ordnance, Third Sea Lord and Second Sea Lord, he was in a position to know. His charges should be investigated, and if his advice were ignored it should be ascertained why he did not resign rather than allow the public to believe that he was satisfied. We want to know who are these politicians?

They are certainly not the members of the House of Commons, of whom I have personal experience. There is nothing that the House of Commons will not do for the navy. Macaulay says somewhere, that the House of Commons, even when most discontented and parsimonious, had always been bountiful to profusion where the interests of the navy were concerned. This was true of the House of Commons in 1906-9 inclusive, a House which came in on a cry for economy. The responsibility for all shortcomings lies between the government of the day and their naval advisers, and in the latter case the government is all powerful in their selection. If behind the scenes the sailors, whether from poverty of argument or lack of character, allowed the provision which was vitally necessary to efficiency to be cut down by the Cabinet or the Treasury, they must share the blame.

Men who enter a profession with the obligation of sacrificing their lives for their country should certainly resign rather than be the instrument of their country's downfall, or the disgrace of the noblest profession in the world. They would have had the backing of all the forces of public opinion had they so acted, and the public always assumes that, in a matter so vital as the navy, the government acts on the advice of the Sea Lords. There is, however, much reason to believe that many of the shortcomings were the direct result of ignorance of the principles and conduct of war through failure to study its problems with an executive War Staff. All the material shortcomings, to which Lord Jellicoe refers in his book, were the outcome of decisions in which his own responsibility as a member of the Board of Admiralty was very prominent.

Take, for instance, the absence of boom defences to the northern ports. The idea of booms is as old as the ancient Greeks, and a recent example is the one commended by Admiral Lord Collingwood which the Turks laid across the Dardanelles in 1808. So little had matters been thought out, that efficient merchant ships were used to block the channels at Scapa, and owing to many of these ships being put down empty, unballasted, the tide drifted them out of position and they failed in their object. The unfortunate politician, whom Lord Jellicoe blames for the state of affairs which resulted in his going elsewhere and losing a new 'Dreadnought' costing over two millions sterling, the *Audacious*, on the north coast of Ireland, surely cannot be blamed for the ignorance and lack of preparation which made the British Navy practically wage a war of its own against the British mercantile marine.

Scapa was decided on as the base early in 1910. A committee, of which Lord Jellicoe was the most prominent member, did consider boom defences and decided against them. The fact, then, that Scapa, Cromarty and Rosyth were without booms, and therefore open to destroyer and submarine attack, was a circumstance for which Lord Jellicoe was himself responsible.

As for the absence of guns from Scapa, Lord Jellicoe says:—

The question of providing gun defences for this base, *which the Admiralty had decided a year or two before the war* was to be the main fleet base, had been discussed on more than one occasion, after an examination by a committee of officers on the spot; but, since finance governs defence, and the Admiralty from year to year had insufficient money for even more urgent needs, no action had been taken.

This dissatisfaction with political control is a kind of running charge throughout the book. Take, for instance, even the personnel, concerning which we are told on:—

I knew also that the German Fleet was in no way short of officers; this was the case with us, owing to the constant political pressure in the years before the war, and I expected that this shortage of officers would be a great handicap to us as the war progressed.

If Parliament ever undertakes an inquiry, it will be ascertained whether the Admiralty ever made out a case for any one of these points, such as the defence of Scapa, which was refused by the Asquith Government.

One popular naval explanation is that provision was made for guns at Scapa in the Navy Estimates of 1914, but in the spring the system which makes administrative convenience supreme began to bring about a change. Dover breakwater was uncomfortably wet. The officers were asking for shelters there, while Scapa was as quiet as the Polar regions. Accordingly, the fiat went forth to divert the money from the defences of Scapa to providing shelters to prevent sailors from getting wet at Dover! Is it to be supposed that any but a handful of lunatics would refuse defences for the Grand Fleet's base in war time? If the Admiralty say Scapa was a great secret and that it was inadvisable to draw attention to its future use by such preparations during peace, in spite of the fact admitted by Lord Jellicoe that German vessels were surveying and sounding there in 1913 and 1914, I shall be happy to send them an article, over a column long, which appeared in the *Glasgow Herald* in 1910.

This article, apparently inspired from the Admiralty, gave a full description of Scapa Flow as the Grand Fleet's base in the coming war. It was almost the only war plan the Admiralty had produced, namely, to select a base as far removed on the east coast as possible, so that the minimum of security would be given to the Expeditionary Force and to the protection of this country from invasion, and then ultimately to forget to place guns, booms, docks or repair facilities to aid the fleet. As regards docks Lord Jellicoe goes so far as to say that all our ships were wrongly constructed with an insufficient beam, in order to suit existing docks. He says:

> Docks, make no appeal to the imagination of the public, and cost a great deal of money. The result was that August, 1914, found us with a superiority in ships but woefully lacking in dock accommodation, and for this reason alone, a fleet action early in the war resulting in considerable damage to heavy ships would have produced embarrassing results.

Again, as in other cases, I could fill pages with the public pressure exercised on the Admiralty to give the navy docks, from 1906 on, and resisted by the Admiralty. When floating docks were urged in 1906-7, the Admiralty representative opposed them as unsuitable. The view that floating docks were unsuitable was even taught as late as 1912.

Special selections are not being made for the purpose of framing an indictment. Similar lethargic thought and action can be found in every direction.

★★★★★★

Even Portland was not considered secure, for a ship was sunk on purpose in the hole in the wall, just as numbers of other ships were purposely sunk at Scapa and elsewhere. The reader should remember that these expensive remedies for lack of preparation in every direction were cumulative in crippling our war effort by diverting men, money and materials to work which the House of Commons would not have hesitated to have performed during peace, had the demand been made. The House of Commons did not know the truth. Even on February 15, 1915, it listened with satisfaction to Mr. Churchill as he told the House that "on the declaration of war" the navy was ready, "supplied and equipped with every requirement down to the smallest detail that could be foreseen."

★★★★★★

Take, for instance, the operations against German Samoa and its wireless station. On August 6, 1914, the Secretary of State for the Colonies telegraphed as follows to the Governor of New Zealand:—

> If your ministers desire and feel themselves able to seize German wireless station at Samoa we should feel that this was a great and urgent Imperial service. . . Commonwealth is being consulted as to wireless stations at New Guinea, Yap, Marshall Islands, and Naru or Pleasant Island.

Thus a "great and urgent Imperial service" was neither foreseen, prepared for, nor suggested to the Dominions concerned until about four days after the delivery of the ultimatum to Germany. It is obvious that the suggested expeditions required armed escort, and that unless such operations formed part of a general plan prepared for during peace, the defence of trade would suffer through the diversion of war ships. This, of course, happened, and serious injury was done to our shipping and trade. Prior to the war, the doctrine had penetrated the Admiralty, for which there is no justification in history, that trade could be trusted to look after itself. The scrapping of cruisers in 1904 and the failure to replace them resulted from this vital error.

When the war broke out there was but one cruiser to defend the whole of our vast and scattered trade with the continent of South America. In addition, the Trade Division of the Admiralty had been abolished a few years before the war, so that the greatest maritime nation was without any organisation for the defence of trade when war broke out.

★★★★★★

The fact is revealed by the Navy List. The list for June, 1914, gives no Trade Division at all; but in July, or the month the European War broke out, there appears the skeleton of a Trade Division, consisting of a captain with the title of acting director, a commander, a major of the Royal Marines, and eight clerks.

This newly-formed division was supposed to tackle the great problem of blockade, contraband, and match itself against the astute brains of the bankers, shipowners and traders of Europe, as well as provide for the defence of our own trade. It is little wonder that the case in regard to cotton and other commodities was so badly argued as to fail to convince the Cabinet until it was too late.

★★★★★★

At a later stage, ignorance of history led to the convoy system being openly derided until the allied and neutral losses rose from about 500,000 tons a quarter to over 2,200,000 tons a quarter, and the war was nearly lost. It was a case of the Admiralty resisting a War Cabinet which was urging convoys, the admirals declaring the convoy system to be "impossible." The lack of cruisers was shown up several years before the war in a general way by Lord Beresford and myself, and in precise detail by Captain Kenneth Dewar's gold medal essay for the Royal United Service Institution, but, in circumstances which beggar comment, the vital part of the latter's essay was suppressed, though the enemy must have been able to work out the problem for himself. The only people to suffer by this secrecy were the British, who were obeying the official precept "to sleep quietly in their beds."

We do not propose to deal further with evidence of this lack of thought beyond saying that it extended from the primaries to the secondaries, and the navy, lacking reserves, had to enter on a mad race with the army to obtain contracts in which the navy naturally obtained priority. This aspect should not be lost sight of in considering the circumstances which led to the establishment of the Ministry of Munitions.

In its fundamental characteristics, war is the same by land and sea, and we learn from the fall that overtook the Prussian Army at Jena, in spite of its former power under Frederick the Great, and the French Army in 1870, in spite of all it achieved under Napoleon, how nothing but unrelenting care is the mother of safety. In Marlborough's phrase, "*the English are famous for negligence*," and such a nation requires continuous criticism of its vital shortcomings, for as a rule it takes a crisis to shake us out of our complacency, and then it is too late to reform except at a great price.

Mr. Asquith's Government staved off all real discussion and criticism by secrecy and falsehood in peace time. Even when the crisis resulted from their own courses of conduct in past years, his self-sat-

30

isfaction was so great as to inspire the speech of June 15, 1915, when he said in the House of Commons: "No body of men, in my deliberate judgment, could have done more or could have done better," Mr. Lloyd George, at the other extreme, said, "We were the worst prepared nation in the world for this war."

The nature of a people can only be changed through the educational system which gradually works with cumulative effect on the propaganda P's, Press, Parliament, Platform and Pulpit. If the nation is imbued with history, with a large sense of the things that we have done and the things that we have failed to do, the whole task of the critic, in all the spheres which make for true imperial greatness, is rendered much easier. He is able to make himself understood as he points to some past lesson which stands out like a finger-post indicating the road of safety, or again as a danger sign which should induce us to go cautiously or retrace our steps. It is only under an autocracy that an army or navy can be nursed into something dwelling apart from the main currents of the national life so that it does not reproduce the characteristic national habits and faults.

The *Samurai*, or military caste of Japan, thus dwelt apart from the nation; but the moment the country was opened, and the attempt was made to adopt liberal institutions, the Samurai themselves took over the educational system, or the Great Safeguard; for people who borrow new religions and new systems stand in danger of taking to the bad and plausible points rather than the good and essential. Unfortunately, in England, the navy and army, except in the days of the Commonwealth, while reproducing the characteristic qualities of our people, both in their strength and weakness, yet dwelt apart from the people though dependent on them for all that constitutes preparation and efficiency.

Reproducing the faults of the people, the study of history in the two services was the work of a mere roomful of officers. Gifted with no historical sense, the people could not be interested in war problems during peace. This accentuated the gulf. The fighting men who felt bitterly—and those who have seen the needless sacrifices in the opening stages of every war and the subsequent sacrifices through their prolongation, had every reason to feel bitterly—yet failed to see that the real remedy lies in the resolute finding of the historical sense in the people by creating a love of the history of the country, much as the Jews clung to their Bible and the Greeks to Homer.

When that is done it will be an easier matter to establish history on a firm foundation in the fighting services, and to make them think and work together, always having the great good of the country at heart, in the service of which on sea, land or air, they are but one team which achieves the greatest results when it most satisfactorily combines together. How often does our history show this absence of team work in our combined expeditions!

We obtained it most under Chatham, when the team work between the civil, military and naval authorities of France was at its worst, and so our Empire was made safe in India and Canada. Yet twenty years later we had lost the sense of team work between the civil, naval and military authorities. This, to some extent, was due to the fact that the war of American Independence was one great sin against all the teaching of our history, a betrayal of principle that could never have occurred had the country been as strongly imbued with the historical sense as was Chatham, who espoused the cause of the colonies.

Many years ago, when, in 1895, Lord Salisbury, as Prime Minister, plaintively exclaimed that naval experts could be found to support almost any view as to what should be done, I wrote attributing the fact to the absence of any kind of historical teaching and study in the navy. Five years previously the Admiralty had acquiesced in Lord Salisbury's blunder of the cession of Heligoland to Germany, from which a trained War Staff, which is in itself the child of history, would have saved them. It was Heligoland which, by protecting the minefields, denied free manoeuvring ground to a British Fleet entering the Heligoland Bight or the Channel by which the Germans returned after Jutland.

The possibilities of sea mines were a subject of discussion from 1891 onwards. My own paper on "The Mediterranean and Suez Canal in War," which the council of the Royal United Service Institution asked me to prepare in 1893, urged their extensive employment, but the paper was suppressed by authority. Ultimately, in 1918, about 200,000 mines were laid by the Allies when 20,000 would have been ample under a prepared plan for rapid laying on the first day of the war. A similar ignorance, arising through want of trained study of history and the principles of war, led to localised naval defences, a sin which never could be charged to bygone Admiralties.

Take, for instance, the localised submarines. It was laid down that they formed an integral part of the local defence. They could not be moved by the local commander-in-chief so that at Malta they could not even be sent to the vicinity of Messina to wait for the *Goeben!* The progress of the war led, as was natural, to the order being rescinded, so that localised submarines were to be found later on attacking the Dardanelles. In other directions, however, the error of localised defences persisted to the end. An account could be given of young officers who might have been gaining the finest experience of war in destroyers at sea who spent years in harbour, on board battleships swinging round a buoy because the battleships were part of the localised defences.

The question may well be asked:

> Does it never occur to the succession of admirals who have controlled naval policy for years that every great leader has been a student of history and has never ceased to be one?

If it has not, let them read the opening chapter of Foch's *Principles of War*, the declared opinions as well as the practice of Napoleon or Mahan's *Maritime Strategy*. It is true that our opponents can cite some historians who have taught like Carlyle, or as Froude indeed said, that history is merely a stage on which the drama of humanity is played by successive actors from age to age. Froude supplied his own refutation to some extent when he declared that "Shakespeare is so great because he is nearest nature." To be true to nature is to be true to a standard which is regulated in accordance with laws. So, in the actions of great commanders, whether by sea or land, we find the same underlying principles whether we are dealing with Caesar, Nelson, Napoleon or Foch.

In England, the navy has hitherto treated the past, except for the voluntary efforts of young officers who work under an almost offensive official discouragement, as though it were negligible wreckage at the bottom of the sea. So, we neglected to ascertain, until a few years ago, how Nelson had fought Trafalgar and whether the operations did or did not correspond with his plan. We disputed about Tegethoff and Persano at Lissa, just as we are disputing about Jutland today, with no assistance from the Admiralty. Important lessons with regard to Jutland hang upon the exact positions of ships. Almost the greatest tragedy of a sea battle is the oblivion that overtakes it. The ships go down and the waters close over them.

One record stood for a few hours in the *Invincible*. On May 28, 1919, a question was asked as to finding the position of the wreck, and a characteristic answer was elicited from an Admiralty which could freely allow the whole fleet to go out for routine exercises from Scapa on the day that nearly every man was ready to bet that the Germans would scuttle their ships, and could yet not spare a couple of trawlers or even destroyers for this most useful purpose. The question put was whether in view of the fact that the exact times at which ships passed the wreck of the *Invincible* at the Battle of Jutland are known, the Admiralty would state the latitude and longitude of this wreck, in order that officers and students who study the battle may be able to check the positions of ships during the battle. To this Dr. Macnamara replied that "measures are being taken to locate this wreck when *the necessary vessels are available.*" Writing in August, or nine months after the Armistice, if anything has been done to locate the wreck, the public has not been informed.

The importance of ascertaining its position (believed to be 57° 6' N., 6° 20' E.) arises from the fact that it stood right out of the water split in two, and that she was the leading ship when the disaster happened. Consequently, every ship passed it to starboard and noted the time and distance. Later, in order to guard against the Germans getting secret documents, a submarine was sent out to torpedo it, but found that the two parts had disappeared under water.

A couple of destroyers employed in sweeping could in a few hours after arrival near the spot settle the whole matter, and enable us better to understand the battle. The Admiralty answer about the *Invincible* is typical. There can and there will be no change, no ardent pursuit of the knowledge of war and its conduct, until the historical school of the navy is in power. Men who have never given a thought to history, whose whole life has become a habit, and that habit the mere handling of ships and the administration of their internal economy, have their minds hopelessly narrowed, so that they are colour-blind in regard to strategy and grand tactics.

They are judged thoroughly efficient officers by their technical work afloat, and their promotion depends on these things and mere examinations. They pass to the control of so-called War Staffs or on to the Board of Admiralty without knowledge, and the result is failure. Successive Cabinets find them convenient in peace time, for, lacking knowledge, they do not press demands for they cannot argue their case. Occasionally there is a crisis which results in an attempt at reform, but the type of men in control persists and a fresh crisis reveals a similar measure of inefficiency.

Take, for instance, the Cabinet Committee report in 1910 on the crisis produced by Lord Charles Beresford's charges. The Committee, consisting of Mr. Asquith, Sir Edward Grey, Lord Haldane and Lord Morley, reported that there were "no substantial grounds" for Lord

Charles Beresford's charge that the Admiralty had no adequate war plans for probable events.

Yet in 1911-12 in the Agadir crisis, the Cabinet found the Admiralty had no thought-out plans for transporting troops to France if Germany went to war and they do not appear to have considered the detailed plans of the general staff of the War Office. On this Mr. Churchill was sent to the Admiralty to form a War Staff, with what success the world can judge. Yet the Committee in their report, in 1910, said:

> The First Lord of the Admiralty furnished the Committee with a *résumé* of the steps which have recently been taken to *develop a War Staff* at the Admiralty and indicated further advances which are in contemplation.

The concluding paragraph is as follows:—

> The Committee have been impressed with the differences of opinion amongst officers of high rank and professional attainments regarding important principles of naval strategy and tactics, and they look forward with much confidence to the further development of a Naval War Staff, from which the naval members of the Board and Flag officers and their staffs at sea may be expected to derive common benefit.

The world is familiar with the struggle Sir Eric Geddes made in 1917-18 to obtain a War Staff. We are decidedly nearer the solution after five years of war in the skeleton of the War Staff, but to make it effective it must have power and cease to be subordinate to men in administrative posts and to mere materialists. The truth may as well be confessed that so long as the latter are in charge we are as little likely to know how to conduct war as we should have been had we depended on the mere seamen in the time of the Commonwealth. The soldier Blake, who understood war and its principles, had to be sent to take charge, for the sailors were colour-blind on the subject of great strategical and tactical principles.

The young navy has done its best to assimilate these principles, but the Admiralty pursue the unfortunate policy of damping down all discussion and refusing all information. The best brains of the navy belong to this young school, which bases all its principles on the teaching of history. It is bound to win, if not today, then tomorrow, for England and England's Empire depend upon the navy, and that navy in turn depends upon *"wisdom's best rule, to profit from the past."* That past is the bountiful mine where all wise men dig who *"with all their getting get understanding."* It interprets golden rules to guide us somewhat as follows, but each student must frame his own:—

(1) The more provident care in peace the less improvident scare in war.

(2) Do not bring your peace mind to bear on war problems. It is as unsuitable as your silk hat.

(3) Do not conjure up pictures to suit either your fears or your wishes. The enemy will act according to his psychology and the probabilities of the situation.

(4) Trust the man on the spot. If you do not trust him change him.

(5) Co-ordination, Co-operation, Consolidation, Comradeship and Concentration are the winning C's of war.

(6) Concentrate. for victory.

(7) The spirit of war is the offensive and the surprise, or Napoleon's *"Frappez vite et frappez fort."*

CHAPTER 2

The Hush-Hush Policy

In the year 1913 I gave a lecture at the Royal United Service Institution solely devoted to showing up the cult of secrecy, and how it prevents discussion and arrests progress. It would be out of place to restate the arguments when we are chiefly concerned with the Battle of Jutland, but the extracts we have already given from Lord Jellicoe's book of the lack of preparation which he considers, as one who was a member of the board up to the first day of war, gravely handicapped the navy and endangered the country, must surely persuade men that these things had much better be known during peace instead of when it is too late. Publicity is the watch-dog of democracy, and secrecy takes the dog off his beat.

As a matter of fact, when attention was drawn to these dangers, they were officially denied by the Admiralty, and the public believed the denials, because they did not imagine that sailors could be found who would acquiesce in endangering the country.

The mischief of the absence of discussion which the Admiralty brought about, and under which the Royal United Service Institution might just as well have been renamed the Deaf and Dumb Institute, extended to all spheres of action. Let me take the most important, such as the tactics at the Battle of Jutland. In the chapter, "Reflections on the Battle of Jutland," Lord Jellicoe gives first place to the question of destroyer attacks in a daylight action, and characteristically devotes all his remarks to the defensive side of the matter. As a mere student of history, I forecasted what this defensive bias would lead to when a battle was fought and controversy followed. My prediction was made as far back as September, 1901, in the *Monthly Review*, in an article entitled "The Navy at School," in the following words:—

Risks there have always been in the wearisome work of waiting for an enemy resting in the security of a fortified arsenal. Some of these, like the lee-shore, have passed away with the advent of steam. New risks, such as the torpedo-boat, have led to the development of destroyers, quick-firing guns, and torpedo nets. My own view of this matter is that we are losing sight of the offensive policy taught by every page in the history of naval war. .... History tells us pretty plainly that when the death-dealing results of a weapon are very terrible, an altogether disproportionate value is attached to its use, and but little regard is paid to those limitations which prevent it from being used.

It was so in the past with the fireship. It has been so in our day with the ram, the torpedo-boat, the Brennan torpedo, lyddite and the dynamite gun. ... So much fuss was made over the destroyer that even the late Admiral Colomb was induced to prophesy in a series of articles that the battleship was doomed. Either this view is right or the British admirals in manoeuvres are sometimes guilty of actions to which a strong term might erroneously be applied in actual war. In any case, nothing could be worse for the moral of the fleet than the knowledge *that the admiral fears to face his work because of the torpedo craft.*

It is time that we should have something to go upon as to the real menace of the destroyer against the fleet. ... The tactical school is too fond of rapid generalisation, *e.g.*, from the known results which follow the explosion of a torpedo to the upsetting of the balance of power by the operations by torpedo craft. ... we have no naval *attaché* in Germany, where there are far greater shipbuilding resources than in France. ... We may commence now for the probable conflict of ten years hence. (The Agadir crisis was in the autumn of 1911.) Our navy as at present organised may be good enough to beat France. He would be a bold man who should say, if we do not introduce progressive changes into our system, that it will be good enough to beat Germany in the second decade of this century.

Here, then, was the complete warning of the future rivalry, war, tactics and the inevitable failure, unless we changed our mode of thought. The warning could in no way affect the navy, for the whole profession lay under the blight of secrecy, so that men hardly dared to discuss anything lest they should injure their prospects of appointments or promotions. Lord Jellicoe winds up his remarks on the destroyer threat by saying that:

> Some German documents which came into our possession early in the war proved the importance which the enemy attached to this form of attack, and emphasised the gravity of the question.

And then is added the only reference to the possibility of our using them offensively:

> It was, of course, fully realised that the question had two sides, and that if our battle fleet was open to this form of attack, that of the enemy was equally so.

If there had been discussion, instead of secrecy, before the war, we think that it would have been so, but just as the one officer, who used his destroyer offensively and fired a torpedo on the occasion of the Hartlepool raid, is said to have been censured, so the defensive role of the British destroyer was emphasised throughout the Grand Fleet until after Jutland. *After Jutland,* our destroyers, which had carried four torpedoes to the German six, had the number of their torpedo-tubes and torpedoes increased. *After Jutland,* they were painted grey to attack by day, hitherto they had been painted black. *After Jutland* it was recognised that the "counter" was futile, but what we needed was a concentrated attack of all arms on the vitals of the enemy fleets, *viz.,* his battleships. Before Jutland, our policy had been the defensive one of holding the destroyers to "counter" the enemy destroyer attack. Lord Jellicoe says:

> The 'counter,' which had usually been favoured by flag officers commanding fleets up to the date named (August, 1914), had

been the obvious one of an attack by our own light cruisers and torpedo craft on those of the enemy, as the latter advanced, or before.

We may dismiss the words "or before" since it is quite impracticable to attack them while sheltered by their battleships, and the slightest study would have shown that our destroyers and light cruisers would have continuously to maintain a position under the fire of the enemy's battle-line if they were to be capable of attacking the enemy's light craft before they reached an effective torpedo range. He then argues that his intention was to turn his fleet either towards or away from the attack. This obscures the fact that the practice of the fleet was the one actually ordered at Jutland, *viz.*, to turn away from the enemy destroyers, which of course meant to turn away from the enemy battleships and victory! The turn away was the defensive measure which lost us a victory at Jutland, for to turn away from the enemy fleet *in the misty North Sea* is a guaranteed means of losing him.

It may be said that though the offensive role of the German destroyers was well known before the war, it is mere assertion to say that had there been discussion instead of secrecy an offensive role for our destroyers would have been introduced into the navy before Jutland. I submit it is fair inference, because, as Herodotus says, "*Free discussion reveals truth.*" One thing, however, is certain. Lord Jellicoe would not have been ignorant of what had happened in our own navy if there had been less secrecy. I may add that he would not have written as in the above quotation as though "the German documents which came into our possession early in the war" conveyed some new information. It only proves that before the war he had not studied contemporary German tactical thought and practice. I now propose to show that he had not sufficiently applied his mind to our own practice. He says:

> It was not, I believe, until the year 1911, during what were then known as the P Z exercises, that destroyer attacks were actually carried out in the British Navy on a large scale.

This is an instance of how little one can depend on Lord Jellicoe's memory. There was another when, in a speech on February 9, 1918, he said that Lord Fisher sent a memorandum to the Admiralty, in 1911, on the use of German submarines against our commerce. Lord Jellicoe later wrote to the *Morning Post* altering the year to 1912, and on investigation, the Admiralty found it to be 1914. In regard to the P Z exercises they were undertaken with destroyers in the fleet under

Sir William May in 1909-11. They were carried out in the Mediterranean fleet in 1900. They had been carried out in the German fleet as regular tactics before 1897.

To say that the "risk attendant on such exercises" had had anything to do with preventing the matter from being made "the subject of thorough practical experiment" is not an accurate statement nor is it complimentary to British seamanship to say that it could not do as much as German. No man doubts the superiority of British seamanship, and the omission was simply due to British carelessness and to the lack of tactical insight resulting from insufficient study. The responsibility lies with the Admiralty, which refused to listen to the warnings of those who saw what was coming, and which abused the confidence that the House of Commons extends to the navy.

The confidence of France in her army administration, in 1870, could only be shaken by defeat, and France inquired after the defeat instead of inquiring before into the warnings given by her military *attaché* in Berlin. Leboeuf boasted that the French Army was ready to the last gaiter button, and Mr. Churchill used similar language about the navy. Leboeuf may have spoken truly in a general sense in regard to material, but the French Army was distinctly unready in its mental preparation, and the result was a surprise to Parliament and People, because it had been kept secret from them.

It is impossible to read the answers given by Mr. Walter Long in Parliament in 1919 without feeling the painful conviction that he was unwittingly becoming entangled in an attempt to prevent the public and the navy from learning important matters from the past events of this war. This is a matter of some interest to a public which was told by Mr. Walter Long, as a Cabinet Minister, in 1902, at the Bankers' Association dinner, that it must share the blame for the needless losses in the South African War, and that:

> If the government had made mistakes it was largely because the people of the country had failed to impress on governments what they ought to do.

It is difficult to see how the public is ever to find out what is wrong when those in high places are determined to defeat them in their zest for knowledge. How can the public be expected to learn anything from past Admiralty statements made up so largely of falsehoods? Take the following from the Admiralty statements of March 19 and March 22, 1915, about the Dardanelles bombardments and what are they worth?

The operations are continuing, ample naval and military forces being available on the spot.

The power of the fleet to dominate the fortresses by superiority of gunfire seems established.

Inflexible had her forward control position hit by a heavy shell and requires repair.

As a matter of fact, the battle-cruiser *Inflexible* was mined and narrowly escaped sinking. So far as the writer can recall, in no single case, where things went wrong, did the Admiralty contrive to tell the truth during the whole four and a half years of war. When they had a stroke of luck, they made the most of it, and an amusing instance is the case of the capture of the *Emden*. (*The Kaiser's Raider! Two Accounts of the S. M. S. Emden During the First World War by One of its Officers,* by Hellmuth von Mücke is also published by Leonaur.)The official announcement indicated that its capture was the result of combined operations which had been in progress for some time. Actually, the *Sydney* was employed on convoy work, and her meeting with the *Emden* was entirely accidental, as the published letters have since revealed.

The Labour leader, Mr. J. H. Thomas, has drawn attention to the evil effects which the secrecy and its accompaniments has had on the minds of working-men. It is not sufficiently realised that the effects were no less surely felt in the fighting services, which remained equally ignorant of events and the lessons to be drawn from them. To the men in power the mishaps and miscarriages were simply scandals to be hushed up. Divine Dora was devoutly to be thanked as a guardian angel whom Lancelot and Guinevere would have given their world to possess lest:

Some evil chance
Should make the smouldering scandal break and blaze
Before the people and our Lord the King.

Mr. Walter Long's persistence in the secrecy policy long after the naval war is over shows how hypocritical was the statement of Mr. Asquith on November 2, 1915, that:

The wish for the fullest information is natural and most legitimate, nor can there be possibly any greater mistake than to suppose that the government has any interest of any kind in concealing anything that is known to themselves, subject to the one overruling condition that its disclosure does not assist the enemy.

What disclosures can assist the enemy today? Why is it pretended that it is in the public interest to hold back the various orders and signals that passed when the *Goeben* escaped? The public interest lies in seeking out the causes of failure. It is only personal interests which are dictating secrecy.

The truth is bureaucratic government has established an unexampled secrecy in regard to the war which cannot be broken down except by half-pay and retired officers whom the regulations cannot touch when once the restrictions of Dora are removed. A free community is supposed to control its own defences, and it cannot do so if the channels of discussion are dammed, for its control will be without knowledge. A community which is not to inquire into its own government's conduct of war when that war is concluded is in no sense a free community. When to this knowledge is added the fact that it required a lawless revelation in almost every case to achieve lasting good, the effect on the public mind is likely to lead to evil results if the government does not reverse its policy. Take the shells controversy and the *Times* telegram; Sir Edward Carson's revelation about the true state of our divisions at the front; the Dardanelles and Mesopotamia revelations, and so on. In each case secrecy was defied in order to win the war, and yet we still act without realisation of the great truth that democracy and secrecy will not run in double harness.

The Admiralty have entrusted the task of preparing a description of the Battle of Jutland to a navigating officer, Captain Harper; but a description by a junior officer, as I pointed out in the Preface, is not a substitute for an inquiry. After the battle, it was obvious that a court-martial should have taken place. Mr. Balfour's most important advisers are believed to have been in favour of this course, and a caustic comment on Lord Jellicoe's tactics was said to have been drawn up by the admiral who would undoubtedly have been in command had the war broken out a few years earlier.

Whether Mr. Balfour dreaded another Buller controversy or feared for the prestige of the navy we do not know; but he decided in favour of a "hush-hush" policy, and circularised the Press, asking for an entire avoidance of all criticism of the commander-in-chief. This he was certain to secure, for so long as Lord Jellicoe was retained in his post, the strength of the country and of his fleet depended in a measure on keeping up Lord Jellicoe's prestige, and no responsible publicist would venture on criticism until this could be done without injury to the interests of the country at war. The fiction of a great victory had therefore to be kept up so long as Lord Jellicoe retained the command afloat. The Admiralty letter of approval of July 4, 1916, and the decorations for officers who never came under fire, must therefore be accepted as part of an elaborate make-believe which deceived nobody except the people of this country.

The people will ultimately resent this pretentious fooling which differed in scale only from the deceptions practised in connection with the loss of H.M.S. *Audacious*. There is no mystery about war at sea, though like all science and art it can be obscured by skilful elaboration. The people can without difficulty deduce from history why decisive victory is sought when one of those rare occasions comes offering the opportunity. They can easily understand why decisive victory is impossible in the misty North Sea if a fleet turns away from a destroyer attack for such a movement involves losing sight of the enemy fleet and throwing away our gunnery supremacy.

They know, therefore, that turning away in the North Sea must be ruled out as Beatty ruled it out when he succeeded to the command of the Grand Fleet. They can also see that the offensive onslaught of destroyers is just as feasible, if not more so, for the destroyers of a preponderant British Fleet as it is for the destroyers of a flying German force. Finally, the public is quite capable of framing the simple question to which it should be possible to give a short clear answer:

> If these things were foreseen in the Battle Orders, why then were they not acted on at Jutland?

CHAPTER 3

The Material and Historical Schools

THE MATERIAL SCHOOL

The constant insistence with which I lament the supremacy of the material school in the navy might lead to a hasty conclusion that, at least in the domain of material, our wants would have been duly met. That was why in the introduction I gave some instances to the contrary. There were other, reasons why we expected to have little to learn. We were the greatest industrial nation, and our technical naval schools were the centres of service talent, while the profession, above all things, prided itself on being "practical." But what a catalogue of deficiencies is revealed by Lord Jellicoe, who had directed the whole of the material, firstly in 1905-7 as Director of Ordnance and Torpedoes, secondly in 1908-10 as Controller of the Navy, and thirdly in 1912-14, as Second Sea Lord in his responsibility for the personnel to which he directed a strong material bias.

Our mine-layers were very slow converted cruisers, inadequate in number, equipment, and sea-going qualities for this work; our mines were entirely unsatisfactory; the elevation of our guns was inadequate; our shell and fuses were bad; our battle-cruisers' magazines were insufficiently protected, for the flash of a shellfire could go down by the ammunition hoist right into the magazine, and hence we lost the *Queen Mary, Indefatigable* and *Invincible* at the Battle of Jutland; our ships were built to fit the docks, and not the docks to fit the ships, and consequently alterations of design both in battleships and battle-cruisers in order to obtain more protection after Jutland resulted in a loss of speed; range-finders had to be fitted for the main armament of many battleships, while those already fitted were too small; and it was found necessary to transfer 6-inch guns in certain ships to the upper deck because they could not be fought on the main-deck except in a flat calm, while in our latest battleships 6-inch guns were removed from the after section of the ships because they had been given areas of training which were quite useless in battle.

Other instances have been revealed in the House of Commons, such as the utterly unseaworthy and slow motorboats ordered early in the war. It is a characteristic sneer of the material school to say that criticism is wisdom after the event. All these things could have been guarded against by clear thinking in terms of war and not of mere technique. Tactics were made subordinate to gunnery by the materialist, if indeed they were not kept separate since he does not understand co-ordination. More attention was devoted to obtaining records in hits than to firing under conditions which were likely to obtain in war, and Lord Jellicoe's influence had been powerful in maintaining this system when he occupied the position of Director of Ordnance.

It is the height of absurdity to suppose that if people had thought in terms of war, they would not have discovered that ships in a fleet could not fire their 6-inch guns on the main deck when steaming at the high speed which is naturally used in battle. Lord Fisher and his school strained after both guns and speed. Since the speed put the guns out of action, does not this show a lack of co-ordinated thought?

Take the mines. Our ships used to be lumbered up with harbour defence mines. In 1894 when I advocated blockade mines for the open sea, I urged the removal of these defence mines, as more dangerous to friend than to foe. It was only with the experience of the Russo-Japanese War that we removed them in a hurry, but we continued to neglect the blockade mines, which were wanted in their thousands and which we did not obtain until 1917-18. The mines in the earlier "Dover barrage" were so useless that there is a fairly authenticated case of a German submarine officer removing one of them to convert it into a punch bowl.

In 1906, I wrote in the Press:

> The pity of it is that the absorption of the Cabinet and Defence Committee in visionary schemes (I was referring to disarmament) tends to exclude the proper consideration of really important concrete questions such as the laying of mines on the high seas, neutral obligations, etc.

On the outbreak of war there was no technical authority to deal with mine developments which had to be even begun. The work was carried out under the official discouragement of a school which did not understand war. As a consequence, 2½ years after the outbreak of war the British Navy was without the weapon which did so much to break the moral of the German Fleet in 1918.

Let me take one episode of Admiralty policy, because it is typical of others, and because it illustrates the inefficiency of public criticism when the blunders are first perpetrated. On November 5, 1914, Lord Jellicoe records how the battle-cruisers *Invincible* and *Inflexible* were taken from his fleet, so that at times there were only three battle-cruisers available. They were very rightly sent to search for von Spee, but few people stop to think why we had to run this risk three months after war broke out. In 1912 we were under agreement with our dominions to station three battle-cruisers in the Pacific.

On July 22, 1912, Mr. Churchill boasted in the House of Commons of his breach of the agreement by bringing the *New Zealand* and *Indomitable* into the home force instead of having them in the Pacific, where, as events turned out, they would very early in the war have accounted for the *Gneisenau* and *Scharnhorst* and saved us from the Coronel disaster. He said: "I should like also on this point to tell the House that we have since I have been responsible for the Admiralty practically added two battle-cruisers to our available resources," that is, for home waters. He meant that he had saved two battle-cruisers on the building programme. The matter was referred to at the time in the Australian Premier's telegram as "unpractical and unstatesmanlike," and it was denounced in the leading New Zealand paper as "the dishonourable pledge-breaking of the Asquith Government." It was a blunder as well as a crime, and it is a little trying to ordinary students, who do not forget it, to find the same First Lord hailing the rectification of this blunder as a master stroke of strategy three months after the war broke out!

Another aspect of policy is the manner in which the airship was dealt with. Airships were built, but met with mishaps, as pioneer attempts were apt to do, and construction was stopped and abandoned. Mr. Churchill takes personal responsibility, but that is an absurdity, unless he regarded his advisers as foolish men. On what advice and on whose advice did he act? Lord Jellicoe, who was a member of the Board which gave up constructing airships, says:

> The German Zeppelins, as their numbers increased, were of great assistance to the enemy for scouting, each one being, in favourable weather, equal to at least two light cruisers for such a purpose.

Lord Jellicoe says that in 1913 he had the Naval Air Service under his supervision. He says that views were then put forward "with emphasis how great would be the value of such vessels for reconnaissance duty in connection with fleet movements"; and that, as regard aeroplanes, "there was no likelihood of their having the radius of action necessary for scouting work in a fleet for some years, whereas the Zeppelin already possessed it." Apparently, these views were put forward by Lord Jellicoe himself, and yet the officer designated for the Grand Fleet was not strong enough to see the thing through. Clearly there is room for inquiry into the way these things were done.

As a matter of fact, Zeppelins would have been of far more use to us than to the Germans, since we had command of the sea and could protect them. Mr. Churchill in his apologia on this matter said we should have had to build so many to rival the Germans, which was not the case, for two Zeppelins in association with naval forces would have been a match in any circumstances for three times that number with an inferior naval force. The case is similar to what obtains in an army where all mechanical contrivances, such as tanks and air planes, depend in battle for their effective use on this close association with other arms. One may possess a less numerous equipment in a certain direction, and yet be able to use it more effectively because of a better foundation or backing.

The main function of all the satellites of a fleet, whether they are mobile like air craft, torpedo craft, cruisers or battle-cruisers, or associated with immobile weapons like mines and booms, is to enable the battle fleet to do its work while hampering and injuring the enemy battle fleet to the best of their ability.

Clear resolute staff work would have led to the conclusion that if airships were decided to be an essential arm of the navy then it was necessary to build them, mishaps notwithstanding. If, on the other hand, they were not an essential arm, it was wrong to build them at all. The half-way measure of starting to build two and then abandoning trials because of accidents was neither one thing nor the other. We are now getting the Zeppelins after the war is over.

The truth is we owe our troubles to the mentality of the naval officer and the educational system on which it is based. First, as we saw in the earlier chapters, is the influence of national characteristics. Next comes the narrow environment of ship life. As far as the navy is concerned, these are more or less fixed. There remains the educational system which, unfortunately, by syllabus and examinations, did everything to foster a mechanical outlook in which the conduct of war was relegated to the background. Not only have we failed to learn the lesson, but the system is being intensified, and there is marked hostility to the direct entry of public-school boys, a system which gave very good results although worked under most hampering conditions. It is not a little significant that the three officers,

Sir David Beatty, Sir Roger Keyes and Sir Reginald Tyrwhitt, who were the survival of the fittest, in the sense that they ultimately had the complete charge of our home forces, passed indifferent examinations. Out of a possible fifteen first-class certificates they mustered only one between them, and among their certificates were a great many third-class. To obtain five first-class certificates, though it means early promotion, involves the clever young officer too frequently in mental servitude to the materialistic aspects of his profession when he becomes a specialist gunnery or torpedo officer.

Sir David Beatty not only escaped this, but by his early promotion for land service was prevented from being unduly cramped by absorption in the details of administrative work, which, important as it is, leaves little or no time and opportunity for higher studies. The system was the direct result of there being no War Staff in control of the training of the navy. It was regulated in accordance with no principles of war, but by two traditions, *viz.*, that an officer must become a practical man, and in order to achieve this object he must go to sea when young. The change from manual to machine labour came much more suddenly in the navy than in civil life, and practical ability was associated to an absurd extent with machinery, although the environment of mechanical work is unfavourable to general education, breadth of view and the psychological insight which has much to do with success in war.

And yet, owing to their inability to think clearly and follow Dr. Johnson's dictum to survey the whole before considering the parts, the materialist, who had full charge of the Admiralty, failed in foresight at almost every point. Naval war, for instance, consists in movement and interference with movements. They failed to anticipate the German withdrawing tactics and the uses of zigzagging. In interference with movements they failed to anticipate smoke tactics, and the uses of mines and submarines. All movement involves rest and replenishment in secure harbours with docks. They failed to provide any on the East coast.

In 1894, in a paper which was suppressed by the Admiralty, I had advocated mining an enemy in with extensive minefields. We entered on this war with no sea mines worthy of the name, and did not get them until 1917. The Americans laid in the northern minefield no less than 5,000 mines in four hours, showing the rapidity with which, we might have acted on the outbreak of war. The reason why the Germans so often chose the right material equipment while we did not was because they went to work in a scientific way. They studied war and its probabilities and exalted it far above mere mechanical knowledge.

Hence, they designed their Dreadnoughts exclusively for war, whereas Lord Jellicoe relates that we built them to suit our docks. Even their chosen moment for going to war was conditioned by the date the Kiel Canal was suited to the Dreadnoughts. They gave their guns the requisite elevation of 30°. Our own elevation, as Admiral Sir Percy Scott relates, was 13½°; in 1907 we increased to 15°; in 1911 to 20°; and a year after the war we decided to increase to 30°. In commenting on this fact, Sir Percy Scott says he drew the attention of the Admiralty, in 1905, after his visit to Kiel, to the fact that the Germans were giving 30° elevation to their guns.

Having realised by the study of war problems that destroyers would attack with torpedoes, the Germans gave 50 *per cent*, more torpedoes and more torpedo tubes for firing from to these vessels than we did.

We altered *after Jutland*. The same study convinced them that to fight at long range they would have to use directors with the very best optical instruments. When Jutland was fought, Sir Percy Scott relates that only six ships of the British Fleet were completely fitted with director firing for all their guns; several battleships were without any director firing; and not a single cruiser was so fitted. Lord Jellicoe says of the German High Seas Fleet at Jutland:

It also appeared that some system of director firing was fitted to the guns of their secondary armament.

The use of the word "appeared" in reference to the 6-inch gun batteries, is somewhat remarkable, for the fact was well known before the war! The real discovery was that we were wrong in failing to reason out the necessity for director firing in order to obtain increased offensive fire. One is reminded of another of Lord Jellicoe's discoveries *after Jutland* which had already been revealed in the various handbooks, including the German, from published records of trial trips. He says of the four *Königs* which led the German Battle Fleet:

On return to Scapa I received a report from the Admiralty which credited the enemy squadron with a speed of 23 knots for a short period, this being the first intimation I had received of such a speed being attainable by them.

He says it was "an unpleasant surprise," as "the information furnished to me at this time gave the designed speed of the fastest German battleships as 20.5 knots only." It is difficult to deal patiently with a statement of this character, in view of the trial trips not only of the four *Königs*, but of the five *Kaisers* of earlier date as well.

Returning to the range-finder question, those who went to see the exhibition at the Central Hall of our scientific products will remember the 30-ft. rangefinder. At 20,000 yards, in clear weather, it had an uncertainty of observation of less than 80 yards. It was proposed by the makers in 1908, and constructed in 1913 for a foreign nation, but not until 1917 was a range-finder of this length supplied to the Grand Fleet. Lord Jellicoe speaks of:

The ineffective range-finders of nine feet length having been installed in the fleet before the great increases in the range of opening effective fire had come about, as the result of experience during the war.

Why, then, did the Germans give 30° elevation to their guns unless they had anticipated this great increase? Our 9-foot range-finder was decided on in 1904 when the range was 6,000 yards, and Lord Jellicoe relates that "pre-war days' battle practice had been carried out at a maximum range of about 9,500 yards." It was not based on study, but on mere slavish materialism of what could be done with the 1904 range-finder and what our materialists taught. In the war the range jumped in a clear atmosphere to 23,000 yards, and Lord Jellicoe mentions 24,000 yards at the Battle of Jutland, though I am unable to trace the occasion. All these things, it should be remembered, were happening while the navy occupied the position of a predominant partner for whom the House of Commons would do almost anything, whereas in Germany it was second to the army.

There is much slipshod statement about unforeseen needs in regard to material, as though the idea was new, rather than that there had been failure of the admirals to see the need of such equipment. Thus, Lord Jellicoe states that:

> There is no doubt at all that the German organisation for night action was of a remarkably high standard. In the first place, the use of star shells, *at that time unfamiliar to us*, was of the greatest service to them in locating our destroyers without revealing their own positions.

It is sufficient answer to say that, if the utility had been perceived, as it should have been, the admiral had only to apply to the army to lend a small supply. The enemy searchlights were "much more powerful." Yet we had over thirty years of naval manoeuvre practice behind to tell us that with the increased power and range of torpedo attack the greatest achievable range of the searchlight was necessary so as to bring the destroyers under fire at the earliest possible moment.

The losses at the Battle of Jutland of the *Queen Mary*, *Indefatigable* and *Invincible* are rightly attributed by Lord Jellicoe to inferior designs as compared with the German battle-cruisers. Our own designs of the *Indefatigable* were stolen while the ship was building in 1908 and there never has been any doubt as to where they found a market. It is characteristic of our secrecy policy that Lord Jellicoe was precluded at the time from giving the reason for the sudden sinking of these ships, namely, that they "were very inadequately protected by armour as compared with the German vessels of the battle-cruiser type." The conference at the Admiralty held it to be undesirable "to draw attention to this publicly while the war was in progress."

As the design of the improved *Invincible* was in German hands, the undesirable feature of publication really was that an Admiralty, which had repeatedly boasted that our designs were far ahead of those of Germany, that we built quicker and could always therefore counter with a better design, had been weighed in the balance by the stern test of war and found wanting. The defects were quickly remedied after the battle had taught us what an efficient war staff or public discussion would have revealed long before. The Admiralty not only held our ships to be far superior, but systematically inspired writers in the Press previous to the war, so that depreciation of the German ships was the order of the day, and any officer who expressed a contrary opinion would have injured his professional prospects. Whenever we argued that our margin in numbers was inadequate, the stock official argument was to point to the individual superiority of our ships. Now Lord Jellicoe tells us quite a different tale, that:

> War experience has since shown that we were justified in assuming that the German naval designers and constructors were not inferior in ability to our own; it was obvious that, taking ships of equal displacement and equal speed, and about contemporary date, if our vessels possessed superiority in gunfire, the Germans must possess superiority in some other direction. It was well known at the Admiralty that their superiority lay in the greatly increased protection, combined with heavier torpedo armament.

Since the one object of the building of our Dreadnought fleet was to defeat the German High Sea Fleet it is strange indeed that the defects should have been "well known" and yet not remedied.

Indeed, we proceeded during the war, prior to the Battle of Jutland, to build battle-cruisers in which the armour defects were still more marked than in the battle-cruisers which sank as the result of gun fire at the Battle of Jutland. The *Repulse* and *Renown*, designed during the war under Lord Fisher, which were completed in the autumn of 1916, had to be sent back to the dockyard for more deck protection, and Lord Jellicoe records that:

> Although the ships were much improved by the alteration, they were still far inferior in protection to the German battle-cruisers.

Now that the war is over there is a proposal to increase their side armour at great cost. Lord Jellicoe does well now to emphasise these defects, for not only did the *Indefatigable, Queen Mary* and *Invincible* blow up through enemy's shell penetrating their magazines, but it is now known that Sir David Beatty's flagship narrowly escaped a similar disaster. The need of armour protection for the vitals was taught by every fight since the *Monitor* and *Merrimac*, and in recent years, the Russian *Rurik* of 11,000 tons was sunk by two vessels the tonnage of which aggregated 7,350 tons, simply because she was unarmoured and they were fairly protected.

Had Jutland been fought in the early part of the war before we got experience in the Dardanelles and battle-cruiser fights, only ten ships in the whole fleet would have had director firing for any guns. And yet Mr. Churchill told the House of Commons that the navy was ready in every detail. He was advised by men for whom material filled the vision, while strategy and tactics were beneath the horizon. They knew how to make the tools of war, and they appeared to know how to handle them as specialists; but they were certainly deficient in the mental processes which make for perfection in the art of handling all the tools in combination with each other.

In 1908 I exposed the fact in the House of Commons that they had actually deprived the Channel Fleet, which was the nucleus of the Grand Fleet, of all destroyers, though a tyro in tactics could have told them that a fleet must practise together in order, to use a popular term, to get the best team work.

I have endeavoured to show elsewhere that all the evils flow from a lack of the historical sense, owing to history being to the majority of sailors like the neglected wreckage at the bottom of the sea. All great leaders have studied the history of war and learned its principles, and the most hateful heresy and cause of offence to them was to subordinate the man to the machine. These ideas were formulated by Moltke in an army order in 1888 at the close of his career:—

> The lectures on military history offer the most effective means of teaching war during peace, and of awakening a genuine interest in the study of important campaigns. These lectures should bring into relief the unchangeable fundamental conditions of good generalship in their relations to changeable tactical forms, and should place in a true light the influence of eminent characters upon the course of events and the weight of moral forces in contrast to that of mere material instruments.

While the mind was absorbed in material it could not but be impressed with the magnitude of the difference between the guns, the hulls, the methods of communication and the motive power of Nelson's ships and those of the Grand Fleet, and was tempted, or one might say forced, to reject the history of the past as having no bearings on the present or the future. The same thought must have passed through the minds of many of those on the banks of the Thames as they witnessed the Thames Pageant in 1919 and the barge carrying the 18-inch gun and Nelson's little gun underneath.

The development of aircraft, the submarines and the torpedo seemed even more to complete the discomfiture of the historical, or as it was called in derision, the theoretical school. Yet the principles of war are as unchanging as the laws of motion, and it is only their application that varies with the development of the material. That was why Napoleon advised soldiers to study the campaigns of the greatest of Greek, Roman and Carthaginian generals who fought before gunpowder was invented.

In the practice of a profession such as the navy, a man needs to be a student all his days if he is to get out of the ordered grooves of that profession. The navy was unable to break itself of the habit of fighting line against line and ship against ship for many years, though a little study of the Anglo-Dutch wars would have taught the navy differently. This study gave the idea to the Scottish Merchant Clerk of Eldin, who preached the manoeuvre of breaking the line in 1782. It is not within the scope of a work of this character to prove over again certain well-defined lessons from history. So, let us lay it down as an axiom that the essence of tactics is offensive action. Everything is concentrated and consecrated to the purpose of victory.

Thus, in our wars with France, in the days of the sailing ships, we chose the weather gage while the French as deliberately chose the lee gage. It enabled us to force an action while the French argued that the lee gage gave defensive advantages through the damage inflicted while the attacking ships were unable to fire their broadsides as they bore down. The writer pointed out in 1913 that the Germans might be expected to take similar advantage with their torpedoes in that a fleet evading action can fire torpedoes at a much higher range than one chasing; for in the first case the target has to be overtaken and in the other the target goes to meet the torpedo. Just as Rodney found the remedy for the French withdrawing tactics of the day by concentrating on a portion of the enemy's line, so the writer ventured to indicate that there was a tactical remedy available through the use of aeroplanes carrying torpedoes, and by their high speed of four or five times that of the enemy's ships, getting into position in advance of the enemy, swooping down to the water, firing their torpedoes into his fleet.

It is due to this want of study that when a change of weapons takes place, it is not seen until long afterwards how it has modified tactics. Its value again is not seen in mass tactics. The surprise is one of the great factors in tactics, and the surprise often consists in the mass use of a new weapon, as we saw with the German siege trains, the British tanks in the war and in the devilish cunning with which the Germans sprang poison gas on us. The invention had to overcome the inertia of a very conservative class, and so it comes about that it is tried on the enemy on a small scale and ceases to be a surprise.

Let us cite a few cases. Captain Holbrook's idea of taking a submarine through a minefield was used on December 13, 1914, or two months before the bombardments, to torpedo a thirty year old Turkish battleship which mattered as little on the surface as it did at the bottom of the sea. The skimming motorboat with its torpedoes was used to torpedo a German destroyer off Zeebrugge after its originator had asked in vain to take his little squadron with, say sixteen men, to torpedo the German fleet at anchor. Prior to the great attack on the ships at Cronstadt the Bolshevist cruiser *Oleg* was torpedoed in the same way, but the method had ceased to be a surprise and the great war was over.

These successful attacks were made long after the boats had ceased to gain any immunity from the fact that their existence was unknown to the enemy; and their success in these circumstances completely justifies the proposal of those who handled them that they should be first used in attacking the German fleet at anchor. The first long-distance bombing air-plane was used as a single unit against Constantinople, and the newly-developed torpedo-carrying sea-plane was also used as a single unit to torpedo a Turkish transport in the Black Sea.

It was the same childish material conception of war, unbalanced by any study, which induced us, two days after the war broke out with Turkey, to give warning to the whole Dardanelles that we were coming, by a perfectly useless bombardment of the outer forts, months before the major operations. It is this sort of futility that the material school loves, and a wider survey and study, in which material is relegated to its proper place, is the only cure. We shall then enlist materialism on an even greater scale in the achievement of victory, but as something to be used by its master and not something to be bowed down to and worshipped.

CHAPTER 4

Tactical Thought—Jellicoe Period

The sea differs from the land in being all road except where the configuration of the land or shallow water interposes as a barrier. One result of this is that an advantage in speed gives the choice of range except where the narrowness of the waters prevents the range from being opened up. At night, or in the mists which are so frequent in the North Sea, this ability to open the range may be of no use except to run away, and its sole offensive value is to concentrate on a position of the enemy line or to close the range. To restrict the fighting area, mines can be used supplemented by submarines.

Thus, there was nothing to prevent the entry of our fleet into the Heligoland Bight through swept channels, but the manoeuvre room obtained would be so small as to make it difficult to fight a successful fleet action since our line would be about seven miles long with flanking cruisers and destroyers.

It was a favourite device of the Germans to attack our coasts, and to flank their line of approach with submarines and minefields, so that forces from the north and south would run into these traps. The paravane was invented to deal with the mines and sweep them clear, and the submarines were held at bay until the fighting formation was taken up, by screens of destroyers.

The difference between the plan by which the Germans intended to raid the trade route to Norway when they came out and were forced to fight at Jutland Bank, and the plan against which the High Seas Fleet mutinied in November, 1918, by which the estuary of the Thames was to be raided, was that for the former it was impossible to place with any degree of certainty a line of submarine boats at close range to the track of the Grand Fleet in an area where the destroyers screen was likely to have been withdrawn. In the latter case, at the narrow end of the North Sea between the Heligoland minefield and our coast, the chances were decidedly better of flanking the route home to "the wet triangle" behind Heligoland, but it is absurd to say, as von Scheer does, that "our plan was carefully worked out and offered *the certainty of success* if the Grand Fleet came out."

The one chance of failure we foresaw was that the British fleet

GERMAN HIGH SEAS FLEET PASSING HELIGOLAND

might not be coaxed out by our Channel attack. The details of the plan are not given, but probably involved a line of the entire submarine boats of Germany along which the British fleet would be led in battle. Such a plan had nothing in the nature of surprise. The Grand Fleet in 1918 was very different in its organisation for battle from the one which entered Jutland without knowledge as to the position of its own ships, and of the enemy, and which found itself, in the early hours of June 1, bereft of cruisers and destroyers. It had become like a fast trailing spider's web in the delicacy of the great combination when the brain in control felt what was trembling on the utmost thread when an enemy vainly tries to avoid the toils. The organisation was the outcome of study.

The submarine derived its terrors from the fact that its potentialities had not been studied and provided against. Under the stress of war, the fleet had been our chief care, and the submarine, though still a terror of the merchant ship, was no longer feared by the fleet. The Germans through lack of the offensive spirit had missed their opportunity at the beginning of the war. What would have been a rude surprise to the Germans, had it not been for the gross error by which we revealed the idea in the small scale operation of sinking a Turkish transport in the Black Sea, was our new counter to the withdrawing tactics.

At the beginning of 1913, in an article based on the fact that the Germans were likely to practise withdrawing tactics, the writer advocated the use on a large scale of aircraft carrying torpedoes to fire from a position on the bow of a retreating enemy. The idea was practicable, for torpedo-carrying aircraft had been proved feasible before the war in 1913 if not in 1912. The Germans would have suffered heavily from these attacks if they had carried out their projected Thames raid as, by 1918, the idea had been developed on a moderate scale.

Von Scheer, of course, accepts the doctrine, which has the support not merely of students but also of Beatty, that the submarine menace depended absolutely on the High Seas Fleet. It is true that the High Seas Fleet depended for its security on the fortifications and the minefields, but the former could have been rendered of no avail, and the latter swept away, but for the existence of the fleet. The Elbe Channel itself is a narrow channel, liable to be blocked by concrete ships out of effective reach of the fortifications, and the submarine could have been jammed in by protected minefields if no High Seas Fleet existed. As von Scheer says:

The fleet was essential to protect the base for our submarine warfare.

He might have added that it enabled many soldiers to be relieved from the defence of the coasts.

From these considerations we see that the opportunities of battle afforded to the Grand Fleet were likely to be few and far between. Indeed, Jutland was an unexpected opportunity, resulting in all probability from the new commander-in-chief wishing to pull off some small success, and a visit the *Kaiser* paid to Wilhelmshaven a few days before the battle. German officers say it was the outcome of a plan for raiding our Norwegian trade. The idea was to give the attacking battle-cruisers and cruisers a secure base against our Battle-Cruiser Squadron by advancing the High Seas Fleet well to the north of the Horn Reef. This then was the event by which the new commander-in-chief of the High Seas Fleet, von Scheer, hoped to leap at a bound into fame. The sinking of the *Indefatigable* and *Queen Mary* tempted him too far.

The last thing in the world which the High Seas Fleet wished or expected was to encounter our Grand Fleet, though they fully expected to meet Beatty's Battle-Cruiser Squadron. So as to avoid giving a warning in advance no exceptional arrangements were made as to submarines, and only the regular destroyer flotillas, seven in number, or seventy-seven destroyers were used. They had underrated the efficiency of our intelligence work in affording early information that a raid was contemplated, though we do not appear to have anticipated it was on so big a scale.

From the fact, then, that the opportunity was not likely to occur again, there arose the simple and obvious necessity to fight a decisive battle when it was given. The whole critical period of the Battle of Jutland lasted a few hours, and a single hour of determined fighting on the part of the battleships in Lord Jellicoe's line would have settled the whole business of the sea war. The only other chance was to intercept the High Seas Fleet on its return off the Horn Reef Lightvessel on the morning of June 1.

Here, then, is the remarkable contrast to the great land battle which the Germans commenced on March 21, 1918, furiously flaring up and then dying down like a fire with its embers still hotly burning, and then flaming up again until the final collapse in the middle of November. In the one case it is quite possible to fire away the whole of the heavy gun ammunition of a battleship in an hour, or in two hours allowing for intervals of smoke concealing the target, while an army gets its continuous supply holding on to its targets all the time, until it is compelled to halt by outrunning its transport arrangements.

On the other hand, while it is altogether undesirable to have a halt in a battle on land, it is a matter of physical necessity both from the point of view of personnel and material. There is no such necessity in a naval battle which must be waged as violently, vigorously and vindictively as possible.

One should never lose sight of the fact that there have been periods in the history of the British Navy when tactical confidence was at so low an ebb that drastic measures had to be taken. We all know that there were fine seamen in the days of the Commonwealth, but the soldiers Blake and Monk had to be sent to take charge of the fleet because the seamen were not informed in the art of war. Equally strong measures in the way of courts-martial had to be taken after the Battle of Toulon in 1744, when eleven out of twenty-nine captains had charges preferred against them. We should not forget the period when it was almost impossible to get an admiral who would risk taking the command of the fleet, though one flag officer, who refused to command, agreed to accept the position of second in command.

This occurred in May, 1780, when the government had the greatest difficulty on the death of Sir Charles Hardy to find an admiral who would accept the command of the Channel Fleet, and the Annual Register for 1781 says:

> To remove this difficulty Admiral Graves, an experienced officer, but who, like his predecessor, had for many years retired from actual service, was prevailed on to abandon his retreat. . . .
> . . . . Upon the return of the fleet to Portsmouth (August, 1781) Admiral Graves chose to resign the command. The former difficulty again recurred.

Admiral Graves was a failure as can be seen from the criticisms in *Mahan's Influence of Sea Power upon History*, and as might indeed have been anticipated in the circumstances. The second in command, Admiral Barrington, refused the command, and Admiral Darby was prevailed on to accept it. Admiral Barrington, who was his senior, agreed to serve as his second in command.

The demands of tactics are far more exacting today than in 1780, and it is astonishing that the Admiralty never recognises any line of demarcation between the strategist, the tactician and the administrator. There is even now a school in the navy which still believes that decisive victory is not the object of a British fleet, but that if it maintains itself without undue losses and cuts the enemy's communications by sea, it has achieved all that can be demanded; and that the material fact of the Battle of Jutland is not that the enemy escaped after inflicting on us greater losses than he suffered, but that we continued to cut him off from the ocean. Such a preconceived notion would lead inevitably to defensive conceptions of tactics, to waiting on the enemy and therefore to an absence of initiative, and to many other evils.

The advocates of this theory neglect not merely the positive advantages which would have accrued to us from a decisive victory, but they forget that the enemy had complete command of the Baltic, so cutting off Russia from allied assistance, and enabling him to obtain iron ore and other supplies from Sweden.

As to how far we had thought out our problems can be roughly tested by the additions we made to our existing instructions concerning tactics *after* war had broken out. It is a valuable test of tactical thought for we have been told that the fleet had been prepared since 1904 for the war with Germany. For over three years the fleet had been under the command of Admiral Sir George Callaghan, an officer who had, as Lord Jellicoe relates, "A unique period of sea service passing from one appointment to another without interval of half pay" for a period of about fourteen years. This being so, it is pertinent to ask whether it can be positively affirmed that all the officers in command, whether of battleships, battle-cruisers, cruisers, destroyers or submarines, knew clearly what their functions in battle were to be? Was there, in fact, any existing doctrine of tactics which was understood by every officer as thoroughly as Nelson's captains understood his intentions and their functions at Trafalgar?

If this is so, then the changes which would have to be made after war had broken out would only represent the advance in thought which might reasonably be expected as time elapsed. Unfortunately, it was not so. Extensive memoranda were issued; it was found necessary to define the functions of every class of vessel, and to change the functions of some; vast additions to the signals were made; methods of battle were introduced for the first time by us, such as minelaying in action and the use of flying craft; all tending to the conclusion that our tactical preparation was, like our strategical and administrative work, very inadequate.

It is not necessary to prove these points, because the admissions are made in *The Grand Fleet 1914-16* by Lord Jellicoe. When Lord Jellicoe tells us that "war experiences" led to drawing up of diagrams of cruising formations, it is necessary to say that at the time of which he writes the fleet had never been in the presence of the enemy, and that it was not war experience, but the stimulus of danger which led to work being done during war which ought to have been done during peace. Neither submarine screens of destroyers to prevent submarines getting at the larger ships, nor zigzagging alterations of courses to confuse submarines had been thought of until the war had been in progress some time. Both were very elementary ideas which could hardly have escaped adoption under any adequate staff system during peace. Let us take zigzagging.

> *Early in the war* the danger of successful submarine attack on warships at sea whether in company or proceeding singly, *had impressed on us the necessity of taking every precaution for safety*, and the practice of the fleet steering zigzag courses was devised and generally adopted in accordance with my directions.... Much theoretical investigation was *instituted* to determine the method of zigzagging, both in a fleet and in a single ship, which gave the greatest protection against submarine attack, and actual experiments took place with our own submarines with a view to forming correct conclusions.

It is difficult, no doubt, for the reader to visualise that all this voyage of discovery concerning submarines,—vessels we had possessed since 1905,—was deferred until the somewhat inconvenient period of war 1914-15, but it is so. To a great extent the fault lay with the Admiralty in separating the submarine service from the general sea service, so fostering a contempt born of ignorance. We have already seen that this ignorance led to a failure to protect our bases. We now see that it led to an even worse failure on the part of the fleet to protect itself, and our Dreadnoughts owe their immunity to the strange inaction of the U-boats up to the sinking of the *Cressy, Hogue* and *Aboukir*, rather than to our own tactical skill.

According to Admiral Sir Percy Scott, even as late as November 24, 1914, *U 18* was rammed by accident off Scapa that morning and the Germans, not knowing the cause, concluded that Scapa was elaborately defended. However, this may be, if the problem had been tackled during peace the fleet would not have lacked destroyers during war.

One could fill a book with the questions which were asked, and the things that were said in the House of Commons from 1906 to 1914 concerning this need of destroyers, which Lord Jellicoe laments in connection with events both before and during the Battle of Jutland.

Among these events one of the most curious was the loss of the battleship *Formidable*. The *Formidable* and her consorts were going at slow speed without outlying destroyers. Inquiry will show whether the former admiral, Sir Cecil Burney, was shifted from his command because he insisted on being supplied with destroyer protection against submarines before proceeding to sea. Was the new admiral, Sir Lewis Bayly, warned as to the danger of submarines in the Channel?

The Admiralty issued a statement treating the loss of the ship as a trivial matter, and yet a few weeks later ships of this class were being employed in bombarding some of the strongest fortifications in the world at the Dardanelles. A much older ship, the *Canopus*, in every respect less efficient, was considered, when it suited the Admiralty's case, of high value in the circumstances attending the Battle of Coronel, and Admiral Cradock was blamed for not waiting for this reinforcement. There is much inconsistency in these views and they suggest instability of thought or wilful misrepresentation.

At the dinner of the National Defence Association on January 20, 1908, I pointed out in a survey of the future situation the alarming position in regard to destroyers and fast cruisers. I concluded by saying:—

> The upshot of our reduction policy is that we have exposed our armoured ships needlessly to torpedo attack. Our cruiser position is worse than the destroyer position. . . . You may lay it down as a golden rule that the absence of small craft involves the loss of big ones . . . the destroyers attack your fleets and probably sink some of your ships; but if you had a sufficient force of destroyers backed by cruisers this would not occur.

It should be added that the Admiralty in their "Statement of Admiralty Policy" in November, 1905, had sounded the death knell of the unarmoured cruiser. My answer was that they would have to build them. No such document as a statement of Admiralty policy would have been issued by a trained War Staff.

We escaped the worst consequences of the folly of the Boards to which Lord Jellicoe belonged because Admiral von Tirpitz lacked enterprise; but even so the *Pathfinder, Cressy, Hogue, Aboukir, Hawke* and

Formidable lie at the bottom of the sea as a consequence of the absence of a real War Staff to think and act before the war.

This lack of foresight was, as we have seen, responsible for the inadequacy of our torpedo flotillas. It was to be expected that enemy submarines would appear in the approaches to our bases, and that security for merchant ships using those ports could only be furnished by strong local flotillas. But the fleet flotilla was insufficient to furnish these patrols. Patrol flotillas of yachts and trawlers, manned by wholly untrained officers and men, had to be improvised in consequence. All suggestions that had been made in recent years for making use of our seafaring population along the coast had been invariably rejected. Proposals, reaching as far back as 1902, had been made for the employment of yachtsmen, fishermen and other small craft seamen in war; but all had met the same fate.

Yet every war in which we have engaged for two hundred years has shown that a very great number of small vessels was always required. Rejecting the teaching of history, and incapable of replacing its service by a vivid imagination, or a high level of tactical thought, we contented ourselves by providing a torpedo flotilla too small in itself and incapable of rapid expansion on an efficient basis of training and experience.

The results in actual practice can be seen in the doctrines of training governing the torpedo flotillas. While the Germans have persistently and steadily for more than twenty years pursued a policy of the offensive use of the torpedo, we have depended less and less on that weapon. For years the Germans, well-known to us, practised the manoeuvre of "*Durchbruch*," which means that destroyers break through their own line to make a smoke screen or to attack the enemy. The object of the manoeuvre is not only to hit the opposing ships, but to cause confusion and to force them to turn away from the torpedoes. Offensive tactics, when taught, have the merit of instilling confidence. Instead of instilling confidence in its powers in the officers of our torpedo flotillas, we instilled something which seems more akin to distrust, leading to neglect.

Anyone who took part in the torpedo prize firing of a few years ago will recollect that in one competition in which destroyers made single night attacks upon a ship, they were penalised for approaching too close, which they did for the purpose of ensuring a hit. If they fired within (so far as can be recollected) 1,200 yards, they could only obtain 60 *per cent*, for a hit, if within about 600 yards they received no marks at all. That is to say officers in destroyer flotillas were being taught that it was of higher importance to save their own skins than to sink the enemy. They were not being continually impressed with the sound truth that safety lies in boldness, and that at all costs they must sink the enemy. No! They must fire at long range and so secure themselves as far as possible against being hit by the enemy's guns, which they ought to have been taught to rate at their true value.

No student of war could ever have drawn up such regulations as were devised by the senior officers, and it is indeed satisfactory to find that in about fifteen or sixteen cases the destroyer captains during the night fighting at the Battle of Jutland claimed to have taken their boats inside the penalised limits.

An example of our tactical views before the war will be found in the prescribed employment of destroyers in battle. The destroyer was looked upon as a defensive unit in day battle, capable only of attacking the enemy at night. Hence, she was painted black, and it was laid down that her duty was to repel the attacks of enemy destroyers. Upon this principle destroyers were designed primarily as gun vessels; their torpedo armament was secondary. It was not until we had gained experience from the enemy tactics at the Battle of Jutland that it was realised by the highest command that the true function of all vessels is offensive, and that the destroyer is no exception to the established principles of war.

But this could have been found out before the war; and it argues a lack of acquaintance with those principles that a wrong formula should have been adopted. It is not that the matter had not been discussed; it had been, and decision had been given in the defensive sense. Beatty alone broke from this practice and, prior to the Battle of Jutland, had ordered his destroyers to attack if a favourable opportunity occurred.

At about the same time a curious doctrine was being taught in the flotillas—namely, that their principal duty off the enemy's coast was, not to attack the enemy's ships, but to report his movements. It was the duty of the battleships to sink the enemy's battleships, and if a destroyer were to attack an enemy's ship, the commander, was by no means sure that he would not be tried by court-martial. In 1901, when Lord Fisher was commander-in-chief in the Mediterranean, he appointed a committee consisting of Captain Prince Louis of Battenberg (afterwards First Sea Lord), Captain C. E. Madden (now Commander-in-Chief of the Atlantic Fleet), and Captain Charles J.

Briggs, a great torpedo expert, to consider the question of the use of destroyers. This committee reported:—

(1) Destroyers are primarily intended to destroy torpedo boats.

(2) To employ destroyers as torpedo boats for attack on ships should not be resorted to while anything remains to be done under (1) except under special conditions, *e.g.*, Gibraltar.

It was this defensive doctrine to which we adhered until after the Battle of Jutland. The strange dogma was preached even in the War College. With such ideas it is not surprising that the Admiralty never bothered about supplying the Mediterranean destroyer flotilla with coal, so that on the night of August 6, 1914, though they were to the eastward in an admirable position to torpedo the *Goeben* or the *Breslau*, they were unable to go to sea because they had no coal!

What, then, was the effect of this stream of thought up to and including the daylight stages of the Battle of Jutland? Two examples may be cited. In the Heligoland fight about forty-eight torpedoes were fired, at ranges sometimes of 5,000 yards at single light cruisers or at other destroyers! The torpedoes were simply thrown away. There is reason, moreover, to believe that more than one was fired simply to get rid of it for fear of its being struck by a shell and exploding in the boat. What officer who had confidence in his weapon would misuse it in this way? And what a comment this affords upon the teaching of sea-fighting which had been inculcated on the officers.

A second example of the same spirit was the refusal to allow the Harwich coastal motorboat flotilla to attack the German fleet at anchor with the skimming motorboats or "scooters." The officers had worked for this object and thought of nothing else for a couple of years. The answer they were given was that the German Fleet was doing no harm at anchor! At the time the proposals were made their attack would have come upon the Germans as an immense surprise. To men accustomed to think in terms of the offensive there was no question of their ability to win success and only a few lives would have been risked. Their proof lies in what has since occurred at Cronstadt, when a number of armoured ships have been sunk by the operations of these little craft, whose existence was revealed several years ago when a German destroyer was sunk off the Belgian coast.

Looking back on those years of war, the wonder is the absolute helplessness in face of so obvious a situation. The personnel was there, the material was there, the one thing lacking was the offensive spirit allied to the knowledge of war in the high places of Admiralty. The offensive had fallen into deep discredit because under Mr. Churchill it had been carried out without plan or method, so that when others came, who had plan and method and the offensive spirit, they found over them the dead hand of the man who had neither the one nor the other.

A third example was the early stages of the Hartlepool raid, when seven Grand Fleet destroyers passed down the line of the enemy's raiding squadron when ten miles ahead of our second battle squadron. The enemy consisted of a cruiser, three light cruisers and a force of destroyers. This was about 4 a.m., when the night was very dark. Out of the whole seven boats only one fired a torpedo—although they were at close range. The remainder opened fire with their little guns. Thus, a destroyer flotilla found itself in the position for which every officer should have prayed, and no use whatever was made of it. It appears that a torpedo attack was perfectly feasible and an opportunity was lost of teaching the Germans that the game of raiding our coasts was not worth the candle.

If the one officer who hauled out of line to fire his torpedo was held by high authority to have acted wrongly, it is a striking example of how the material school, through lack of a true historical perspective, adheres to mere precedent and the eighteenth-century tradition of the unbroken line. Inquiry should elicit why attack was not made with the torpedo and whether the officer who fired a torpedo was held to have been right or wrong. There is no finer fighting material in this world than the crews of our destroyer flotillas, and the whole episode can be traced to wrong conceptions of tactics through lack of proper study of war. Lord Jellicoe, in his account, suppresses all mention of the crux of the whole fight. He says they engaged the enemy, but neglects to mention that they failed to use what, in such a fight, taking place at night against a superior force at close range, was most certainly their primary weapon.

The skill, seamanship and endurance of the destroyer crews and their marvellous bravery at all times, of which no more remarkable display has been given in war than at the Battle of Jutland, would make the mention of this episode ungenerous if it were not part of the general proof that there was much to be desired, in the doctrine governing the war training of torpedo flotillas. It was the fault, not of the officers in command, but of a system which did not keep war singly in its eye. For one word about war in the destroyer manual there were about one hundred about peace. Leave regulations, clothes, exercises, discipline, gunnery practices, routine and other matters of internal organisation formed the bulk of the contents, but one might turn over its leaves from beginning to end without finding any clearly expressed views as to the employment of the vessels in war.

In all military organisations the training is treated as a function of the Staff. The end kept in view is fitness for war. A Naval War Staff was instituted in 1912 as a result of the Agadir crisis, but when it was brought into being no idea was entertained of the training of the personnel as being part of its duty. War was nowhere taught to the young officer. He picked up his knowledge at haphazard or not at all. He had no centre of discussion to make him think, for lectures and papers at the Royal United Service Institution, under the deep discouragement of the Admiralty, had become a dead letter. Some of the younger officers banded themselves together to found a confidential review for the discussion of war among themselves.

The dead hand of Admiralty nearly blighted it in 1919, because a writer discussing the escape of the *Goeben* and the Battle of Coronel ventured to quote signals that passed, and made some comments on the movements which were not to Whitehall's tastes. The popular idea held by many admirals was that all there is to be learned about war can be learned at sea. It was the precise answer which Lord Goschen gave to Sir Charles Dilke when I armed the latter with a question proposing a War College on shore some twenty years before the war.

The fact that study is needed to develop a habit of thought which leads to correct action was not understood by those who considered that an officer should give his whole attention to the narrow compass of his daily duties. The result was that war became largely guess-work, and singularly bad guess-work at times if we merely judge by such a fact as that the First Lord of the Admiralty was informed by his advisers in 1917 that one submarine could not torpedo another.

The Admiralty had to issue five reminders during the war of the importance of keeping plans secret. This inability to understand what is vitally secret, both in the Admiralty and afloat, arises through the term being brought into contempt owing to its habitual use when publicity would have been a clear gain. Officers were never taught what is essentially secret. Similarly, they were never instructed in the importance of clearness in reports and signals, and conciseness in instructions. Lord Jellicoe finds fault with his information several times in his description of the Battle of Jutland. Training in the writing of reports or drafting of intelligence formed no part of any naval officer's education, except for the small number who happened to go to the War College.

Again, and again in this war important instructions have been entrusted to, and vital information has been acquired and passed on, by quite junior officers in small craft. This was obviously inevitable, for the small craft are the outlying vessels which see the enemy first, and though in contact by connecting ships, are perhaps forty miles away from the commander-in-chief. Lord Jellicoe had twenty months in which to train his force. If his information was defective, there is no escape from the inference that his dispositions or his system of training were at fault.

The navy, as a consequence of the absence of a Training Division to the War Staff, had no manual corresponding with the Field Service Regulations of the Army. It had nothing to guide its ideas and it was furnished with no principles. It was therefore unprepared for war in most of its higher aspects. It resulted that the Cabinet and our Allies never had any clear guidance on naval affairs. There was guesswork, as when Mr. Balfour said in 1915 that the submarine danger was at an end, or when Mr. Lloyd George said it in 1918, or again when the Admiralty resisted the adoption of the convoy system which in the latter part of 1917 saved us from defeat. But guess work is not staff-work.

In many obvious tactical problems, it will be found that our foresight compared badly with that of the Germans. They developed obscuration or smoke tactics, whereas we did not even anticipate the probability of their use. They reasoned from the fact, repeatedly drawn attention to in the 1906-10 Parliament, that most days are misty in the North Sea. They argued that this necessitated approach within 15,000 yards; and therefore, the torpedo to a retreating fleet would become a potent weapon against a chasing fleet.

Anticipating these retreating tactics, the writer publicly advocated in 1913 an immense development of aircraft carrying Whitehead torpedoes which, covering 75 miles an hour on the horizontal in still air, would dive down at about 150 miles per hour on the bow of the retreating enemy and fire their torpedoes. Nothing was done because the life training of our admirals had not included any study of war, nor the history of war, but relied wholly on detail knowledge of material, experience and the tradition of precedents. In fact, the first complete realisation of the German withdrawing tactics appears to have come after the action on January 24, 1915, for Lord Jellicoe says that:

After the experience of the engagement on January 24, 1915 ..
... the conviction became stronger that in any action between
the two fleets, the enemy would fight a retiring battle. . . since
a retiring fleet is in a position of great tactical advantage in the
employment of these weapons (mines and torpedoes).—(*The
Grand Fleet.*)

CHAPTER 5

The Offensive

We have always had a naval controversy between the historical and
material schools at the outset of every war, and the latter, who are
most suited to administrative convenience, have usually been found
firmly entrenched, so that nothing but the most wounding crisis could
bring the historical school into a position of power to retrieve a bad
start. In this war, so far as the Admiralty was concerned, the exponents
of the historical school were brought only as far as a planning division
which submitted plans to the judgment of the First Sea Lord, and this
concession simply came about through the inability of the existing
staff to answer the questions of our new Allies, the Americans. The
navy suffered from no Unseen Hand, but from an Unseeing Brain.

How plausible was the argument of the material school under
Lord Howe when the French War broke out in 1793. You keep your
fleet in harbour in the pink of condition, with clean bottoms and
unworn spars and sails, and you do not have to divide your force by
sending ships in to refit, revictual, and replenish with water. Then the
American convoy got through and rescued France from famine, and
the French invading force was not intercepted on its way to Ireland.
So we got the wounding blows, and St. Vincent's school came into
power. At the very outset, the fleet was dispersed by a gale, and it was
hailed by the materialists as proof of the correctness of their views.
But there is only one test, and that is decisive victory, and it was St.
Vincent's policy that drove Napoleon to his doom.

All the arguments based on mere preservation of forces in 1793–
1802 were with Lord Howe's views, in favour of keeping the ships in
harbours in the best condition. The one demand of war inexorably
asking for contact with the enemy when he put to sea, was "impossible." The storms, the lee shore, the loss of ships refitting, and countless
other arguments were and could be urged against St. Vincent, and yet
because his was the supreme demand which victory made his policy

won against the defeatist policy of Lord Howe.

Examine Lord Jellicoe's actions as Commander-in-Chief and First Sea Lord, and it is easy to identify the school to which he belongs. Granted that highly-skilled forces must fight by daylight, then the time that remained to him at the Battle of Jutland, from 6.16 p.m. to 9.0 p.m., was all-important; but considerations of the preservation of his force made him throw away the surprise which is all-important in battle, made him turn away from and lose the enemy, made him dispose of his fleet so that he never regained contact the next morning, though his subordinate's masterly manoeuvres had given him the vantage position between the High Seas Fleet and their base.

Lord Jellicoe in his book searches for material details by which to weight the scales against his own force, and paints in heavy colours the risks of offensive actions. A man indeed of tearful yesterdays and fearful tomorrows! A man who never gets to grips with the broad salient fact that both on May 31 and June 1 he had at his disposal as targets a demoralised enemy utterly inferior in fighting power.

This overwhelming advantage, when great superiority is combined with the offensive, is shown by the brief spells when the Grand Fleet was ventured within offensive range of the enemy, and inflicted punishment on that enemy. Lord Jellicoe always boggles with the fact that in the whole action, from the moment he formed a line of battle with the twenty-seven ships in his line only the Colossus was hit. He speaks of the immunity of the ships of this or that squadron at this or that period. With the exception of that one shot which wounded four men, they were immune to gunfire all through the battle! Thus, we find Lord Jellicoe saying of Sir Cecil Burney's squadron (the rear ships):

> Both at this period, and earlier in the action, the ships of the First Battle Squadron were afforded more opportunities for effective fire than the rest of the battle fleet, and the fullest use was made of the opportunities.... The immunity of the ships of the squadron from the enemy's fire, whilst they were inflicting on his vessels very severe punishment, bears eloquent testimony to the offensive powers of the squadron.

One would have thought that if this immunity was obtained by the excellence of the gunnery of a portion of the British Fleet in the First Battle squadron then, on the principle that "the more you hurt the enemy the less he will hurt you," instead of allowing eleven destroyers to drive the whole line of twenty-seven battleships out of action the whole twenty-seven would have been pressed into the service to complete the "severe punishment" which was being inflicted by the First Battle Squadron. This would be done the more resolutely, for the destroyer attack had but one obvious object, a sort of forlorn hope that, combined with smoke tactics, it would enable the heavy 2 ships to escape from the guns of the British Fleet.

All the British ships were immune because not only was the visibility in our favour, but what is far more important, the enemy were still labouring under the panic of the Grand Fleet's unexpected entrance into battle. It is not necessary to argue that point now, for we have the evidence of German officers, since it has been no longer necessary for them to gasconade in order to make propaganda. For instance "A Member of the Inter-Allied Commission" in Germany contributed an article to the *Times*, January 14, 1919, in which he quoted a Zeppelin officer who was gunnery lieutenant of the *Deutschland* as saying to him:

> They (the men) are not fools about the things they can see, and the way we were utterly crushed from the moment your battlefleet came into action took the heart out of them. Another hour of daylight would have finished it.

As for the destroyers' attack which drove Lord Jellicoe's twenty-seven battleships out of action, the German gunnery officer said:—

> Torpedo attack in the daylight was almost hopeless, because the English destroyers averaged faster than ours, and I do not need to tell you that their guns were very much heavier.

Yet such is the psychological possibility of an offensive action, on a mind predisposed to defensive measures, that the forlorn hope was successful in relieving the German battle-line.

What the weather gage was to the sailing navy the advantage of speed is to the steam navy. To the weak it is an opportunity to escape, and to the strong to force the battle. At Jutland, owing to the presence of the German pre-Dreadnoughts, Lord Jellicoe had a 3-knots advantage in speed over his enemy and an even greater advantage if he had availed himself of his preponderance of strength in order to shed some of his slower battleships. To a flying enemy, to shed a ship is to lose a ship, as the Germans found with the *Blücher* at the Dogger Bank action; but to the pursuers it is merely a delayed reinforcement which by wireless can be directed to finish off the damaged ships of the enemy.

Lord Jellicoe elected not to use the extra speed because he wished to have it in hand to avoid the torpedoes. His conduct now as in all his measures on the afternoon and night of May 31 to the final loss of the enemy on the morning of June 1 was governed by defensive considerations. He deployed his fleet away from the enemy when he formed his line, partly because of the torpedoes and partly because of a supposed gunnery disadvantage. He thereby enabled the enemy to get over the first shock of surprise at his arrival. He then, at later stages, twice allowed his whole fleet, with the exception of Sir David Beatty's inferior battle-cruisers, to abandon the action, because of destroyer attacks.

From first to last he fought a defensive battle. And why? His actions have got to be sifted and explained. They are in the same class as the failures of Byng and Mathews, which resulted in courts-martial. They differ from Calder's battle in 1805, which achieved far better results in that Calder was able to plead to the court-martial which severely reprimanded him, that though his force was of inferior strength he had captured two enemy battleships. No such plea could be advanced by Lord Jellicoe. His force was overwhelmingly superior in gun-power. The alleged inferiority in destroyers has not been substantiated.

The inferiority of British shells in penetrating armour, for which Lord Jellicoe's administration at the Admiralty must bear a large share of responsibility, was only discovered weeks after the action as a result of investigation carried out on the insistence of Sir David Beatty. This drawback, therefore, had no influence on his mind on the day of battle, and he himself has stated that he was unaware of the loss of the British battle-cruisers until the day after the battle.

The true spirit of the offensive was shown in the little action of the *Broke* and the *Swift* with six enemy destroyers at another stage of the war. They rushed into close quarters and made the action two against two, for the four other destroyers could not risk firing at their own side. They accounted for their two opponents, and the remainder fled. That was a practical fulfilment of Cicero's demand for a threefold audacity: "Audacity, audacity, and always audacity," which centuries after was repeated by our own poet Spenser and by the French revolutionary Danton, to whom with Napoleon it is generally attributed.

It is impossible to discover any principle on which Lord Jellicoe acted except that of avoiding losses, one which leads to nothing but the evasion of action. His black destroyers proclaimed aloud their defensive role by day. Had they been intended to be used offensively they would have been painted grey like the ships. In his chapter of "Reflections on the Battle," Lord Jellicoe places in the forefront considerations of what would have happened if he had been beaten. Thus, Byng worried about what would happen to Gibraltar if he were beaten. Marshal Foch says in his *Principles of War:*

Defensive battle, never brings about the destruction of enemy forces.

And again:

The will to conquer: such is victory's first condition, and therefore every soldier's first duty; but it also amounts to a supreme resolve which the commander must, if needs be, impart to the soldier's soul.

Elsewhere Foch goes so far as to say that the commander who is thinking of what will happen if he is defeated is already overthrown. Byron's reference to the thunderbolt in the reluctant hand has a clearer application to a man fearful to use it, than to Napoleon, who was fearless in its use, because he had full knowledge of the measure of its power.

If one sits down to record all that the offensive does in the hands of a great leader, one would put it down succinctly somewhat as follows:—

(1) It is the only winning policy.

(2) The only method of enhancing the moral.

(3) The only way to start with the surprise.

(4) The only way to gain the initiative.

(5) The only way to save a long drain on one's resources by a wasting defence.

(6) The only way to get concentration of effort.

(7) The only way to enhance the prestige of one's country and one's profession.

The whole spirit of war is the offensive, for the more you hurt the enemy the less he will be able to hurt you. Experience may indeed be the best of schoolmasters, but the fees may be beyond our capacity to bear, and it is useless to go to school too late. Think, for instance, of the amount of experience we had to undergo before we blocked up Zeebrugge and Ostend. I wrote on July 28, 1917, repeating what I had often said before, about the submarines:

> Surely, it will be found that in stopping the bolt-holes no loss is so terrific as the day-by-day loss of vital shipping and cargoes, and the waste of a defensive system such as I have hinted at.

The system I had pointed to was that the Allies provided many thousands of armed ships of one kind and another against about 25 to 30 submarines operating at a time.

It is very doubtful if the Admiralty ever knew the distinction between offensive and defensive measures. About July, 1917, the War Staff issued a memorandum in which it was stated that the offensive measures being undertaken against the submarines consisted of depth charges, torpedoes, etc.

Two things are noticeable here:

(1) They are thinking only in terms of material.

(2) The idea that patrols, depth charges, nets off Ireland, etc., were regarded as offensive measures. They were purely defensive measures, taken after the submarines had arrived at their operating ground. Let us consider how we had troops to defend England against invasion and a barrage against air raids. Would any man with a knowledge of war describe these precautions as offensive measures? Yet the Admiralty issued a publication to the fleet describing such like things as offensive measures.

I remember, some years ago, commenting rather freely on an article written as far back as the *Naval Annual* of 1901 by Admiral Bacon, who was the predecessor of Sir Roger Keyes in the Dover Patrol. My antagonism to the doctrine has grown with this war, for I felt in regard to this central doctrine of the material school that it was something akin to—

> *The young disease, which must subdue at length,*
> *Grows with its growth, and strengthens with its strength.*

The writer stated his doctrine very frankly:—

> Should we not apply to strategy the old rule in navigation of, when in doubt as to the ship's position to place her on the chart in the worst possible situation, and study future action from that point? In our strategic forecast we should give to every opposing aim its highest value, and attempt to forestall success by our

preparedness, and not by our *dicta*.

It was precisely the argument of visualising a situation at its worst which led Man to take his squadron home from Gibraltar, so reducing the force of Jervis (afterwards St.Vincent) by one-third. It was the true spirit of war which induced Jervis, with the disheartening influences of the loss of five more battleships through storms and grounding, to see the stress and strain his country was passing through in the light of his exclamation that "a victory is very essential for England at this moment." And so, he fought and beat twenty-seven Spanish line of battleships with his fifteen. His example lives on.

And so, we turn on this theory of the materialist school, and say that in navigation we avoid danger while in battle we plunge into it, only seeking to make it much more dangerous for the enemy than for ourselves. In fact, our will is to make him see the situation at its worst, if need be by camouflage, but in any case, make *him* see at its worst while our own chief acts on probabilities and seizes opportunities.

Instead of considering the situation at its worst, a great chief takes the probabilities and the opportunities and acts swiftly. Drake's drum plays him into victory, for the great chief is never punished like the Israelites who wandered away to material gods.

CHAPTER 6

The Command in War

Lord Jellicoe was born December 5, 1859. As a junior officer he passed brilliant examinations, obtaining first-class certificates in all subjects. He was a gunnery lieutenant under Captain Fisher, and in after years Lord Fisher lost no opportunity of advancing his career. With all his abilities Lord Fisher was a poor judge of the qualifications of men on any but the merely administrative side, and never understood that a man might be a good administrator and yet a poor tactician and strategist. It is a melancholy reflection how all the men whom the navy knew as Fisher's men have failed to come anywhere near the high standard set by the navy's two most conspicuous successes in Beatty and Roger Keyes.

Both Lord Jellicoe and Beatty experienced war service in Egypt and China; and both were severely wounded on shore in the Boxer rebellion. Lord Jellicoe was a lieutenant in 1881; commander in 1891 under Sir George Tryon in the *Victoria*; and was promoted to captain in 1897. He was assistant to the Third Sea Lord from February,

1902, to August, 1903, and subsequently commanded the *Drake* until January, 1905, when he began the long period of administrative work which was most suited to his qualifications as a master of detail, Sir John Fisher having selected him for the post of Director of Ordnance and Torpedoes. In August, 1907, as rear-admiral, he took a post attached to the Atlantic Squadron.

In October, 1908, he joined the Board of Admiralty under Sir John Fisher in the administrative post, Third Sea Lord and Controller, responsible for carrying out the shipbuilding programmes and the maintenance of the material. On December 20th, 1910, he was appointed in command of the Atlantic Squadron, and subsequently of the Second Division, nucleus crew Home Fleet, returning in 1912 to the Admiralty as Second Sea Lord responsible for the personnel. Unlike Sir Arthur Wilson, who repeatedly commanded fleets in the Naval Manoeuvres, Lord Jellicoe only obtained this experience once when he went afloat for the 1913 manoeuvres, still retaining his Admiralty post. On August 5, 1914, he took over the command of the Grand Fleet from Sir George Callaghan in circumstances requiring the utmost tact, and which he felt deeply.

It is characteristic of the lack of foresight in our arrangements that it should have been necessary to change the command at all on the outbreak of war, since long habits of association and interchange of ideas between Admirals, their staffs and the captains of the ships, are essential to the smooth running of a fleet and its effectual use on the day of battle. It was an obvious forecast, made by me repeatedly in past years, and by Lord Fisher among others, I understand, in private conversation, that the Germans would go to war after the completion of the improvements of the Kiel Canal, which would enable the largest Dreadnoughts to pass through its four locks.

This great undertaking, completed in June, involved locks greater than any in the Panama Canal and the widening of the Channel bed from 72 to 144 feet, an increase of depth from 29 to 40 feet, and a surface width improved from 220 to 334 feet. The high level bridges had all to be pulled down and reconstructed and the whole undertaking was ready by June, 1914. The fact that other preparations synchronised and that Germany gathered her crops and then mobilised in 1870 fixed the probable date for the end of July. Happily, the lack of enterprise of the German Navy on the outbreak of hostilities gave us a long period of preparation during the war which was largely utilised in doing a great deal that ought to have been accomplished during peace.

Much of it was done wastefully owing to the absence of a trained war-staff at the Admiralty and the lack of any war doctrine permeating the Service afloat. The delay, however, gave the new commander-in-chief and the Admiralty about twenty months to prepare before any action was fought except by the battle-cruisers.

If a more exact analysis of Lord Jellicoe's services is made, it will be found that during 12½ years before the war he was 7 years 10 months in purely administrative posts. Either he was a master of war or he was not. If we assume him to have been regarded as a great leader in war, we were taking the very course to ruin him as such by keeping him to administrative posts. His appointment to the Grand Fleet indicates the belief of Mr. Churchill that Lord Jellicoe was a man fit to take the mantle of Nelson. As a matter of fact, that was never the view of the writer, but those who held that view showed almost criminal carelessness in not preparing Lord Jellicoe for his great task by placing him in positions where he would always be studying the problems of war rather than the routine and details of administration. He was given no opportunity of familiarising himself with merchant shipping and blockade work.

The blockade only became moderately effective after about two years of war, and as First Sea Lord it took a long time to convince him of the need of interfering with the German trade round the Texel. They not merely handicapped him to this extent, but as we have seen, Mr. Churchill confronted him with the task the day after war broke out. The result was exactly what might have been expected. The Grand Fleet was nursed and prepared for the day of battle, and the blockade work was done, with an administrative care for which Lord Jellicoe deserves great credit, and yet on the day of battle it was like a broken sword in his hands.

Lest it should be thought that this method of choosing and preparing men for their tasks was exceptional, it should be stated that it was customary and remained so after the war, because the war's real lessons had not been revealed. Take the chief of the War Staff at the Admiralty, Sir Henry Oliver, a most painstaking and conscientious man and one of the finest seamen and navigators in the world. He was a man who never spared himself in his country's cause. His training had been entirely in the specialist duties of a navigating officer, valuable in the training which it gives in accuracy and attention to detail. He was a favourite of Lord Fisher, who made him captain of the Navigation School in 1905.

In December, 1908, he was brought to the Admiralty as naval assistant of Lord Fisher for three years. On November 1, 1913, he was brought back as Director of Naval Intelligence. Mr. Churchill took him as his naval secretary on October 14, 1914, and then, with Lord Fisher as First Sea Lord, made him chief of the War Staff, November 5, 1914. He was successful in all methodical, plodding and routine work which he undertook, but through the lack of a staff he was overburdened with work, and it is doubtful if he had any genius for the conduct of war.

The training of a navigator is to avoid danger; his reputation is built up on it. It is a bad training in every respect for the conduct of war which demands the utmost energy, enterprise and initiative, coupled with very broad views of the war situation as a whole. In spite of this handicap, however, Sir Henry Oliver brought to bear on our war problems a strong fund of common sense. It was not his fault that the study of war had been neglected in his training and that he had not been given adequate opportunity to develop himself as a strategist.

In other directions things were not quite so bad as they used to be. In the series of articles on the navy for the *Times* in 1901, I pointed out that of twenty-two seconds-in-command of our Main or Channel Fleet, who ought presumably to be training for high command and who had occupied the post during the previous twenty years, not one arrived at the command of either of the two fleets embracing battleships, *viz.*, the Channel and the Mediterranean Fleets. The articles resulted in improvements, but changes are always difficult to make in the navy, for the reason given by Lord Haddington in 1842, that:

> In doing what might be needful for the public interest they would be sorry to distress the feelings of officers.

This is a familiar difficulty. In reality the only safe course is to appoint men without much regard to age or rank, but almost solely for their qualifications.

Sir David Beatty, owing to two early promotions for land service, became a flag officer at thirty-eight years of age. By passing bad examinations he escaped the fate of clever officers who became specialists in gunnery and torpedo work, and whose minds are so directed for years as to be absorbed in details and the worship of mere material. He also escaped almost the worst period of a naval officer's career, when he learns nothing about the business of fighting, but as executive officer of a ship is engrossed in a soul-destroying routine work connected with the internal economy and discipline of a ship. Some such experience is both useful and necessary, but the trouble was that it became enormously exaggerated.

Beatty's time as commander of the *Barfleur* was very short, for he was promoted for service in China after only two years in the rank of commander. His time subsequently on the captains' list was so short that, with the period of enforced idleness by reason of his wound, he was unable to complete the regulation service of six years in command when he became due for flag rank, and a special Order in Council was issued to enable him to be promoted. On becoming rear-admiral he was younger than nine-tenths of the officers on the captains' list.

Though promoted for land services in war, Beatty was always a sea service officer. The only two shore appointments he has filled were of short duration as naval adviser to the War Office, and as Secretary to the First Lord of the Admiralty, Mr. Winston Churchill. It was Mr. Churchill who has the credit of selecting him for the command of the Battle-Cruiser Fleet. Two years later, at under forty-seven years of age, he arrived at the command of the Grand Fleet, the youngest of all the Allied fighting leaders by sea or land.

If the character of a fighter were at its best in compromise; if knowledge of war were familiarity with mechanical details of weapons and their use; if courage were merely physical; if skill were the product exclusively of drill and parade movements, it is possible that Lord Jellicoe was the superior of his successor. History and biography show that this is not so. The command in war requires immense energy, concentration and determination, directed towards the one object of swift and decisive victory. It requires untiring patience both in forcing and tempting the enemy to afford an opportunity. The last thing in the world it needs is that character of compromise which fears loss, which by its formal methods of approach loses all the advantage of surprise, and which conforms, to the enemy's initiative and therefore to his wishes.

Moral courage is more necessary than physical, but it is a far more rare quality. Beatty exulted in responsibility and would strain all to the limit to ensure it, and the men under him were exalted by the strain. Lord Jellicoe's end was not victory, but the preservation of our communications and their denial to the enemy which he believed could be attained without a decisive victory. With the one the smashing of the enemy's force was the supreme demand which gave us the command of the sea, and with the other the preservation of our own force sufficed. Hence things were achieved with the one which under the easier rule of compromise were held to be impossible. Lord Jellicoe knew far more of gunnery, and yet under Beatty's inspiration the "impossible" in regard to fire control was accomplished.

Under Lord Jellicoe it was held to be impossible to co-ordinate completely the movements of separated squadrons or divisions. Under Beatty it was worked out because it was essential to victory. Lacking the technical knowledge, he yet had the instinct of the born leader, who demands what victory requires, and spurs on an enthusiastic staff to help him in his difficulties.

"Nelson was no seaman," said Codrington.

"His ship was always in bad order," said St. Vincent.

The answer is that he was the greatest leader the sea has ever produced, and he stands on a pinnacle today for those qualities of leadership which Beatty has made manifest again. The French admiral and historian, Jurien de la Gravière pointed out how the circumspection of the British admirals and formal tactics in the war of the French Revolution favoured the continued existence of the French naval threat, and that this state of affairs was only broken when Nelson was given his first independent command and fought the Battle of the Nile. The Germans were well aware that the strongest refitted fleet they could send out after August, 1916, would never be able to return successfully from an encounter with the Grand Fleet under Beatty, so they gave him no opportunity.

It is among the disadvantages of working in a room in an administrative capacity, dealing with sea affairs from a town environment, that insensibly one thrusts psychology more and more into the background. If one's work absorbs the mind in the material side of the navy, then the process is much accelerated. The earlier attention devoted to passing examinations with all their false perspectives prepares the ground for the evil crop in the first instance, and though ship life corrects it in some men it accentuates it in others. Nothing struck me more, in reading Lord Jellicoe's book, than this absence of any consideration for the psychological factor, as though there were no soul in war. Because Nelson gave first place to psychology, he had one plan for attacking a French fleet and another for a Russian.

Lord Jellicoe quotes the German writer, Captain Persius, as "a reputable and informed writer on naval affairs," but he does not quote this officer's statement that the German fleet escaped because there was not "a resolute commander on the enemy side," or his statement that the High Seas Fleet "was preserved from disaster" through "the unskilful handling of the British Fleet under Admiral Jellicoe." Nelson's plan for a Russian fleet was to confuse the line by attacking the van. Was it a dossier on the psychology of the British admiral that taught the newly-appointed German admiral von Scheer that a British line of twenty-seven ships could be driven out of action by attacking its tail with eleven destroyers? That this should happen to a man whose physical courage had been proved again and again, whose cleverness as a young man was beyond any dispute, affords much ground for thought and inquiry.

We have already drawn attention to the fact that the best men we have had in command, Beatty, Keyes and Tyrwhitt, could not muster more than one first-class certificate in examinations out of a possible fifteen that they could have attained had they been clever at these tests. Napoleon's attainments in examinations were such as to draw the adverse comments of the Inspector of Military Schools, who thought he would do for the navy! As for the Duke of Wellington's mathematical knowledge Sir John Burgoyne said:

> It is very likely that he could not have solved a problem in Euclid, or even worked out a question in simple equations or logarithms.

Even if examinations could give us Newtons, the Nelsons could not be replaced by Newtons. Huxley declared that he forgot all he knew about drugs a week after the examinations and sarcastically suggested that medical men should belong to the Iron and Steel Institute, and learn about cutlery because they used knives. The waste of time over material details and what is called knowledge in the navy, has resulted in the neglect of the study of war, and it is a very grave matter that lives should be lost and ships endangered by this neglect. The so-called dunces escape the specialist training in material such as falls to the lot of gunnery and torpedo lieutenants.

They further escape to a large extent the subsequent immersion in administrative work on shore. Here, then, is the clue as to why the three admirals we have named were not spoiled by the navy's training system. The seven years and ten months which Lord Jellicoe spent over administrative details at Whitehall which had nothing to do with the conduct of war were as ruinous to his mental outlook as were the years Lord Raglan spent at the War Office before he went to the Crimea. If both are bad, it matters little whether the system produces the type of man or the men produce the system. It is equally important to criticise the men in order to end the system, and to show up the system in order to mend the men.

Successive statesmen have been implored to inquire into the system. They refused, for it is their method to wait for a crisis and even then, to cover up failure if it is possible to do so. Between the statesman and the sailor or the soldier the process is one of shelving rather than shouldering responsibility. The great thing appears to be to have something on paper. So, it was with the Russian Admiral Stark, whose ships were torpedoed at Port Arthur the day before the declaration of war by Japan against Russia. He sent in a report advocating preparations.

On it was noted by the viceroy, "No, not yet." When people wanted to put the blame on him, he tapped his pocket and said: "I can show this paper to everybody." What is written on the scroll the public never knows. It intrudes into the escape of the *Goeben*; we hear of it in the Dardanelles fiascos; our curiosity is brought to a high pitch over the battle orders of Jutland, and it leaves the situation as obscure as any North Sea mist. When the wrong man is proved by events to be in command, the statesmen are afraid to make a change. They quote Lincoln about swapping horses whilst crossing the stream. They forget that Lincoln changed the chief command six times before he arrived at Grant. There is nothing inconsistent in that fact with Mr. Choate's description, speaking in Edinburgh in 1900, that:

> Lincoln was true as steel to his generals, but had frequent occasion to change them, as he found them inadequate. This serious and painful duty rested wholly on him, and was, perhaps, his most important function as commander-in-chief.

In the navy, it appears to rest on the First Lord of the Admiralty, and probably the navy would like to know something about his selection as well. It is inclined to say to the statesman that the changes are bewildering, and that it has been ruled in succession by a courtier, a financier, a journalist, a philosopher, a lawyer, a railway man and a landowner, and it asks whether our system is any better than that of the French Revolution, which entrusted the direction of naval affairs to a mathematician because the sea has to do with navigation, just as the previous king's government had handed over finance to a dancer because he was careful of his steps.

Not one of them has been animated by a great idea, which was Disraeli's conception of a statesman. Disraeli's remark is equally true of the soldier like Foch and the sailor like Beatty. They were both animated by great ideas. The preservation of his ships, which was the idea animating Lord Jellicoe, is an idea, but it is not a great one. So also, the tabulation of numbers of small material defects may show a mind for detail, but not a grasp of principle. After all, von Scheer went into action with pre-Dreadnoughts, and does not appear to have complained. He went into action with 11-inch guns, and he makes no murmur. It does him credit. Chatham said to Boscawen:

> When I apply to other officers respecting any expedition I may chance to project, they always raise difficulties: you always find expedients.

CHAPTER 7

Final Reflections on Preparation

Before we now pass to the actual handling of the naval weapon at the Battle of Jutland the question must be answered as to why there were so many defects, strategical, tactical, administrative and material, as we have outlined. It should be remembered that in regard to any weapon, it is not so much the actual defect that matters as the dry rot that brought it about, and this is what we have endeavoured to emphasise throughout. At Jutland we had overwhelming material superiority. It was in the use of that superiority that we failed.

The causes are to be sought in the slothfulness of thought and action which accompanies a long period of peace, and in the exaltation of the administrative side at the Admiralty with its routine and formalities which are so utterly unfavourable to initiative, to imagination, and to the study of anything but rules and regulations. If Mr. Asquith's Cabinet Committee had pondered deeply and gone deeply into the situations revealed to them when they investigated Lord Charles Beresford's charges, they would have seen that something more was demanded from them than the mere hint of a dangerous situation which they gave in their report of August 12, 1909, in the following words:—

> The Committee have been impressed with the differences of opinion amongst officers of high rank and professional attainments regarding important principles of naval strategy and tactics, and they look forward with much confidence to the further developments of the Naval War Staff, from which the naval members of the Board and flag officers and their Staffs at sea may be expected to derive common benefits.

We have spoken of national characteristics and of the indifference to historical study in our educational system. We dine to celebrate events, but we do not study them. Without study, there is no profit from the past except the mere properties it hands down. If we will not think of the past, we are hardly likely to think clearly of the future, and we find, indeed, that a dislike to face the future is a national characteristic. We can see it in the wars of the past, as we see it today. Abstract reasoning is distasteful, particularly to the class of persons who call themselves "practical men." The navy is essentially a practical profession, and it is only natural that the national characteristics should exist in a pronounced form. War demands continuous study and abstract thought. War did not stare us in the face, and with the exception of the Agadir issue, there had been no crisis until July, 1914.

Indeed the navy did not even recognise a crisis until the continental armies were already in process of mobilisation, and so, though the First Fleet got to its war station in the nick of time, the only enemy ships shadowed were the *Goeben* and *Breslau*, which were met by pure accident on their return from bombarding the French North African ports. Matters of technique were obtrusive, they were immediate and pressing in the departmental correspondence, and they clamoured for solution. They received attention accordingly, as Members of Parliament attend to matters in proportion to the clamour of their constituents. Poor Scapa was a neglected port, except for the visits of the German survey ships, and no appeals come from the desert and the wilderness.

And yet the story is in some respects a libel both on the country and the navy. There was a distinct disturbance in both, as a historical leaven was fermenting. But the pity of it was that it worked only in the young navy, and the young navy had pushed only two of its officers near the higher ranks in Rear-Admiral Beatty and Captain Roger Keyes. Promotion to flag rank has been throughout kept rigorously to seniority, if we except the acting rank of rear-admiral conferred on Sir Reginald Tyrwhitt after some pressure in the Press and Parliament, and that officer has since been informed that he must revert to his former seniority. Consequently, the young navy was not able to press its ideas at the Admiralty, which, by discouraging discussion, closed the sources of inspiration.

However, this change for the better among the students of history in the young navy had come in spite of the fact that, from 1904 onwards, there was a steady centralisation of ships under a single command in home waters. To a large extent centralisation was necessarily brought about by the rise of the German Navy, but the evil result was that it offered no independent responsibility, such as service in foreign parts often gave, to the junior officers. Such service develops independence of character, whereas the habit of waiting for orders, or acting by rule, tends to undermine it. One has only to read Foch's *Principles of War* to see that all his War Staff training aimed at promoting independence of judgment by discussion, for it is only by constant examination and straight challenging that truth is set upon her throne.

The study of history had tended to promote this independence of judgment among the young naval officers to whom we have referred. Their positions are not so assured as is the case with Earl Beatty and Sir Roger Keyes who have won through as the only naval chiefs who have shown both strategical and tactical insight, so it is undesirable to mention any by name. If ever full inquiry is made into the fight which these young officers made to get things done, then justice will be done to them, and let us hope justice will also be done to those others who, having power, sinned against the light.

As already pointed out in the chapter on the command in war, Lord Jellicoe had only held one independent command in the Atlantic Squadron for less than twelve months, from December, 1911, to December, 1912. He had also been in charge for a brief period of naval manoeuvres in 1913-14. He was second in command of the Atlantic Fleet earlier in his career, from August, 1907, for one year. Excepting these two years, one may say that from February, 1905, when he was Director of Naval Ordnance, he spent all his time in administrative posts. The last thing in the world one could picture him doing was to resign his position as a member of the Board of Admiralty when, as he alleges, politicians refused money for vital services. Assuming that he protested, which is by no means certain, for ministers were always able to state that they acted on the advice of the Sea Lords, it is evident that he did not possess the independence of character of Admiral Berkeley, afterwards Lord Fitz-Hardinge, who resigned from the Board in 1845 when certain necessary expenditure was struck out.

After the matter had been dealt with in the House of Commons, the expenditure was granted and Admiral Berkeley rejoined the Board. Take, again, the two junior Sea Lords who, in 1867, sent in their resignations but were induced to resume their posts on the government promising to concede their demand for a programme of seven ironclads. Their strength lay in the fairness and justice of the House of Commons, which would no less surely have backed up Prince Louis of Battenberg and Sir John Jellicoe, the two senior Sea Lords, in the years before the war, had they possessed moral courage.

War was coming, and nobody doubted it who had made any study of history. We had seen quite recently in South Africa the prolongation of a war with much loss of life and treasure because we were unable to provide more than 8,000 men immediately the crisis broke out. Instancing this and other wars in our history, I wrote in 1904 that:

> The assertion holds good in every case that if a fraction of the increase made in war had been incurred during peace, in all cases the war would have been avoided or considerably shortened, always predicating that the expenditure is in the right direction, for otherwise the money were far better left to fructify in the banks of the nation.

Again, in 1906, I said that:

> One vessel in the hunt at the beginning of a war is worth two at the end . . . . The problem of commerce protection can only be satisfactorily met by relatively preponderating forces enabling us to envelop the raiders at the outset.

These were elementary truths, and men who had been through the Agadir crisis of 1911 ought to have been the last to forget them, still less men who were aware of the extraordinary demand made by Germany in 1912 that we should pledge ourselves not to assist France. It is hardly conceivable that the Cabinet concealed this demand from the Admiralty.

The truth is that the weakness of the Sea Lords lay not merely in lack of moral courage, but in what contributed to that weakness, the inability to argue their case. In other words, they lacked what a War Staff is meant to do. General Sir Henry Wilson, who works with a staff, would never complain of the handicap of being unable to express his ideas. Lord Jellicoe has frequently done so, and in his book he says of soldiers and sailors:—

> They are as a rule accustomed to carry out ideas without having first to bring conviction to the minds of men who, although possessing great general knowledge and administrative experience, have naturally but little acquaintance with naval and military affairs which in themselves form a lifelong study.

★★★★★★

This esoteric plea is a favourite device. I well remember the indignation of one who was present when he related how an admiral burked an inquiry from Mr. Lloyd George in conference as to whether torpedo-boats could be spared for convoys, by saying that "they were not suitable." He must have known that Mr. Lloyd George meant destroyers. In the German Navy destroyers were known as torpedo-boats to distinguish their primary weapon, and it is a far more suitable title. Napoleon's opinion of his admirals is well known, and they used to baulk him with the same plea about "a life-long study" which one is unable to explain to the uninitiated! They even persuaded him to enter children of eight years old to embark on this life-long study!

★★★★★★

The question may well be asked whether the statesman was not infinitely more to be pitied in being unable to obtain advice owing to the professed inability of the "Jellicoes" to express their ideas. One cannot imagine Anson and Ligonier, who were the naval and military advisers of Lord Chatham, putting forward such a plea. The first thing Chatham had to do was to make the sailors and soldiers work together or, in other words, pool their ideas. The expression of ideas is what staff training ought to achieve. In 1918-19 proposals came before the Sea Lords for War Staff Colleges of the navy and army to work in close association. They were resisted by the Sea Lords with ingrained prejudice. If this object cannot be achieved in any other way it may be necessary to place a minister, if one can be found as powerful as Chatham, in charge of the Navy, Army and Air Services in order to establish the close coordination which is so necessary to an Island Power with vast interests across the seas in every continent in the world.

Many war questions which come up to be considered before the Cabinet are questions affecting all our war operations, and should be argued as strongly as possible by combined effort. Right at the outset of the war for weeks the German reservists were allowed to return to Germany because the case was badly argued by the Admiralty, and for many months a similar condition of affairs existed in regard to the neutral trade through Scandinavia and Holland. Foolish assertions in regard to Germany's dependence on cotton supplies could have been exposed in the first week of war by a really efficient War Staff.

The absence of a War Staff to study events, and draw from them every helpful detail in the conduct of war, rendered it all the more necessary that we should not lose what little machinery we had inherited from the past for profiting by our experience during the war as it progressed. This is why at all times I have kept the question of courts-martial so prominently to the front. As a War Staff gradually permeates the navy with its body of doctrine based on the offensive and the highest standards of fighting, it may be possible to look less and less to the court-martial to keep up the great ideals of the navy. In this war, in the absence of the War Staff, it was imperative that we should have held to the court-martial. It has more than once saved us in the past, as can be seen by the following examples.

After his defeat, Blake, in 1652-3, was given complete power to purge his fleet on the reports of three commissioners sent to investigate. He dismissed his own brother after court-martial, and a number of captains were put under arrest. The results were a succession of victories. Tromp, de Ruyter and de Witt fearlessly told the deputies of the State that the English were the masters of the sea. Blake was told to appoint whom he liked to the Mediterranean when he left, and he appointed Captain Stoaks as vice-admiral in the Spanish Seas, so showing the navy another standard which it does not recognise today of promotion by selection from the captains' list.

In the court-martial on Lord Gambier the charge contained the words "neglect or delay in taking effectual measures to destroy the enemy." That was in strict accordance with the Articles of War which are intended to direct the mind of the navy to victory. Was there neglect or delay on that day of great opportunity of May 31, or on the following morning to seek a decisive action? It was an occasion on which an admiral might well have echoed what old Jervis (St.Vincent) said, as he took his numerically much inferior force into battle with the Spaniards:—

A victory is very essential for England at this moment.

Our army was sore pressed, and there was much anxiety about Russia. We did not reach the high mark of man power until ten months later, and as Sir Douglas Haig said in his last despatch:—

It was not until midsummer 1916 that the artillery situation became even approximately adequate to the conduct of major operations.

How much we lost on that day I have endeavoured to estimate elsewhere, and yet Mr. Balfour is said to have rejected the advice of the high admirals who gave him reasons for bringing Lord Jellicoe before a court-martial, and he procured for the latter the title of viscount. Did Mr. Balfour think he was thereby helping the standards of conduct and ability of the navy? What, indeed, was the main count on which Byng was found guilty but that of not having done his utmost to take and destroy the ships of the enemy. The reward of Lord Jellicoe simply affirmed as a standard of conduct that a man should do his utmost to preserve his own force.

In the case of Sir Robert Calder in 1805, he was loudly praised by ministers, especially by Lord Castlereagh in Parliament, but he was subjected to Press criticism. On September 30, 1805, he wrote a letter to the Admiralty demanding a court-martial. A court consisting of six flag officers and seven captains was assembled:

To inquire into the conduct and proceedings of the said Vice-Admiral, Sir R. Calder, with His Majesty's squadron under his command, on the said 23rd day of July last, and also into his subsequent conduct and proceedings, until he finally lost sight of the enemy's ships, and to try him for not having done his utmost to renew the said engagement, and to take or destroy every ship of the enemy, which it was his duty to engage accordingly."

We are in this difficulty in the navy. There is the very highest standard in regard to courage. There is a high standard in regard to seamanship. There is really no standard at all, enforceable by court-martial, in regard to skill in strategy, staff work, and tactics, especially in regard to the two former. There is no conception such as General Sir Charles Napier, who saved the situation in India by going against the advice of his officers, gave voice to when he said that the officer who does not make himself master of his profession is a murderer. We have to find some means of attaining the same high standard in regard to staff work and strategy as in regard to seamanship, so that if the enemy escape, or our own ships are endangered through faulty staff work, the inefficient may be made an example of.

What is needed is a great War Staff which will help to form a body of doctrine throughout the navy, of which courts-martial must take cognisance, and which will help to give full significance to that portion of Article 2 of the Naval Discipline Act reading:

If he has acted from negligence or through other default, he shall be dismissed from his Majesty's service with or without disgrace, or shall suffer such other punishment as is hereafter mentioned.

The defence which Mr. Churchill put forward in the House of Commons, February 15, 1915, for not holding courts-martial to inquire why things went wrong is now seen to be wholly false. The court-martial to inquire conveyed no imputation of guilt, though Mr. Churchill asserted that it did. On the contrary, some of our greatest sea-officers had their merits revealed by court-martial. Nelson in justifying disobedience of orders on occasions when the orders militated against what he called "the great Order" of the destruction of the enemy, expressly stated that there ought to be a court-martial "to inquire" into the circumstances. As the result of Mr. Churchill's action the court-martial now does convey the presumption of guilt. Mr. Churchill was very emphatic that courts-martial would lead to naval officers refusing to take risks, he said:

> I would especially deprecate anything being done which tends to make officers, whether afloat, or at the Admiralty, play for safety and avoid responsibility for positive action.

Jutland is the answer. The man of action, full of the knowledge that he is doing right, exults in the thought that come what may, he can prove himself before his peers. This is no idle assertion, for it has the history of several centuries of war at sea behind it, the history of which Mr. Churchill has not shown himself to be a student.

Great responsibilities should always involve full power to act and the commander-in-chief should not be called on to continue in his office any officer in whom he has no confidence. He should be allowed to supersede such officers, it being left to the Admiralty to take what further action they may deem necessary. In the instructions of 1816 the last one read as follows:—

> If there should be a captain so lost to all sense of honour and the great duty he owes his country as not to exert himself to the utmost to get into action with the enemy, or to take or destroy them when engaged, the commander of the squadron or division to which he belongs, or the nearest flag officer, is to suspend him from the command, and is to appoint some other officer to command the ship till the admiral's pleasure shall be known.

The reward of merit is of even greater importance than the punishment of demerit, though the two depend on each other to a large extent. The reward of merit means promotion by selection and appointments without regard to seniority. The danger, especially in peace time, is that the power will be abused, or what is known as favouritism will be established and comradeship between officers will be lessened. There is little to choose between an admiral who has got on because he is a courtier and one who has climbed because to leading politicians he was known as a man of tact who would shape his naval policy to suit their party exigencies.

That the navy has some of the latter type is shown by the support given to the Declaration of London, and by the neglect of vital preparations prior to the outbreak of war in August, 1914, while those who indicated the danger were subjected to a Press campaign in which they were stigmatised as disappointed or disgruntled critics.

CHAPTER 8

A Summary of the Chief Moves

In order to assist the student and the reader, I have given in the appendix as complete and accurate a chronology of the Battle of Jutland as is possible with all due care. This is the first attempt that has been made to supply a long-felt want, and since there does not seem to have been throughout the British Fleet a rigid standardisation of time by watches with ship's clocks, there are necessarily discrepancies, and some of the times may be disputed. These uncertainties occur in the official documents as well. We may take as an example the fact that Lord Jellicoe gives the time for turning on the signal to deploy as 6.16 in the text of his book, whereas in the official chart it is given as 6.14, and this chart is reproduced in the book.

Such discrepancies are not as immaterial as at first sight appears. There are controversies about the positions of the ships dependent on bearings. As a fleet moving at the speed of Lord Jellicoe's fleet, or 20 knots, covers about 1,340 yards in two minutes that interval makes a considerable difference in such cases. The reader is recommended to glance through the chronology, as well as the general summary of this chapter, before reading the more critical survey which follows.

The British fleet of battleships and battle-cruisers had an immense gunnery advantage in which the weight of projectiles from a single discharge of heavy gun-fire was 420,600 lb., compared with 226,074 lb. for the High Seas Fleet. This does not bring out fully the British advantage, on which so much stress was laid by the Fisher school before the war, as so much depends on the concentrated weight fired from guns

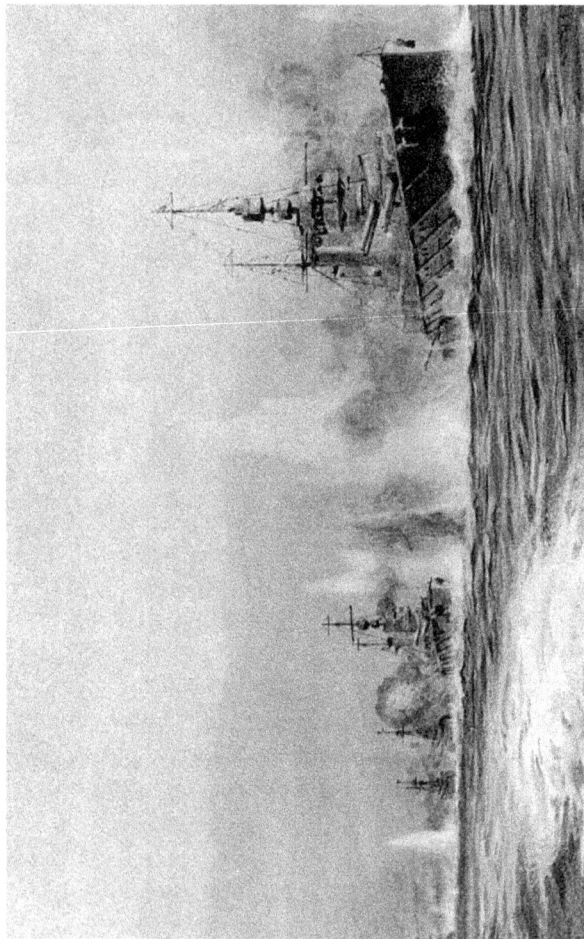

British battleships opening fire in the opening action, 31st May

of the highest calibre. The Germans had no guns greater than 12-inch calibre, whereas the Grand Fleet had 48 of 15-inch, 10 of 14-inch, and 142 of 13½-inch. So great an offensive superiority is of no avail unless it is used to the best advantage by one who has the will to conquer, and this point is fully discussed in the succeeding chapters.

The essential features of the Battle of Jutland were as follows:—

(1) On the night of May 30, the British Battle Fleet under Lord Jellicoe proceeded to sea from Scapa and Cromarty, and the fast scouting squadron from Rosyth, under Sir David Beatty. There was little doubt that something was known of enemy movements. Some big move was expected following the appointments of a new head of the German Navy and of the High Seas Fleet in Admirals von Capelle and von Scheer respectively. There had also been a visit to Wilhelmshaven of the *Kaiser* himself to stir up enthusiasm.

For reasons which are not known, the two British forces were not ordered to rendezvous or establish visual contact until the afternoon of the next day, a fact of some importance, as will be seen later. Before that could happen the Rosyth force under Beatty sighted the enemy, and in pursuance of the general policy steered to cut him off from his channel through the minefield to the Heligoland Bight known as the Horn Reef Channel. The enemy proved to be the five German battle cruisers with accompanying small craft.

(2) The fast scouting groups of the British and German fleets operating at a distance from their battlefleets met, and the German group retreated to the South towards its battle fleet. In the course of this action the *Indefatigable* and *Queen Mary* were blown up through inadequate armour protection to their magazines, and Beatty's flagship, the *Lion*, narrowly escaped a similar disaster. Attention is drawn to the fact that the designs of the *Indefatigable* were stolen in 1908 and passed into the possession of Germany. The secrecy policy continued to be maintained against the British public so that there was no criticism of the designs at the Society of Naval Architects or Royal United Service Institution.

The danger of this absence of criticism of the designs was pointed out by the writer before the war, when he stated that we owed the loss of the *Captain* to a similar policy of secrecy. All attempts to elicit information as to our designs in the House of Commons had failed, and the responsibility for the terrible losses resulting from deplorable errors in the designs is a very onerous one seeing that the public interest was pleaded for not giving information which was already in the possession of Germany.

On the four *Barhams*—battleships of the *Queen Elizabeth* class—drawing into action the German gunnery fell off, showing a loss of moral in spite of their successes, whereas the British gunnery improved in spite of our losses.

(3) On Beatty sighting the enemy's main force he turned north, drawing the enemy after him towards the Grand Fleet, so that actually, when the Grand Fleet came into sight at 5.50 p.m., Beatty was at a point about fifteen miles further north than when he started after the enemy. The visibility varied from different directions, but by 5.50 p.m., when the Grand Fleet drew near from the North, it was in our favour, as is proved by the battle fleet sighting the *Lion* to the South several minutes before the *Lion* sighted the battle fleet to the North, the enemy being to the Southward of our Rosyth force.

On the enemy being first reported in sight, the three battle-cruisers of the *Invincible* class under Hood, which were stationed twenty miles ahead of the battle fleet, were ordered by Lord Jellicoe (2.30 p.m.) to cut off any retreat of the enemy by the Baltic. At 4 p.m. they were ordered to steer direct to reinforce Beatty. Much time had been lost and they got into action at 6.15 p.m., turning in at once ahead of Beatty's battle-cruisers at 6.21, the *Invincible* being sunk at 6.33 from the same cause of defective construction as had lost us the other two battle-cruisers.

(4) From the reports which were made to him, Lord Jellicoe had expected to meet the enemy twelve miles further to the east and twenty minutes later than he did, and was much disturbed in his mind over the question of deployment from his formation in five divisions into single line. The cause of this discrepancy in information arose from the information sent from the Rosyth force being based on the calculations as to position on the chart made in the *Lion*, whereas had our two forces come into visual contact before Beatty chased the enemy they would have been based on the *Iron Duke's* reckoning as to position. The importance of the dispositions of the ships before deployment is discussed in the chapter on the "Theory of Deployment."

Lord Jellicoe rejected deployment towards the enemy astern of the Rosyth force already in action, or deployment on his starboard division, in favour of deployment away from the enemy on his port division. He turned to port at 6.14 or 6.16, the whole line being formed

The explosion of H.M.S. Queen Mary

on a southeast course, with the enemy to starboard, by 6.38 p.m. The *Iron Duke* opened fire on the enemy line at 6.31, or 41 minutes after she had sighted the *Lion*. Owing to the deployment being to port, and as time had to be allowed for the Battle-Cruiser Squadron to pass along to the head of the line six miles further to the eastward, the speed of the battle fleet was reduced to fourteen knots. In addition, the battle orders provided that the fast division of battleships (the *Barhams*), known as the Fifth Battle Squadron, were to occupy the head of the line when the deployment was towards Heligoland and the rear of the line when the deployment was away from Heligoland (*vide* Jellicoe).

The deployment to port might appear to have been construed as away from Heligoland as these battleships which had been following Beatty made a wide turn to form astern instead of ahead, and for all practical purposes were taken out of the battle just when they were most needed. The probability is that the *Barhams* were taken astern because their speed did not admit of their crossing the front with deployment to port. The result of this movement and the reduction of speed of the leading ships was a considerable bunching up of ships in the rear and some actually had their engines stopped.

Other incidents were a break-down of the *Warspite's* helm, so that she turned 16 points towards the enemy and was so severely punished as to pass out of the battle. Two of Lord Jellicoe's armoured cruisers, the *Defence* and the *Warrior*, prior to the deployment had been engaged with enemy cruisers, and in the endeavour to pick up their station turned to starboard inside our battle-cruisers, coming under the fire of the enemy line and blanketing the fire of our own battle cruisers. The *Defence* was sunk at 6.16, and the *Warrior* seriously damaged. The result of the *Warspite's* accidental turn was to relieve the *Warrior* from the attention of the enemy.

The outcome of Lord Jellicoe's decision as to deployment was to leave the battle-cruisers only in action, except for a few shots fired from the rear of the line, and to lose all the advantages of the surprise, which might have very speedily decided the issue. He claims that there was both a gunnery and a torpedo disadvantage in following the battle-cruisers by a deployment to starboard towards the enemy. On the other hand, psychological factors such as the surprise, the time limit imposed by the approaching darkness, and the all-important gunnery advantage of the light have to be considered. On this point Beatty's despatch states:—

The *Iron Duke*, Admiral Jellicoe's flag ship opening fire approximately 6.15 p.m., 31st May

It is interesting to note that after 6 p.m. although the visibility became reduced, it was undoubtedly more favourable to us than the enemy. At intervals their ships showed up clearly, enabling us to punish them very severely and establish a definite superiority over them. From the reports of other ships and my own observations it was clear that the enemy suffered considerable damage, battle-cruisers and battleships alike. *The head of their line was crumpled up, leaving battleships as targets for the majority of our battle-cruisers.* Before leaving us the Fifth Battle Squadron was also engaging battleships.

The diagram which Lord Jellicoe submits is subjected to criticism in a succeeding chapter, but diagrams, however clever, cannot explain away the state of affairs to which Beatty's despatch points.

(5) The enemy cruisers had mistaken the sudden onslaught of the three *Invincibles* coming from the north as the head of the line of our Grand Fleet, and at once began to turn away to the south, but owing to the Grand Fleet deployment to port our battle-cruisers had to steer about six miles further to the west to take up their positions at the head of the British line. As stated, we had lost a great deal of the effect of the surprise and consternation which the arrival of the Grand Fleet caused in a fleet in which the slow 17 knot pre-Dreadnoughts were present and which could not therefore escape by speed.

(6) The Grand Fleet had to turn towards the enemy in order to close the range, the rear of the line having better opportunities for action than the rest of the fleet, but the original course was resumed on it appearing that a torpedo destroyer attack was to be delivered. At 7.21 course was altered two points and then a further two points, making 45 degrees in all, away from the enemy, though before doing so it had been observed that the enemy was steering away almost in the line of their fire. The attack of the German destroyers was actually delivered against eight of the ships in the rear of the line and eleven torpedoes were observed, but none of them hit.

Some of these ships in the rear turned away as much as eight points. Beatty made a signal to the admiral in the *King George V.* leading the line of twenty-seven battleships asking him to follow the battle-cruisers to defeat the enemy, but this division turned with the others in obedience to the signal from the commander-in-chief's flagship, the *Iron Duke*, which was the ninth ship in the line. The battleships did not again get into action for, though they sighted a detached part of the

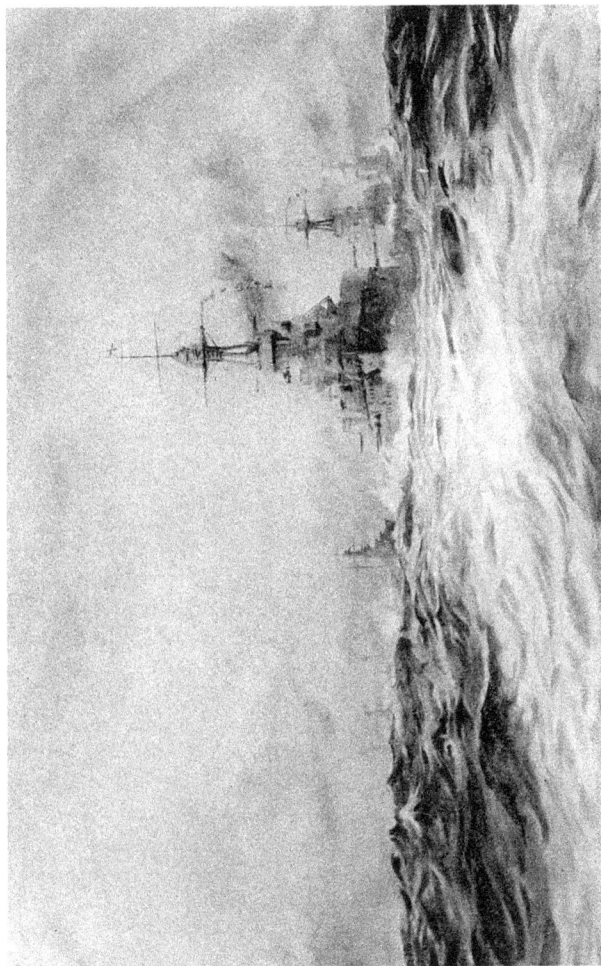

British battleships led by the flag ship *Iron Duke*

enemy fleet after eight o'clock, another destroyer flotilla moved out from the enemy and both sides turned away from each other.

(7) Lord Jellicoe decided not to risk a night action, so he turned south at the speed of 17 knots, which had been maintained ever since single line had been formed. The fleet was formed in divisions and the destroyers were disposed astern at about five to ten miles distance. Sir David Beatty concurred in the decision not to fight a night action as the enemy was cut off from his base and he considered that our strategical position was such that the High Seas Fleet could be brought to action the following morning. This considered opinion was given by Sir David Beatty in his despatch as the reason for ceasing action at 8.38 when he found that the battle fleet was no longer in sight of the linking cruisers and, in conformity to orders, he turned south:—

> In view of the gathering darkness and of the fact that our strategical position was such as to make it appear certain that we should locate the enemy at daylight under most favourable circumstances, I did not consider it desirable, or proper, to close the enemy battle fleet during the dark hours.

During the night our destroyers were in action with the enemy fleet, which turned to the south-east at dark, steering for the channel by the Horn Reef. The course of the enemy towards the Horn Reef Channel was roughly indicated by the destroyer divisions sighting the enemy from west to east so that those most to the westward came into action first. The fighting could be seen from some of the battleships. The destroyers got somewhat scattered by these attacks. The failure to assemble them at dawn operated in Lord Jellicoe's mind to prevent him going to the neighbourhood of the Horn Reef Lightvessel to intercept the enemy, who passed the lightvessel well after dawn on June 1.

Lord Jellicoe steamed 97 miles to the south and then, after dawn, at 2.45, turned north for 15 miles instead of going in the direction of the Horn Reef Lightvessel to intercept the much-battered German ships. The result was that the Germans retrieved all their modern big ships except the battle-cruiser *Lützow*, and all their other large armoured units except the pre-Dreadnought *Pommern*, which was torpedoed during the night, while we lost six large armoured units, of which three were battle-cruisers. Separate chapters are devoted to the night action, the torpedo and to the losses at Jutland. Another matter which is discussed is the failure of the Admiralty to send out the Harwich force, and the Third Battle Squadron of the ships of the King Edward

VII. class until after the battle was over on the forenoon of June 1, these forces having remained in harbour by Admiralty orders.

The following represents the relative forces engaged, the armaments of which are discussed in Chapter 13.

	BRITISH.		GERMAN.	
	Jellicoe.	Beatty.	Von Scheer.	Hipper.
Dreadnoughts .	24	4	16	7
Pre-Dreadnoughts	—	—	5	—
Battle-Cruisers .	3	6	—	5
Light Cruisers .	12	14	6	5
Armoured Cruisers	8	—	1	—
Destroyers . .	51	27	55	22

The *Roon* was the only surviving armoured cruiser of the German Navy at this period and is included as present at the battle.

CHAPTER 9

The Threshold of Battle

In the spring of 1916, there was a great undercurrent of expectation afloat. Von Tirpitz had been dismissed, and von Capelle had succeeded him on March 16, 1916. In May, von Scheer became commander-in-chief of the High Seas Fleet; With the visit of the *Kaiser* to Wilhelmshaven and the attempts to inspirit the men, it was more than ever felt that operations were being planned which would give the Grand Fleet a longed-for opportunity of attacking the enemy outside the heavily-defended Heligoland Bight. It was known that Germany was exceedingly anxious to prevent supplies from reaching Russia, both through Norway and by Archangel, and that her policy was by some means or other to detach Russia, or what was nearly the same thing, profoundly to discourage her.

On the morning of May 30, 1916, the Grand Fleet was stationed at its three main bases, Scapa, Cromarty and Rosyth. The general policy had been for the battle fleet with its attendant destroyers, two cruiser squadrons and a light cruiser squadron to be stationed at Scapa and Cromarty, whilst the Battle-Cruiser Fleet under Sir David Beatty, consisting of the battle-cruisers, three light cruiser squadrons and attendant destroyers, were at Rosyth. This great port was, in fact, the advanced base of the Grand Fleet, and the fast squadrons stationed there were favourably placed for action if advance information was obtained of enemy raids on the East Coast, or attempts at invasion.

GERMAN BATTLESHIP *FRIEDRICK DER GROSSE* ADMIRAL SCHEER'S FLAG SHIP

On the day prior to the Battle of Jutland the three ships of the Third Battle-Cruiser Squadron of *Invincible* class were with Lord Jellicoe, and their places had temporarily been taken by the powerful force of four 24-knot *Barhams* of the Fifth Battle Squadron, armed with a total of thirty-two 15-inch guns. The Rosyth force under Beatty therefore consisted of the battle-cruisers *Lion, Princess Royal, Tiger, Queen Mary, New Zealand*, and *Indefatigable*; the four battleships of the *Barham* class (the fifth ship of the class *Queen Elizabeth* was away refitting); three light cruiser squadrons aggregating thirteen ships; twenty-seven destroyers, and the *Engadine* carrying sea-planes.

The information on which the sudden orders were given to raise steam for full speed with all dispatch was received about 6 p.m. on May 30. We have not been told its exact nature, but the fact that eight destroyers from the Harwich force were in Beatty's fleet was evidence that the developments expected from the *Kaiser's* visit to Wilhelmshaven were about to take place. Time may show that we ought not to accept the account put forward by Lord Jellicoe that the fleet was merely out on one of its periodical sweeps, a statement which does not do justice to our intelligence work. As it was known that the enemy were out, the visual contacts between the fleets ought to have been arranged for daylight the following day.

We shall see this was not done, and visual contact, even if the enemy had not been sighted, could not have been obtained until well into the afternoon under the arrangements made. In the meantime, the wireless messages passing conveyed to both sides the presence of fleets at sea, and in a fair number of cases, in spite of codes, something of the meaning of the messages. The Germans are stated to have sent an actual message to the Rosyth force, purporting to come from the *Iron Duke*, to steam at twenty-three knots, in the hope that this would be obeyed!

Normally, in any sweep in the North Sea, the advanced squadron constituted a very powerful scouting force, capable of pressing home an attack or a reconnaissance. Whenever it has been detached so as to be out of sight of the battle fleet the accuracy of its information depends on it having been kept in visual contact by a chain of ships with the battle fleet until there was a definite purpose for the fast force to achieve by increasing speed. This precaution becomes necessary because of the fact that it is quite possible for two ships which have been at sea for many hours to arrive at estimates of their positions which do not correspond.

BRITISH BATTLE-CRUISER H.M.S. LION, VICE-ADMIRAL SIR DAVID BEATTY'S FLAGSHIP

The error will then vitiate all reports of an enemy subsequently encountered by the one, and transmitted to the other. Lord Jellicoe records that an error of twelve miles too far to the eastward in regard to the position of the enemy was thus made, but regarding it as inevitable he fails to see his own responsibility. Its importance will be seen later, for it resulted in the Grand Fleet arriving late in action when every minute of daylight was of the utmost value.

In order to understand how this contact is maintained after it is once made by establishing a rendezvous, say thirty miles away for the fast fleet, let us take a supposititious case where A is the battle fleet and D the battle-cruisers.

.   .   .   .   .

A   B   C   D   E

A, B, C, D, E are at equal intervals of ten miles and the line joining them constitutes a line of bearing forty miles long. A is the battle fleet with cruiser and destroyer screen reaching to B ten miles ahead, linking, ships reach to C, and beyond is first a linking ship and ten miles from C is the Battle-Cruiser Squadron, or thirty miles ahead of the battle fleet, still further again is D's cruiser and destroyer screen reaching to E. All these vessels then plot their position according to the signalled latitude and longitude of the flagship of the commander-in-chief of the Grand Fleet, and all reports of enemy sighted from D and E can be exactly plotted for the admiral's information at A.

These figures are merely given to explain the idea by which visual contact is maintained over a distance of, say, forty miles. In the actual cruising formation by which Lord Jellicoe maintained visual contact in his own force on May 30, 31, he had the Third Battle-Cruiser Squadron of three *Invincibles* twenty miles ahead with the *Chester* as linking ship, six armoured cruisers spread eight miles from each other at right angles to the line of advance, with the *Minotaur* in the centre fifteen miles ahead of the *Iron Duke*, and the linking ship *Hampshire* six miles astern of the *Minotaur* and nine miles ahead of the *Iron Duke*.

The battle fleet was spread in six divisions, each in column with the *Iron Duke* leading, the third from the left or near the centre, and three miles ahead of it was the Fourth Light Cruiser Squadron. In the chain on the line of advance along which the Grand Fleet zigzagged at a general rate of progress of 14 knots there were intervals from the *Iron Duke* to the *Invincible* of 3, 6, 6 and 5 miles, while the spread sideways of the armoured cruisers was forty miles. All these ships then worked in visual contact and plotted their position according to the signalled latitude and longitude of Lord Jellicoe's flagship, the *Iron Duke*.

Lord Jellicoe's general orders made no arrangement for contact between the Scapa and Cromarty force on the one hand and the Rosyth force on the other until after 2 p.m. on May 31, or nearly twenty-four hours after the two forces had left their respective bases. If, therefore, as happened, an enemy was encountered at or about 2 p.m. on May 31, before his divided fleet had established contact, it was possible and even probable that the position from time to time of the enemy as reported by the Rosyth force would not be accurate according to the reckoning in Lord Jellicoe's flagship, since different reckonings as to their positions on the chart had been kept by the separated forces. His anxiety after 2 p.m. concerning this visual contact was evidenced by his signals. He had risked and lost it by his general orders in the first place, and, in the second, by allowing trivialities such as economising the coal of one or two destroyers searching vessels *en route* to delay the progress of the whole fleet.

The actual order was for the Cromarty force under Admiral Jerram to meet Lord Jellicoe's Scapa force at 2 p.m., May 31, in lat. 57° 45' N., long. 4° 15' E. Sir David Beatty's Rosyth force was directed to steer so as to be in lat. 56° 40' N., long. 5° 0' E., about 2 p.m., May 31, and then to stand to the northward to get into visual touch with the battle fleet. In other words, a vital junction was deferred to about twenty hours after the Grand Fleet had gone to sea. When it was 2 p.m. the Grand Fleet was eighteen miles from its ordered position and seventy-seven miles from the Rosyth force, partly owing to Lord Jellicoe's anxiety to spare destroyers examining vessels met *en route* from burning too much fuel in regaining their positions with the fleet.

At 2 p.m. the Rosyth force had placed itself nearer the Grand Fleet's rendezvous than had been ordered, as it was in lat. 56° 46' N., long. 4° 40' E., and was steering to the northward with the view of getting into visual touch with the Grand Fleet. Twenty minutes later the enemy was sighted and all idea of getting into visual touch had to be abandoned. There was one more chance arising from the accidental fact that the Third Battle-Cruiser Squadron, capable of six knots' greater speed than the battle fleet, was with Lord Jellicoe and stationed twenty miles ahead. If this squadron had been pushed forward at once, a reckoning based on that of Lord Jellicoe's flag-ship would soon have been in possession of the Rosyth force. Instead, however, of following the safe rule of concentration, a fanciful picture of ships escaping to the Baltic was conjured up by the commander-in-chief.

The three *Invincibles* were ordered to steer to intercept the enemy in case they did try to so escape at a time when it was not even known whether the enemy were battleships or cruisers, for the first ships sighted may always be mere outlying vessels. This message was not cancelled in favour of one directing them to reinforce Beatty at once until one and a half hours later at 4 o'clock, and the outcome of the false move was that Hood's Squadron did not enter the battle until 6.15 p.m. when, without a second of delay, they gave a splendid display of what a powerful reinforcement they constituted.

The presence of the three *Invincibles* with Lord Jellicoe, and of four fast and powerful battleships with Sir David Beatty, was an accidental variation from the general disposition due to the fact that the *Invincibles* were at Scapa carrying out exercises, and while doing so their places were taken by the *Barham, Malaya, Warspite* and *Valiant*, of the *Queen Elizabeth* class. It was a fortunate accident in every respect, and might have been of still greater use if the *Invincibles*, which were one hour nearer the enemy than Lord Jellicoe and gained a quarter of an hour in every hour on the battleships in racing for the enemy, owing to their speed, had been used in the way I suggest. Apart from any reinforcement, their presence in the fight, at the earliest possible moment, would have meant absolutely reliable information for Lord Jellicoe as to the enemy's position well before he came into action himself.

The moment Hood, in the *Invincible*, obtained visual contact with Beatty, he could have signalled his position, based on the navigating officer's calculations on board the *Iron Duke*, and after that all information transmitted to Lord Jellicoe would have been accurate in every respect. It was the nemesis of Lord Jellicoe's arrangements that the first vessels he challenged at about 5.45 p.m., after signal was made to engage the enemy, should have been our own three fast *Invincibles* which did not get into action until 6.15 p.m. They were the victims as we have stated in the first place of a fanciful picture. In the second place they had been unable to steer a direct course when ordered to reinforce Beatty because they were working on false ideas as to the position of the enemy through no visual contact having been obtained at a rendezvous with the Rosyth force.

The fault then by which an error of twelve miles too far to the eastward was made in the estimate of von Scheer's position which resulted in Lord Jellicoe finding himself in the presence of the enemy twenty minutes earlier than he expected, obviously did not lie in the reports of the advanced force, but in the fact that the general orders did not allow for sufficiently early contact between the two separate bodies. Lord Jellicoe, it is true, gives a different version:—

> Owing to the constant manoeuvring of the ships of the 2nd Light Cruiser Squadron during the engagement, the position of the Southampton, as obtained by reckoning, was somewhat inaccurate, as was to be expected. This fact detracted from the Value of the reports to me, the position of the enemy by latitude and longitude, as reported from time to time to the *Iron Duke*, being consequently incorrect. The discrepancy added greatly to the difficulty experienced in ascertaining the correct moment at which to deploy the battle fleet, the flank on which to deploy, and the direction of deployment. Such discrepancies are, however, inevitable under the conditions.

Lord Jellicoe here attributes the discrepancies as to position to the constant manoeuvring. Presumably this refers to the interval between the battle-cruisers beginning the action at 3.48 p.m., and turning to southward, steering a general direction of S.S.E., with the enemy on a parallel course, and 4.38 when the *Southampton* reported that the enemy's battle fleet was in sight. Few will be found to agree that a discrepancy of twelve miles could occur in a period when about twenty miles were covered on a general S.S.E. course. The true state of affairs was that these ships had been out from Rosyth since 10 p.m. the previous evening or an interval of nearly nineteen hours, and the main fleet had been out three-quarters of an hour longer, when the *Southampton* reported the position of the German Battle Fleet. During the whole of this time no visual contact had been established between any ships of the Rosyth force with the Main force, and it was due to this oversight that the discrepancy in reckoning arose.

Lord Jellicoe has also stated that:

> The junction of the battle fleet with the scouting force after the enemy had been sighted was delayed owing to the southerly course steered by our advance force during the first hour after commencing action with the enemy battle cruisers.

Elsewhere he had been complaining at arriving in the presence of the enemy twenty minutes earlier than he expected. It is, however, difficult to see the use of the remark, for actually from the time the enemy was sighted to the time the battle fleet effected its junction, the

BRITISH 2ND DIVISION OF BATTLESHIPS

net result had been to draw the enemy about sixteen miles further to the northward. Had the distance between the two fleets been kept at thirty miles until an enemy was sighted, then the junction would have been effected much earlier and without any anxieties such as occurred because Lord Jellicoe met the enemy twelve miles further west and twenty minutes earlier than he expected.

But when all is said, the question must still be asked: Where was there any very great handicap to Lord Jellicoe in arriving in the presence of the enemy, when daylight would soon be lost, twenty minutes earlier than he expected? What real disadvantage was there in sighting the enemy on the starboard bow instead of ahead? If Lord Jellicoe really regarded it as a disadvantage to be too much ahead, why does he harp in other chapters on the undoubted advantage such a position gave the Germans in torpedoes? The truth is that in battle if you insist upon knowing too many things before you are willing to act with vigour and determination, you are likely to find that most of the action is on the side of the enemy. It must also be remembered that Lord Jellicoe was accompanied by eighteen cruisers, excluding the *Chester* and *Canterbury* with Hood, and ten of these were of very high speed.

It was their chief business to provide him with exact information long before the entry into action of his own ships. If gun flashes are seen and the boom of heavy guns comes from the starboard bow, it is their duty to find out exactly what is the cause, even at some risk to themselves, though the risk could not have been very great when the enemy was on the other side of the Rosyth force. Thus, earlier in the day at 4.38 p.m. the *Southampton* with the Second Light Cruiser Squadron pushed her reconnaissance right under the guns of the German High Seas Fleet in order to obtain the essential information.

CHAPTER 10

Beatty Delivers the High Seas Fleet to His Chief

At the moment when the first indication of the presence of the enemy was obtained, Sir David Beatty, in compliance with his orders, was steering N. by E., as in diagram A, from the rendezvous. The object was to establish visual contact with the Grand Fleet which had been delayed by waiting for destroyers examining vessels met *en route*. At 2.20 p.m. the *Galatea* which, as in diagram A, was at the easterly end of a twenty-five mile line of cruisers, sighted two enemy vessels to

Diagram A.

Course and Formation of Rosyth Force at 2.20 p.m.
--- when Galatea sighted Enemy Ships
Speed 19½ Knots

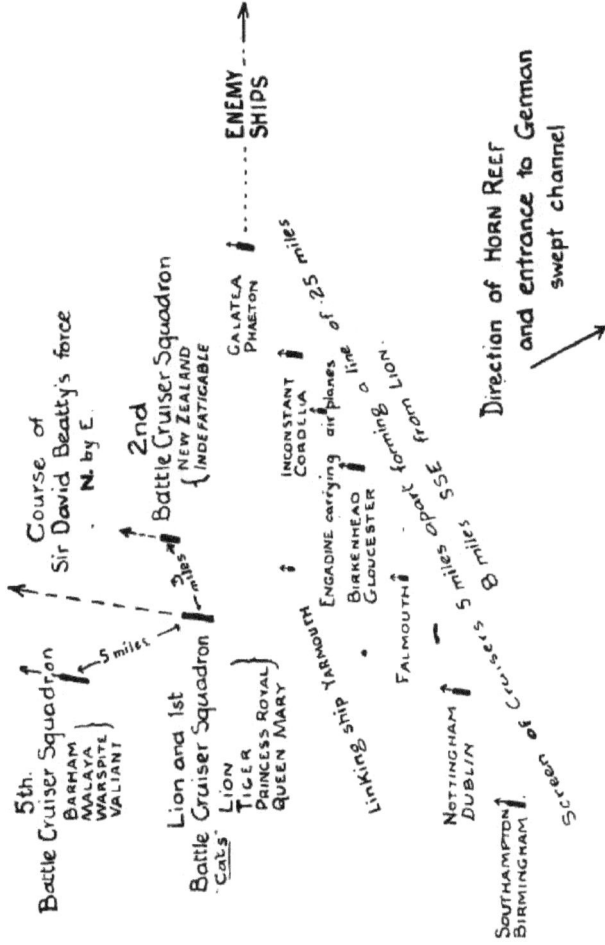

5th.
Battle Cruiser Squadron
BARHAM
MALAYA
WARSPITE
VALIANT

5 miles

Course of
Sir David Beatty's force
N. by E.

2nd
Battle Cruiser Squadron
NEW ZEALAND
INDEFATIGABLE

Lion and 1st
Battle Cruiser Squadron
"Cats"
LION
TIGER
PRINCESS ROYAL
QUEEN MARY

2 miles

GALATEA
PHAETON

INCONSTANT
CORDELIA

ENEMY
SHIPS

ENGADINE carrying airplanes

a line of 25 miles

BIRKENHEAD
GLOUCESTER

Linking ship YARMOUTH

FALMOUTH

forming a line SSE from LION.

5 miles apart

NOTTINGHAM
DUBLIN

8 miles

Direction of HORN REEF
and entrance to German
swept channel

SOUTHAMPTON
BIRMINGHAM

Screen of Cruisers

the eastward, which report was received by wireless in Lord Jellicoe's flagship the *Iron Duke*. Beatty, acting in conformance with the main policy of cutting off the return of the ships by the swept channel of the Horn Reef, at once turned his whole force in the direction of that channel.

Lord Jellicoe at 2.30 p.m. directed the three 26-knot *Invincibles*, which were twenty miles ahead of his fleet, to steer so as to intercept any escape of the enemy to the Baltic, which order was countermanded at 4.5 p.m. (see chronology) after it was known that the smoke sighted was that of the five enemy battle-cruisers. They were then directed to steer for the calculated position of our battle-cruisers. Owing to a difference of reckoning between the *Iron Duke* and the *Lion* this calculated position was about twelve miles too far to the eastward, and, together with the time lost in steering east, resulted in the *Invincibles* not getting into action with the enemy's battle-cruisers until 6.15, or the time when our battleships commenced the movement to deploy into line. To substitute a mere supposition for an actual fact is an error into which an admiral should not fall.

A message was received at 2.20 p.m. that the enemy lay in a certain direction, and it was not known whether the two enemy vessels were isolated ships or outlying cruisers of a fleet. The report was cruisers and Beatty's thirty-knot cruisers could take care of them, but if the major supposition proved correct that they were outlying cruisers how can one find any excuse for adopting a fanciful picture of two small cruisers escaping to the Baltic, so that three great battle-cruisers were sent to prevent it. He could have got there by the Kiel Canal and he came from the Heligoland Bight. Steering for the enemy was the Rosyth force, with which no portion of Lord Jellicoe's Fleet had established contact, a matter of great importance in view of the necessity of all ships working to the same plotting on the chart as the flagship *Iron Duke*. If the vessels proved to be outlying cruisers of a battle fleet or a squadron of battle-cruisers, then the *Invincibles* in addition to establishing visual contact would have been a welcome reinforcement.

Our North Sea strategy, it should be stated, was conditioned by the fact that it was known that our one objective, the enemy fleet, was in the habit of using a channel swept clear of mines in the vicinity of the Horn Reef as a main exit and entrance into the Heligoland Bight. It was, therefore, the primary object of our warships, encountering German ships north of the Horn Reef, to place themselves so as to cut the enemy off from the entrance to this channel, and so prevent his return to the mined waters and fortified coasts of the Heligoland Bight. Our first care, in order to achieve this purpose, was to obtain early information of the enemy proceeding to sea, and as to the extent of his force.

The acquisition of this information was hampered by two bad errors of the Admiralty as to the material required, in both of which Germany had produced the necessary equipment before the war broke out. The first was the development of lighter than air craft which could scout over the North Sea. The dirigibles, building in 1914, were abandoned by Mr. Churchill's orders. The second error was that no submarines were equipped, until late in the war, with a long range wireless, so as to transmit the information they acquired while in the Heligoland Bight and its vicinity.

On the other hand, Germany's Zeppelins had performed North Sea voyages before the war, and her submarines were so well equipped with wireless that when the *Formidable* was torpedoed in the British Channel, the information at once went to Berlin. On this occasion, when the whole Grand Fleet swept over the northern section of the North Sea, we were aware from certain indications that German ships would be met, but we did not know in what strength the move would be made. We were also aware of the German Fleet's wireless messages.

A quarter of an hour later, or at 2.35 p.m., the report was received from the *Galatea* that a large amount of smoke, apparently from a fleet, was observed to the eastward, and, after a few minutes' interval, that these ships were steaming to the northward. On receipt of this report Beatty altered course to E.N.E. towards the smoke, and at 3.30 p.m., or seventy minutes after the first report, five enemy battle-cruisers accompanied by two light cruisers and fifteen destroyers were sighted.

At the time of this second report from the *Galatea* the position of the ships was as shown in diagram B. The visibility was good, the sun behind the British force, the wind S.E., and the position favourable for cutting off the enemy from the Horn Reef Channel. Nothing was known of the German Battle Fleet being at sea. The four fast battleships of the *Queen Elizabeth* class, armed with eight 15-inch guns each, were 10,000 yards, or 5 nautical miles, away and out of range. They did not come into action until twenty minutes after the battle began, or at 4.8 p.m., at 19,000 to 20,000 yards' range, the battle-cruisers of both sides having opened fire simultaneously at 3.48 p.m. Beatty having brought the enemy to action in a position advantageous for cutting them off from the Horn Reef, now reduced speed from 27 to 21 knots to enable the four *Barhams* and their small craft satellites to come up.

The German fire was accurate, three of the 1st Battle-Cruiser Squadron being hit several times in the first twelve minutes of action, the *Lion* being hit twice in the first three minutes. Both squadrons pursued zigzag courses for the purpose of confusing the fire-control of the opposing side, so that the range had opened to 23,000 yards at 4.12 p.m. (this is not shown in the official diagram, which makes the range 18,000 yards), and course was again altered to close the enemy. Beatty had given a general direction to his destroyers to attack when they thought the moment favourable, and a division of twelve destroyers proceeded to get ahead of the enemy at 4.16.

About the same time an enemy cruiser and fifteen enemy destroyers moved out for a similar purpose. The object was in each case to obtain a favourable position on the bow, and then turn to the north or the opposite course to the enemy, and fire their torpedoes. The two flotillas met and the Germans lost two destroyers, the British destroyers having much superior gun armaments. The enemy destroyers succeeded in firing some torpedoes at our four *Barhams* without effect, and we also fired several torpedoes. The *Nestor* fired three torpedoes, two about 4.48, and one about eight minutes later.

Captain Bingham of the *Nestor* believed that the *Lützow* was hit, and he states that the *Nestor's* survivors, who were subsequently taken prisoners, had confirmation of this from the *Lützow's* crew, who said that their speed was much reduced. The German cruiser disabled the *Nestor*, and she, with the *Nomad*, which was disabled about 4.45, were subsequently sunk by the German Battle Fleet, but not before the *Nestor* had discharged her fourth and last torpedo. The attack was handicapped, like subsequent destroyer operations in the daylight battle, by our vessels making easy targets through being painted black.

It is worthwhile at this stage to point out that an attack such as the one we have dealt with may last half through a battle in spite of the speed of the assailants, which is a mile or more in two minutes. They have first to draw well ahead of any enemy moving at 26 knots, and it may take half an hour to do so on a somewhat converging course. They then turn towards the enemy to deliver the attack on the opposite course, and the rate of approach is that of their combined speeds, or as much as an express train. It is then very difficult for the defending guns to get good aimed shots, owing to the rapidity with which the bearing changes, and the torpedoes are fired soon after at the line, which in this case was about two thousand yards in length,

DIAGRAM B.

AT 3.25 ENEMY BATTLE-CRUISERS SIGHTED
VISIBILITY GOOD FOR THE BRITISH FORCE.

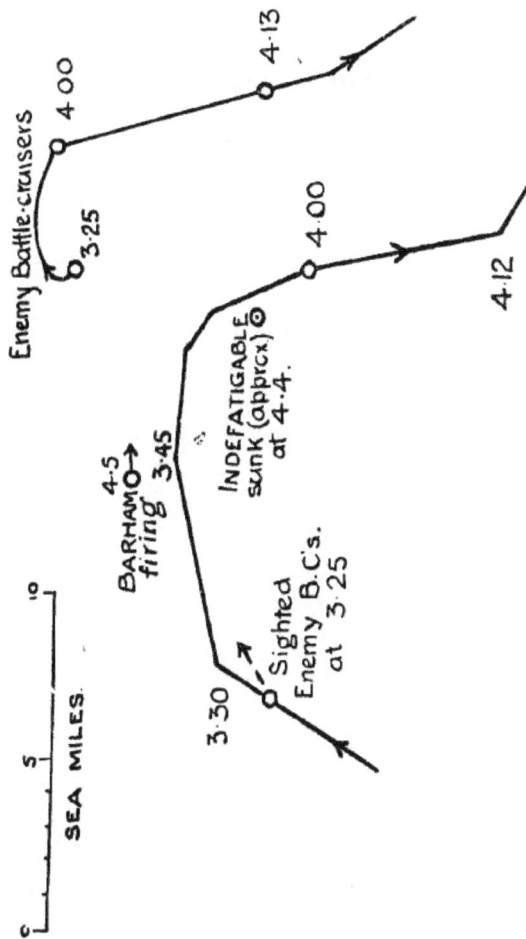

Enemy Battle-cruisers

4·00

4·13

3·25

4·00

4·12

BARHAM_O→
firing 3·45

4·5

INDEFATIGABLE
sunk (approx)⊙
at 4·4.

Sighted
Enemy B.C's.
at 3·25

3·30

SEA MILES.

0   5   10

of which about half would be actual target. In this particular attack, before even our torpedoes were fired, our own battle-cruisers had turned in succession to north at 4.42 on sighting the enemy High Seas Fleet of 22 battleships. While our torpedoes were speeding to the enemy battle-cruisers they turned four points away, and subsequently to north, making the complete turn in the opposite direction to Beatty. The *Barhams* turned up astern of our battle-cruisers so as to act as a rear-guard.

It is necessary now to note some of the results which had been achieved in the first stages of the action before even the High Sea Fleet had, been sighted. These results were due to the excellence of the German gunnery, and indirectly to the defective construction of the British ships. At 4 p.m. the roof of one of the four turrets of the *Lion* was blown off, and the ship was saved from utter disaster by the presence of mind and bravery of an officer, who lost his life. Subsequently at 4.6 p.m. the *Indefatigable*, armed with eight 12-inch guns, and at 4.26 the *Queen Mary*, armed with eight 13½-inch guns, blew up through the flash of shells getting to the magazines.

The latter ship, it will be seen, was totally destroyed eighteen minutes after the four great *Barhams* had come into action, so that the five German battle-cruisers with sixteen 12-inch and twenty-eight 11-inch guns accomplished this feat when subjected to the fire of four battleships with thirty-two 15-inch guns, and five surviving battle-cruisers armed with thirty-two 13½-inch and eight 12-inch guns. Our battle-cruisers were firing from a position before the beam of the enemy, and the four *Barhams* some distance astern from a position abaft the beam. It is said that owing to the bad light and to smoke screens made by the enemy, not more than two of the enemy could be seen at a time from the *Barhams*, but this cannot account for so astounding a result.

The intelligent use of smoke screens is not an accidental matter, nor was it in any respect new. It had been a practice of the Germans at the beginning of the war. The ships sunk were the victims of single well-directed salvoes, and there is no other explanation than errors of design, for the Germans were, as we have seen, taking punishment from a far more powerful and numerous artillery. It was a remarkable feat, for which a variety of errors in the peace preparation of the navy have been blamed. These include defective construction of British ships; a superior delay action German fuse so that the shells burst inside the armour; improved armour-piercing shell, and a better system of fire-control.

In all respects great improvements were made after the Battle of Jutland, and proposed developments that had been vetoed as impossible were accomplished. The Germans had inflicted a surprise on us owing to the secrecy policy which prevented criticism before the war. Having once inflicted the surprise, the Germans were well aware that we would profit by the experience. They had taught us the one great flaw in our designs which the Fisher advertisement policy had presented to them at the same time as it was concealed from this country.

In all probability the stolen *Indefatigable* designs, referred to elsewhere, had revealed to Germany the weak points of our battle-cruisers of which we exhibited such profound ignorance. This defective construction is dealt with elsewhere. Beatty had lost two battle-cruisers in circumstances far more sudden, dramatic and surprising than the blowing up of the great French ship *L'Orient* at the Battle of the Nile. Yet in the spirit in which Nelson held on when he lost one-fourth of his force on going into action at Copenhagen, Beatty raced on to the southward and the British fire gradually began to tell on the five well-armoured battle-cruisers of the enemy.

At 4.18 p.m. the third battle-cruiser in the German line was on fire. The effect of our gunnery was evidenced by a depreciation both in the accuracy and rapidity of the enemy's fire. Unfortunately, the visibility was beginning to lessen looking to the eastward, and the outline of the enemy ships was indistinct, while to westward it improved for the enemy, giving them the advantage in gun-control. Two hours were to intervene before the Grand Fleet could render any assistance. Ships had been lost, but no ship in the British force had been disabled or reduced in steaming powers. Had this happened one can well imagine the controversy which would have raged round the Battle Orders which placed the Rosyth force at the start so far apart as 50 miles from the Main force. Risks must be run for definite strategical and tactical purposes; but in this case one is unable to perceive the object which would justify the risk. There is a definite reason in concealing the main force, but this is fully achieved, except against air craft, by screening at a distance of 30 miles.

The light-cruiser *Southampton* was scouting ahead of the four battle-cruisers, and at 4.38 p.m. her report that the entire German High Seas Fleet was in sight altered the whole situation. This report necessitated retirement on our own Grand Fleet, and Beatty's role now became one of scouting rather than attacking.

Diagram C.

From 5·00 to 5·45 Visibility bad for us and good for Enemy

SEA MILES.

Lat. ·56° 37′ N.
Long. 5° 58½ E.

4·13

4·00

4·30

5·00

4·52

Enemy destroyers.

13th Flotilla Attack

Queen Mary 4·20 blew up

4·12

5·00

5·15
2nd. L.C.S being
shelled by enemy
Battleships.

4·37

4·45

Sighted Enemy Battle Fleet
at 4·40

2nd. Light Cruiser Squadron
altered course to Northward at 4·45

4·38
Enemy Battle Fleet
(approx.)

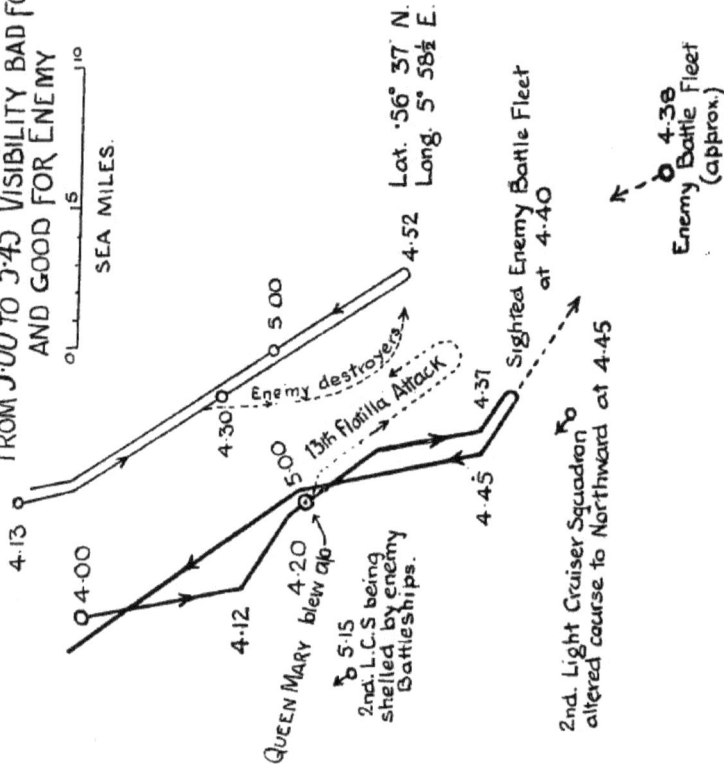

Diagram is based
on official plot German
Squadron zigzagged.
Range was 23,000 yds.
at 4·12 (not 19,000 as in
diagram) so positions are
only approximate.

He maintained contact with the enemy, reported his movements, and so manoeuvred as to draw the enemy into a position where the battle fleet could surprise him. He had therefore to avoid loss and keep to the primary object of preparing the situation for the advent of the heavy fleet. Consequently, a complete turn to the northward was made as soon as the enemy fleet had been sighted, the four *Barhams* turning astern of the four battle-cruisers at 4.57 p.m., and the enemy battle-cruisers turning at 4.52 p.m., ahead of their battle fleet. The general position at the time of these turns is sketched in diagram C. The action then continued on a northerly course at a range of about 14,000 yards. During this time the enemy received severe punishment, and undoubtedly one battle-cruiser quitted the line in a very damaged condition.

As the enemy High Seas Fleet was following, the main purpose of a Battle-Cruiser Squadron had been achieved. Beatty had fought the battle-cruisers, found the enemy's battle fleet and was drawing it north, and it only remained for him to manoeuvre his Rosyth force so as to hand over the enemy ships for targets to the Grand Fleet while cutting off that enemy from the sanctuary of his minefields. Thus, he continued in action with the enemy battle-cruisers, the four battle-ships of the *Barham* class occasionally drawing the fire of the leading *Königs* of the enemy's battle fleet. The great majority of the enemy battleships were out of action and trailing far astern. The event showed the wisdom of Lord Fisher's policy in increasing the speed of the battleships and battle-cruisers.

The *Königs* were steaming well, and the Fifth Battle Squadron only drew ahead gradually, but the result must have been to leave the 17-knot pre-Dreadnoughts far behind, a circumstance which may explain the slowness of the enemy movements at a later stage after 6 o'clock, and the complete turn then made by his battle-cruisers and probably by the *Königs* as well. It was evident that he did not believe our battle fleet to be out or he would not have thus risked separating his forces. The atmospheric conditions were unfavourable to the use of Zeppelins or he might have been undeceived.

In spite of the advantage of light from 5 p.m. to nearly 6 p.m. on this northerly course, the gunnery of the enemy had fallen off. Our own ships were silhouetted against a clear horizon, as shown by a photograph taken of our destroyers to the westward at 5.15, at least 16,000 yards away, whereas we had to cease fire from 5.15 until 5.40 p.m., when three or four enemy battle-cruisers could be seen indistinctly at about 14,000 yards. In the next ten minutes the *Lion* fired 15 salvoes.

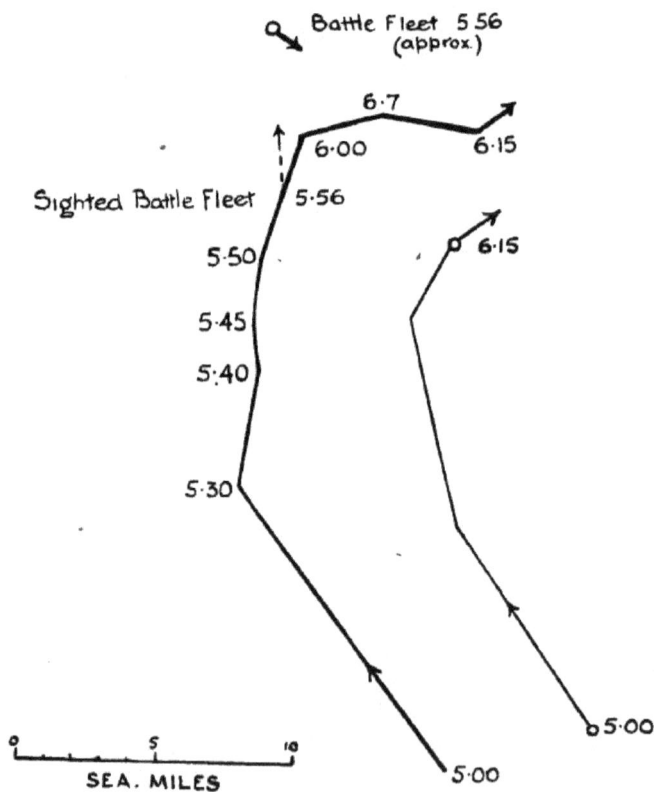

DIAGRAM D.

FROM 5·45 VISIBILITY GOOD FOR US AND BAD FOR ENEMY.

Battle Fleet 5·56 (approx.)

6·7

6·00

Sighted Battle Fleet

5·56

6·15

6·15

5·50

5·45

5·40

5·30

5·00

5·00

SEA. MILES

At 5.35 (see Diagram D) the course of battle was changed by Beatty to N.E. from N.N.E., the range being kept at 14,000 yards.

The enemy about 5.55 accentuated this movement to the eastward possibly on information from his cruisers which had come into contact with the Third Battle Cruiser Squadron of *Invincibles* at that time steering due south. At 5.50 Beatty sighted Jellicoe's advanced cruisers on port bow, and at 5.56 the starboard division of the battle fleet bearing due north. He thereupon altered course to east, proceeded at utmost speed and brought the range down to 12,000 yards, there being three enemy battle-cruisers in sight closely followed by the *Königs*.

One hour's hard steaming must have left the pre-Dreadnoughts well behind. In fact, we do not hear of them at any stage of the daylight battle, but only in connection with the night attacks when the Germans acknowledge that the *Pommern* was lost as the result of a torpedo attack.

I have commented elsewhere on the fact that, in a fleet so well supplied with cruisers and destroyers, when information should have been the more zealously sought because of the uncertain visibility, Lord Jellicoe obtained his first knowledge of the position of his battle-cruisers by sighting them himself at 5.50 from the *Iron Duke* in the centre of the Fleet. As there was firing astern of our battle-cruisers, the presumption was that the *Barhams* were engaging the enemy battle fleet. This was twenty-five minutes before the actual deployment. Even if he still hesitated about making the front of the line of leaders of divisions at right angles to the probable bearing of the enemy, why did he wait until 6.8 before signalling to the destroyers to take up their battle stations (see diagram of intended battle positions)? It appears that the delay was once again, due to defensive considerations predominating over vital offensive requirements.

The three *Invincibles* under Hood, once in sight of the enemy, were brought into play by this admiral with a swiftness of onset for which Beatty in his despatch expresses unstinted admiration. At 6.19 Beatty had the mortification of seeing the 5th Battle Squadron turning away widely to port to form astern of the twenty-four ships of the Grand Fleet. At 6.20 he sighted his own *Invincibles* ahead and within five minutes they were 8,000 yards from the enemy's line. Beatty thereupon altered course to E.S.E. to support them. The surprise to the enemy on finding the head of his line checked was so great that, combined with the bad visibility from his position, he was firmly convinced, and remained for days firmly under the battle's impression,

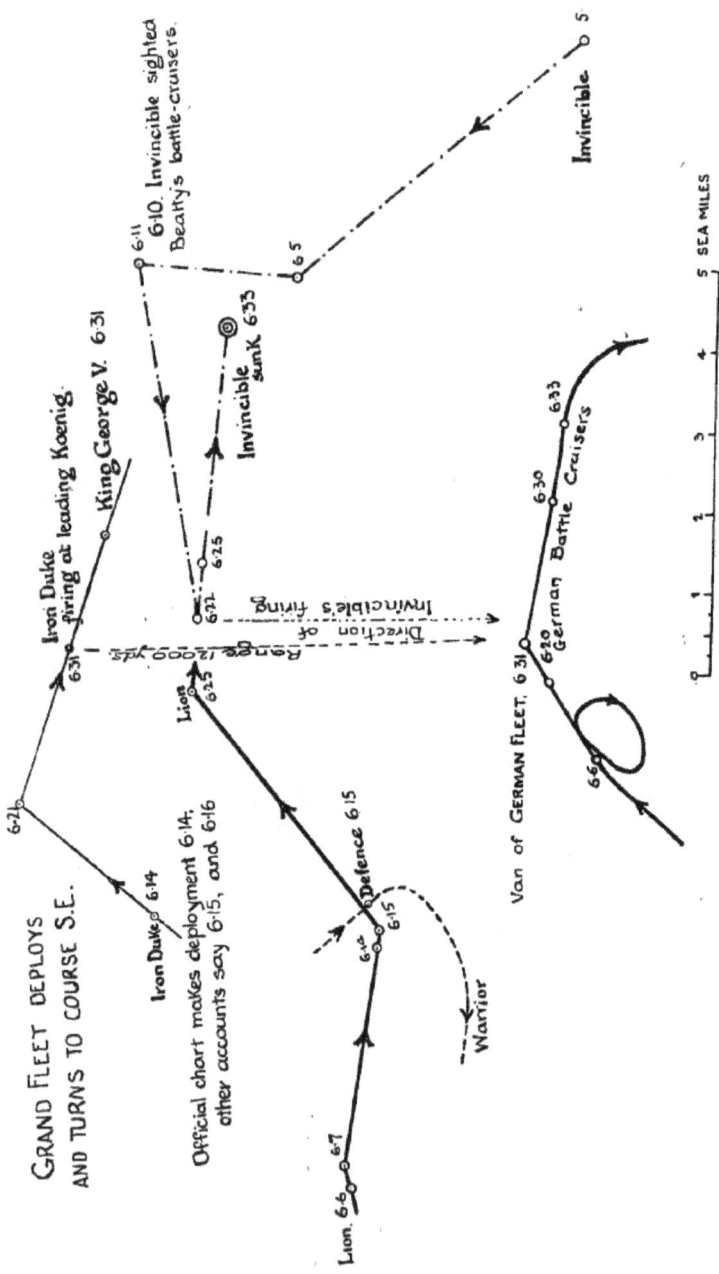

THE THREE INVINCIBLES ENTER THE BATTLE.

GRAND FLEET DEPLOYS
AND TURNS TO COURSE S.E.

Official chart makes deployment 6.14,
other accounts say 6.15, and 6.16.

6.10. Invincible sighted
Beatty's battle-cruisers.

Invincible sunk 6.35

Direction of Invincible's firing

Range 12,000 yds.

King George V. 6.31

Iron Duke firing at leading Koenig.

Lion 6.25

Iron Duke 6.14

Lion. 6.6

Defence 6.15

Warrior

Van of German Fleet, 6.31

German Battle Cruisers

Invincible

5 SEA MILES

that the three *Invincibles* were battleships and leading the Grand Fleet's line into action.

This can be seen by the enemy diagram officially issued some days after the battle. The German battle-cruisers and possibly the *Königs* had made a complete turn of 16 points between 6 o'clock and 6.16 p.m. towards their main support, the German Battle Fleet, then turned back again, and thus the armoured cruiser *Warrior* had actually come under the starboard guns of the enemy. We say "possibly the *Königs*" because one shell that hit the *König* struck her starboard side and at no other time could she have exposed her starboard side to gunfire.

The sixteen point turn then was actually completed, or completing, at the moment the Grand Fleet was entering action on its right, and, bearing in mind the simple rule that one should manoeuvre as little as possible in sight of the enemy, it is difficult to imagine a more favourable time to engage him, than with his leading ships dominated by our battle-cruisers and steering in a circle to join forces with the slower battleships, while pounding away, already in action, were the four *Barhams* with thirty-two 15-inch guns and the *Marlborough's* division at 18,000 yards range firing eight 15-inch, twenty 13½-inch, and ten 12-inch guns.

Against the five German battle-cruisers carrying sixteen 12-inch guns and twenty-eight 11-inch guns, assuming, all were still fighting (though the information points to only three continuing in formation) there were now seven battle-cruisers carrying twenty-four 13½-inch guns, and thirty-two 12-inch guns, and in addition we held the van position, which gives the advantage to the torpedo, and enables a fleet to threaten a movement across the head of the enemy's line and thereby enfilade him. If discount for the wear and tear of a fight has to be applied to the above, it will only take away two of the *Lion's* guns which were disabled about 4 o'clock, and probably two enemy battle-cruisers for fighting purposes.

Against this mass of heavier artillery what was there to fear in the enemy's 12-inch and 11-inch guns? What was the burden of the materialist's song before the war, when some of us were pressing so hard for the margin which would give us the swift victory of annihilating the enemy? He said the German 11-inch shell weighed only 700 lb., the 12-inch shell 980 lb., while the British 15-inch weighed 1,950 lb., that is, nearly three times as heavy as the German 11-inch shell and nine times as destructive. He told us that the effect of the burster of a shell varies as the square, so that if three times as large there is nine times

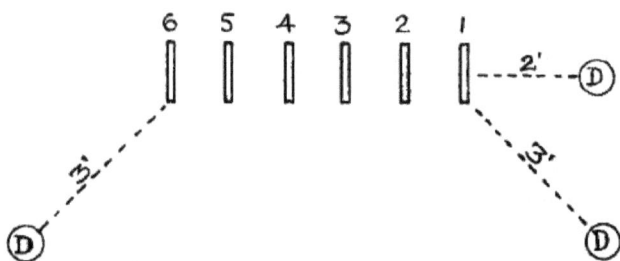

GRAND FLEET WITH DESTROYERS' INTENDED BATTLE POSITIONS.

The movement to these positions was ordered too late, and destroyers were all moving across front at moment of deployment.

GERMAN SEMI-OFFICIAL DIAGRAM.

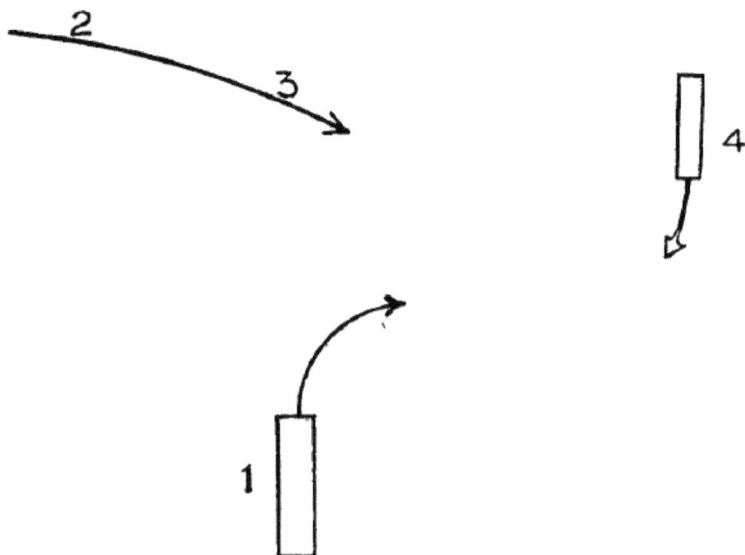

1.   German Fleet.

2 and 3.   Described as " 4 Battle Cruisers and 5 Queen Elizabeths."

4.   " Meanwhile there approaches from the North, presumably coming from Norwegian waters, the English main force (4) consisting of more than 20 battleships."

the effect. He expatiated on the much greater power of the heavier projectile at long ranges against armour; the ease with which one gets the range owing to the huge splash made by the big shell when it falls into the water, the greater accuracy because of the flatter trajectory, so that the danger space at long range was twice as great for the 15-inch gun as for the German 11-inch gun; and the absence of spread in the fall of the heavier projectiles so that ships are not straddled, but hit.

The public was deluged with Dreadnought talk by the active Press campaign of the Admiralty, the whole tendency of it being that the German designs were inferior, that nothing else mattered but Dreadnoughts, and the public might "sleep quietly in their beds." This kind of thing persisted well into the war. When Mr. Churchill spoke on the Navy Estimates on February 15, 1915, he certainly gave the House the views of his naval advisers, and this is what he said:—

> Now, I come to the battle-cruiser action on the Dogger Bank. That action was not fought out, because the enemy, after abandoning their wounded consort, the *Blücher*, made good their escape into waters infested by their submarines and mines.
>
> ★★★★★★
>
> This statement was incorrect. The flagship *Lion* dropped out of action owing to impaired speed as the result of being hit. The second-in-command abandoned the chase when far away from the German minefields, and the submarines were no menace to vessels going 26 knots flanked by destroyers.
>
> ★★★★★★
>
> But this combat between the finest ships in both navies is of immense significance and value in the light which it throws upon rival systems of design and armament, and upon relative gunnery efficiency. It is the first test we have ever had, and, without depending too much upon it, I think it is at once important and encouraging. First of all, it vindicates, so far as it goes, the theories of design, and particularly of big gun armament, always identified with Lord Fisher. The range of the British guns was found to exceed that of the German. Although the German shell is a most formidable instrument of destruction, the bursting, smashing power of the heavier British projectile is decidedly greater, and—this is the great thing—our shooting is at least as good as theirs.

The navy, while always working very hard—no one, except

themselves, knows how hard they have worked in these years—have credited the Germans with a sort of super-efficiency in gunnery, and we have always been prepared for some surprises in their system of control and accuracy of fire. But there is a feeling, after the combat of 24th January, that perhaps our naval officers were too diffident in regard to their own professional skill in gunnery. Then the guns. While the Germans were building 11-inch guns we built 12-inch and 13½-inch guns. Before they advanced to the 12-inch gun we had large numbers of ships armed with the 13½.

It was said by the opposite school of naval force that a smaller gun fires faster and has a higher velocity, and therefore the greater destructive power—and Krupp is the master gunmaker of the world—and it was very right and proper to take such a possibility into consideration. Everything that we have learnt, however, so far shows that we need not at all doubt the wisdom of our policy or the excellence of our material. The 13½-inch gun is unequalled by any weapon yet brought on the scene. Now we have the 15-inch gun, with which the five *Queen Elizabeths* and the five *Royal Sovereigns* are all armed, coming into line, and this gun in quality equals the 13½-inch gun, and is vastly more powerful and destructive.

It is clear that no representations had come from Lord Jellicoe to cause the First Lord to pause over such a boastful utterance. It is *after* the event that one gets, the depreciation of British material! The event was a battle, when these Dreadnoughts, with the German Fleet at their mercy, were held to be so valuable for ulterior objects that a flotilla of eleven German destroyers, attacking the rear of the line, drove twenty-seven of them out of action! How could von Scheer have anticipated such luck? He had been tempted north by the hope of annihilating Beatty's force already reported as having lost two main units. He would never have ventured into the trap if he had thought there was any danger of contact with the Grand Fleet, and their arrival came in the nature of a great surprise.

He was, in the first instance, given time to recover from that surprise; in the next, he was able to shake this terrible menace off by the simple and well-known expedient of launching a destroyer attack. The persistence of the weak force under Beatty harried him up till 8.38 p.m., when it left him seven to eight hours' steaming from his swept

Horn Reef Channel, so that he could be intercepted at daylight. So far as the Grand Fleet was concerned, he was left free to return through that channel by daylight with no other risk than some mines scattered during the night by the *Abdiel* in the Horn Reef Channel.

CHAPTER 11

The Theory of Deployment

The cruising formation to be adopted by a fleet of 100 to 150 vessels when it may meet an enemy at sea depends upon visibility. While small craft are of the greatest importance in obtaining information, and in action must be placed in a position from which they can attack the enemy with torpedoes, or overwhelm enemy vessels of their own type, they must not impede, by their proximity or their smoke, the gunnery of the battleships and battle-cruisers. Altogether insufficient attention was devoted on May 31 to these matters. Not only did the small craft which drew on to the scene of battle after 5.30 fail to supply the commander-in-chief with information, but they were so used and disposed as repeatedly to interfere with the gunnery of the primary units.

It is difficult to understand the situation when the *Defence* (which was sunk at 6.16 just after crossing the bow of the *Lion*) and the *Warrior* circled across the path of the battle-cruisers in the endeavour to take up their westward station on the Grand Fleet. They thus came between our battle-cruisers and the enemy and blanketed the fire from Beatty's ships while sacrificing themselves.

When, as in this war, the enemy, by his weakness, is forced to avoid battle, it becomes of the greatest importance to organise the fast ships apart from the slowest. It was possible in the Grand Fleet, not merely to organise the fleet in two fast divisions of battle-cruisers and the Fifth Battle Squadron of *Barhams*, but to create a 22-knot division as well. It was of overwhelming importance to prevent the enemy's escape and to counter any advantage he obtained with the torpedo from turning-away tactics. If, for instance, it is desired not to lose relative position, a four point, or 45°, turn towards the enemy would require a relative speed of 14 to 10, which the *Barhams* could easily provide. In parallel courses a 3-knot advantage of speed is a gain of 300 yards a minute.

One other fact has to be carefully considered in North Sea warfare. When the *Dreadnought* designs were under discussion in the House of Commons, I pointed out that it was quite impossible for us to say we were going to build a ship which was to fight outside torpedo range. The Sailing Directions gave one a clear idea of the number of misty days in the North Sea, and since it was the business of the British Fleets to fight decisive battles when they got the chance, they would, from time to time, have to go inside torpedo range.

The mistake in the first Dreadnoughts, which were provided with an entirely insufficient secondary armament for protection against destroyers and submarines, was rectified in later vessels; but owing to the ships being designed with insufficient beam in order to adapt them to existing docks, they were needlessly vulnerable to torpedo attacks. Points such as these derive their chief importance because of the effect they have in swaying the conduct of men who bow down before material considerations, and who do not press the advantages they possess because they are morbidly anxious about the risks they encounter.

To effect, on entry into action, the most effectual surprise with the means at his disposal, an admiral has to bear in mind, first, the approach, and then the deployment. The enemy's position changes rapidly, and as the reports are received the course and line of bearing of leaders of divisions have to be adjusted so as to secure the most favourable approach with the least loss of time. The formation, on drawing near to the enemy, must lend itself to rapid deployment so as to have the greatest number of guns to bear with the least possible delay against a section of the enemy.

Before entry into battle, a rough idea is obtained as to the visibility in different directions by sweeping all round the horizon with the range-finders to get the maximum ranges at which ships can be seen. If the weather had been clear, as it was on the occasion of the Dogger Bank action, it would have been the correct intention to fight at first at over 14,000 yards, provided there was time in hand, because that range not only discounted torpedoes but gave the full advantage to our heavy projectiles. We had exactly 200 guns in the British Fleet of over 12-inch calibre, a large proportion of them firing shell of 1,950 lb. weight, as compared with 981 lb. for the German 12-inch gun.

The Germans, on the other hand, had not one single ship with guns greater than 12-inch calibre, and the majority of their ships had 11-inch guns firing 760 lb. projectiles. The advantage of the heavy projectile at the long ranges is very great, but all such considerations on May 31 were discounted by the fact that the conditions of light did not permit the guns to be used at such distances. Hence the next point to be appreciated was that the range-finder revealed that the advantage of light was with a force to the northward and eastward, and the advantage of light means the multiplication of whatever gunnery advantage you possess. There was then a distinct premium on refusing to allow the torpedo to dominate the movements of the British Fleet.

Unfortunately, the very reverse was the thought in the mind of Lord Jellicoe. Apart from this, the theory on which Lord Jellicoe obviously worked on going into action was sound if he knew for certain the exact position of the enemy. In other words, his plan was based on conditions of good visibility not usually found in the North Sea. It was to bring his fleet into action with all guns bearing. Take an ordinary cruising formation such as the six divisions in which he formed his fleet, the line AB joining the leaders of divisions will be at right angles to the course of the fleet.

The important thing then is to manoeuvre so as to get the line AB at right angles to the bearing of the enemy instead of being at right angles to the course of the fleet. The result is given in the second diagram.

The manoeuvre of bringing all guns to bear is a simple one from this formation, involving merely the turning of the ships into the line AB. Thus, to form the line of battle, the leading ships of columns would turn at once to the line AB, while the other ships of the divisions would follow their leaders in succession.

But on May 31 the conditions were entirely uncertain, and Lord Jellicoe states there was insufficient information to justify the alteration in direction of the line AB as explained above. The cruising order adopted was consequently not satisfactory for the particular conditions when the enemy would probably be sighted from an unexpected direction. It might have been atoned for if Lord Jellicoe had made better use of his cruisers and destroyers for the purpose of obtaining information. But in the circumstances the formation was distinctly bad, as can be seen by the following examples. The battle fleet is in six columns on the course S.E. by S., with the line AB at right angles to the course. Let us suppose the enemy is unexpectedly sighted in the direction X.

Then to get the fleet into battle line on a line OZ at right angles to OX, and so to get all guns bearing, is a complicated manoeuvre, and would take a considerable time, being accomplished by turning either the wing column A or B on to a line parallel to OZ, the other columns turning towards the wing column and following up in the wake of A or B. In such circumstances the risk is that the wing columns will suffer severely through concentrated fire before the other columns could come into the line of battle.

From the foregoing it will be seen that the cruising order of the battle fleet was not suitable for the conditions of low visibility when the enemy might be encountered suddenly from an unexpected quarter. Lord Jellicoe says nothing on this point, and it can only be inferred that despite the misty Conditions which constantly prevail in the North Sea, the important question of bringing the battle fleet into action in the shortest possible time in such circumstances had received insufficient attention. Tactical investigation had apparently been lacking.

Up to the last moment Lord Jellicoe remained uncertain as to the position of the enemy. He states:

> The first definite information received onboard the fleet flagship of the position of the enemy's battle fleet did not therefore come in until 6.14 p.m., and the position given placed it 30° before the beam of *Iron Duke* or 59° before the starboard beam of *Marlborough*.

Is not this an extraordinary confession of failure from an admiral possessed of the great superiority of 36 cruisers to 11 for the enemy, since the main function of cruisers is to act as the eyes of the Fleet? Lord Jellicoe goes on to say:—

> There was no time to lose, as there was evident danger of the starboard wing column (that is, the column led by *Marlborough*) being engaged by the whole German Battle Fleet before deployment could be effected. So at 6.16 p.m. a signal was made to the battle fleet to form line of battle on the port wing column (that is, the column led by *King George V.*) on a course S.E. by E., it being assumed that the course of the enemy was approximately the same as that of our battle-cruisers.

Lord Jellicoe had therefore decided to form his line on the column led by *King George V.*, that is, the column away from the enemy, *vide* diagram, so that during the formation of this line columns of the battle fleet would be turning away from the enemy. In any action he took he was hampered by the fact that the battle fleet was not initially in a suitable cruising order for the conditions. Apart from this, however, it is pertinent to ask:

A   MARLBOROUGH   COLOSSUS   BENBOW   IRON DUKE   ORION   KING GEORGE V   B

Course SE by S.

(1)

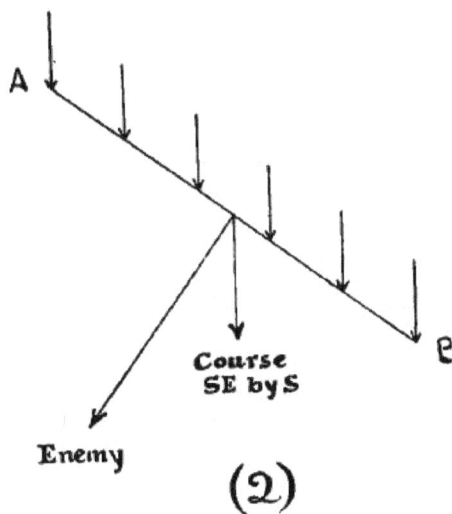

A

Course
SE by S

Enemy

(2)

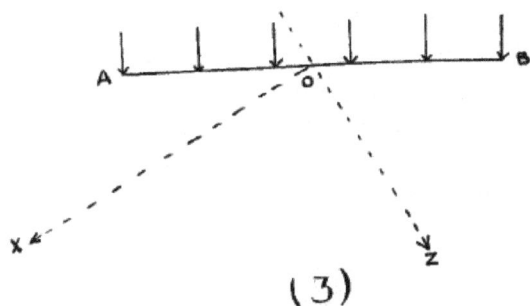

A   B

X   O   Z

(3)

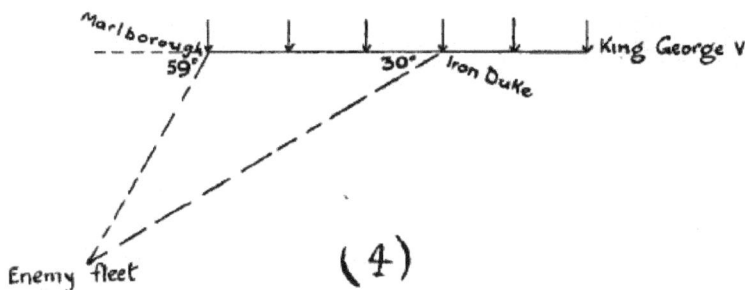

Marlborough   King George V

59°   30°   Iron Duke

Enemy fleet   (4)

Was the decision to deploy on the port column away from the enemy as opposed to the starboard column, that is, towards the enemy, a correct one?

Lord Jellicoe himself states that his first and natural impulse was to form on the starboard wing column in order to bring the fleet into action at the earliest possible moment. But he goes on to say that he deliberately sacrificed this tremendous advantage in view of the risks, which he considered too great to be run.

These risks included the possibility that in forming on the near column, divisions of the battle fleet as they came up to form into line would be subjected to a concentrated enemy fire and would be over-whelmed, and also that enemy destroyer attacks would be launched against the British Fleet whilst deploying, and that heavy losses might be sustained. Considerations of caution, therefore, urged deployment on the port column away from the enemy, but considerations of early action with the enemy urged deployment on the starboard column. Caution won the day.

The arguments for caution are very fully set forth in Lord Jellicoe's book, and have been dealt with in these pages. The arguments deal only, however, with material factors and include the development of gunfire and the effect of torpedo fire. But the far larger moral question of joining action early in view of the failing visibility and few hours of daylight is left unconsidered. No account is taken of the factor of surprise and its effect on the German command. Material considerations alone weighed with Lord Jellicoe, but in the final issue history shows that it is the moral forces to which a commander must pay the most heed, for these exercise the decisive influence in battle. In the will to conquer, to take risks, to make sacrifices for the supreme end of victory, he was deficient. His own *apologia* is his strongest condemnation. He thought, like Byng, of what would happen if he were beaten, and the preservation of his force was his chief end and aim.

One has only to think if Foch had been the admiral instead of the general, how he would have handled such marvellous concentration of force as the Grand Fleet afforded. What importance he would have attached to the surprise which Lord Jellicoe threw away; to the element of fear which comes from both moral and material causes, and of which Lord Jellicoe had the best evidence in that his ships were never even hit by the enemy; and to the fullest use of the advantage of light!

One can imagine how horrified he would have been by the suggestion that such a secondary weapon as a few German destroyers, much inferior in speed and in guns to our own destroyers, could drive all our heavy units, save the battle-cruisers, out of battle! One can imagine how he would reason from his profound knowledge of military history that in all the best tactics will be found simplicity and flexibility. They are the servants of the great fighter, who never allows the system to be his master. The system gives the opportunity of victory, but not the victory itself. The single line offered both flexibility and simplicity in the broadside gunfire.

In bad hands it was as rigid as a poker and resulted only in indecisive battles. No great naval leader ever said that the single line at every moment must bring all its gunfire to bear. All he would say is that a concentration of gunfire at a vital portion of a battle justifies its loss at another time, such as the approach to breaking the line in the old days and in the deployment today, especially when the enemy is taken by surprise and is already engaged by a detached force.

The cautious policy is one which essentially plays into the hands of German methods of gunnery, which are to concentrate on one ship at a time so as, by a dramatic destruction of a ship, to create the maximum of horror and loss of morale. It is the old-fashioned principle of *"Fight neither with great nor with small, save only with the King of Israel."* Thus, we find the *New Zealand* escaping altogether, the *Queen Mary* and *Indefatigable* sunk, and the *Lion* nearly sunk. In the Third Battle-Cruiser Squadron we see the *Invincible* sunk, while the *Inflexible* and *Indomitable* escape without a single casualty and with only a small hole in a funnel. And yet the *Inflexible* and *Indomitable* at one time were within about 6,000 yards of enemy battleships (8.26 p.m.).

If now the tactics of the British admiral had been to bring what gunfire he could into an action already raging, at the earliest possible moment, with the rest of his ships coming in as soon as feasible, the concentration would have been so much against the enemy that he would have had little chance of developing anything like the gunfire which sank the *Invincible*. Von Scheer's main preoccupation was his own escape. As it was, the *Warspite*, with her helm jammed, turned to starboard towards the enemy alone and unsupported. If deployment had been to starboard she would have had the help of her three sister ships and the *Marlborough's* division of four ships. Hence one of the most valuable units was driven out of the battle after the arrival of the Grand Fleet, and this is attributed to bad luck instead of to the true cause!

The loss of H.M.S. *Indefatigable*

A further consideration which suggests itself is a criticism both of the position in which Lord Jellicoe placed his flagship, and the formation in which he chose to approach. As regards the centre position it is only possible in practice if the subordinates have,

(1) A complete knowledge of the chief's intentions.

(2) Freedom to act.

In Lord Jellicoe's arrangements the all-important provision for initiative was lacking. They suggest a too-rigid adherence to the line of battle with provisions by which the leading ships could reduce speed to correct distances. It cannot be too plainly stated that a firm adherence to the single line is a denial of free action to the subordinate commanders whether of squadron or divisions. It is a defensive conception. To attack one needs the power to seize opportunities which may be invisible to the chief, and whereas a line of twenty-seven ships cannot be moved quickly enough for this purpose, the whole line can avail itself of the situation which a subordinate has created by a rapid stroke.

If it was so dangerous to deploy to starboard it was because of the smallness of the initial front which would be exposed to the enemy, which he believed to be six battle-cruisers (he did not know of our losses until the next day), four *Barhams* and the four ships of the *Marlborough* division. That arose from the abreast formation. It was in no way necessary, and with the *Iron Duke's* division in the centre it meant that whichever way we deployed the flagship could not lead. To gain the lead and yet be able to show a wide front to the enemy from the start, a very old formation, sometimes spoken of as "the wedge," or in former times in land and sea battles as "the *Phalanx*," suggests itself, and in the diagram at the end of this chapter the two methods are contrasted. It is the mass formation of wild ducks flying.

Deployment would thus bring fourteen ships at once into action with the flagship leading whichever way was turned. The importance of the flagship leading lies in the fact that she ought to see the situation of her own engaged ships first and set an example of keeping contact with the enemy. It is the golden rule in tactics that whatever else lets go the van should hold, and as the enemy turns, turn with him. The *Barhams*, being capable of 24 knots, should, for the same reason, have remained in the van, and at a later stage we shall find that Jerram's division in the van altogether lost sight of the Battle-Cruiser Squadron as well as the enemy. With the speediest ships in the van this would have been less likely to happen, and when it did happen, it would have been easier to rectify.

Whatever system one adopts, a long line of ships is bound, however, to be barren of decisive victory if that line is rendered rigid through subservience to the signals and motions of the flagship. Briefly, we may say that history is dead against such a conception of the line and most of all in the presence of a fleeing enemy.

The sailors' adherence to the line against the Dutch lost us the chance of victories, and it was the military men, Monk and Rupert, who freed the fastest ships to act independently and to concentrate on the enemy in the best manner known.

In spite of the lesson, the sailors reverted to the parade ground methods and persisted in them well into the Seven Years' War. Boscawen and Hawke introduced greater latitude. The maximum of flexibility was introduced by Nelson, who broke out as a subordinate at St. Vincent; and at the Nile and Trafalgar gave out his general idea, conceding complete responsibility to each in execution. For instance, at Trafalgar, the battle order stated that:

> The second in command will, after my instructions are made known to him, have the entire direction of his line.

If such had been Jerram's instructions, surely, he would have leapt to Beatty's assistance on receiving the famous signal about 7.15, begging him to follow the battle-cruisers and cut off the enemy. It was not to be. The rigid line turned as one from the destroyer attack conforming to the *Iron Duke's* movements and signals. The story is told elsewhere in these pages, and again in the chronology I have compiled.

It is a story difficult to match in the history of the world for the difference it would have made to the world's future if, in that fateful minute, natural impulses had triumphed over the discipline of the rigid line.

As to how Nelson would have acted is shown by what he did at the Battle of St. Vincent, and it is not a little significant of the effect of standards of conduct in warping the mind that Calder, who held a very influential post under Jervis (afterward Earl St. Vincent), was outspoken in his condemnation of Nelson's action.

The difference between the two men persisted to the very end in that Calder played for safety and Nelson played for victory, and the relative measure of their utility is to be seen in the battles they respectively fought in 1805.

GERMAN BATTLESHIPS TURN AWAY AFTER COMING UNDER FIRE

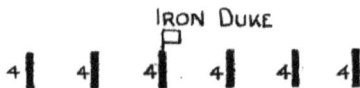

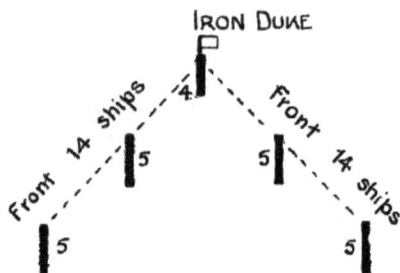

IRON DUKE

4| 4| 4| 4| 4| 4|

IRON DUKE

Front 14 ships   4| Front 14 ships

5| 5|

Front 14 ships   Front 14 ships

5| 5|

CHAPTER 12

The Grand Fleet Nibbles but Does Not Bite

The speed of the *Marlborough's* division was 21 knots and of the *Barham's* division 24–25 knots, so that concentration on the van with a 4-knot advantage of speed over the 17-knot German Fleet was simplicity itself. All of this was lost; the full advantage of surprise was lost; some of the precious time of remaining daylight was lost; and finally confusion was introduced by the determination of Lord Jellicoe to turn his fleet into line away from the enemy and form on the port, or left hand, division over five miles away.

At 6.16 p.m., when the German battle-cruisers were on the opposite course to their battleships and were turning back again, or the precise moment when the armoured cruiser *Defence* was being sunk, and her sistership the *Warrior* disabled by the enemy's battle fleet, the deployment away from the enemy was commenced. This left the starboard wing division of four battleships a brief encounter with the enemy, as it formed the tail of a line it ought to have led.

Thus at 6.20, the third ship in this division (*Hercules*) opened fire on what she believed to be the second enemy battle-cruiser, though this makes it a little confusing, as her leader, the *Marlborough*, opened fire three minutes before from 1,000 yards ahead of the *Hercules* at the leading *Kaiser* by his own account, and Lord Jellicoe's diagram is based on the latter only assuming it was the van battleship *König*. The *Iron Duke*, number 9 of the line, opened fire on enemy battleships at 6.31, in a light by no means so good as at 6.14, and ten minutes after she had turned up astern of the *King George V.*, which led the line.

Had the deployment been to starboard all ships would have fallen naturally into their place just as the four *Barhams* would have turned into the gap between the battle-cruisers and the four ships of the sixth division led by the *Marlborough*. In a similar way, without signal Hood prolonged the line ahead of the battle-cruisers at 6.21 when he came into the main action. But with the deployment to port all became uncertain. Not only was speed reduced to 14 knots but Jellicoe was uncertain as to the position of ships. At 6.20, he says:—

Owing to smoke and mist, it was most difficult to distinguish friend from foe...The identity of ships in sight on the starboard beam was not even sufficiently clear to me to permit of fire being opened; but at 6.30 p.m. it became certain that our own battle-cruisers had drawn ahead of the battle fleet, and that the vessels then before the beam were the battleships of the *König* class. The order was therefore given to open fire, and the *Iron Duke* engaged what appeared to be the leading battleship at a range of 12,000 yards on a bearing 20° before the starboard beam: other ships of the Third and Fourth Divisions opened fire at about the same time and the van divisions very shortly afterwards; these later ships reported engaging enemy battle-cruisers as well as battleships.

The loss of so many minutes can well be appreciated, especially in view of the gradual setting of the sun. It is necessary to dwell at length on our failure in the all-important preparation for the surprise, which is nine-tenths of the victory in battle, because very important conse-quences resulted, which we will now summarise.

(1) It was not until 6.14 p.m. that Lord Jellicoe was able to say with certainty where the German Battle Fleet lay, and then he at once took his fateful decision to deploy his six divisions into single line away from the enemy instead of towards him, as expected by the ships al-ready in action. Thus, the whole advantage of surprise was lost.

(2) The battle-cruiser *Invincible* was sunk during this lost time.

(3) The Fifth Battle Squadron, which had fought so splendidly, was taken out of the fighting, and the *Warspite* was not supported, so that she was so disabled as to go out of action. This squadron sighted the *Marlborough's* division (the westward division of the line) and Admiral Evan-Thomas believed that deployment would be made towards the enemy. He therefore came in ahead of *Marlborough's* division when he sighted it at 6.6 p.m. At 6.19 he realised that deployment was being

made to port, so he turned widely away from the enemy to port so as to form astern of *Marlborough's* division. The *Warspite's* helm jammed and she turned 16 points to starboard or towards the enemy. She came under the fire of the enemy and was so severely punished that she had to return to the base.

With reference to Admiral Evan-Thomas's action at this juncture, which appears so different from the earlier handling of his squadron and the subsequent persistence with which he kept his division inside the line towards the enemy, it is necessary, in the first place, that we should have before us Lord Jellicoe's battle orders, so that we can study them as a whole. Lord Jellicoe tells us that Evan-Thomas had sighted the *Marlborough* at 6.6 p.m. and the remainder of the Sixth Division of the battle fleet a few minutes later.

> Not seeing any other columns, he concluded that the *Marlborough* was leading the whole line, and decided to take station ahead of that ship. At 6.19 p.m., however, other battleships were sighted, and Admiral Evan-Thomas realised that the Fleet was deploying to port, the Sixth Division being the starboard wing column. He then determined to make a large turn of his squadron to port, in order to form astern of the Sixth Division, which by this time had also turned to port to form line of battle.

We are given no indication as to whether the movement was right or wrong, but earlier in the book, when Lord Jellicoe mentions the Battle Orders there is suggested a criticism. He says:

> The Fifth Battle Squadron was ordered to take station ahead of the remainder of the battle fleet in the case of a deployment *away from* Heligoland.

The italicised words "away from" are Lord Jellicoe's, and it is difficult to understand why they are emphasised unless he had in his mind what took place at Jutland. If so, it is necessary to say plainly that the source of the trouble was his unfortunate decision to deploy away from the enemy, a decision he had prepared for at 6.8 when he ordered two torpedo flotillas to battle stations on his port front and only one to starboard. We do not know if Evan-Thomas was informed of the battle fleet's speed, which had been 20 knots and was reduced to 18 knots at 6.2 p.m.

The decision to deploy to port, however, meant that if the four *Barhams* were to lead the line they would have to traverse the whole six mile front of Lord Jellicoe's fleet in order to form ahead, and would blanket the fire of that fleet during the operation. We can form an estimate by what happened because of the 26 knot battle-cruisers well ahead of the *Barhams*. To enable them to pass to their positions the Fleet's speed was reduced to 14 knots, and the ships in the rear were as we shall see badly bunched up, some ships even having their engines stopped! This then was the probable explanation of Evan-Thomas turning his 24-knot ships to port to form in rear, and it was the outcome of Lord Jellicoe's decision to deploy to port.

The determination of the Admiralty to whitewash the commander-in-chief, if they were not prepared to supersede him, was correct. It was, however, somewhat clumsily done in the official communication issued through the Press Bureau with the despatches, and published on July 1, or a month after the battle. Here we were told of Lord Jellicoe:—

> To the last moment he kept his Fleet in steaming order so as to preserve up till the end the utmost freedom of deployment, but by what precise manoeuvres the deployment was carried out must for obvious reasons be left in a mist as deep as that which was hiding from him all that was most important for him to know. Suffice it to say that the junction was effected with consummate judgment and dexterity. So nicely was it timed that the deployment was barely completed when at 6.15 p.m. the First Battle Squadron came into action with the enemy, who had by that time turned to eastward and was already attempting to avoid action.

Of course, all this was a fairy tale, a mixture of mystery and error. At the moment when the thing is a nine days' wonder and the public is interested, it is fed from all quarters with this sort of stuff. Then it does not matter two or three years later. It is an out-of-date tale. But somehow or other the democracy is dismayed, disquieted and disgusted at being played with like this, and the bureaucracy goes about shaking its head and says it is all due to after-war nerves.

One of the most amusing instances of the fairy tales was the account of how the *Warspite* put the whole German Fleet to flight and appeared in the *Times*, June 6, 1916, from "Our Portsmouth Correspondent." It is amusing reading, but too long for quotation, and I will summarise it. The pity is that nobody made a film story of it.

It begins, after suitable headlines:—

The manner in which the *Warspite* fought the whole of the

German Battle Fleet, and beat them, when she went to the rescue of the *Warrior*, provides one of the most thrilling battle stories of our annals.

Then comes the story which the Press Bureau did not correct.

(1) First Admiral Jellicoe sends the *Warspite* ahead to rescue the *Warrior:*

At full speed she arrogantly sweeps into the fray... Crash went a salvo from the *Warspite's* 15-inch batteries. A German ship got the full force of it and sank.

Then it tells how the *Warspite* fought the whole fleet, circling round the *Warrior* four times, a shell damaging her steering gear:

All this while punishing the enemy terribly with her great guns. "Come back, you are sacrificing yourself," signalled Admiral Beatty . . . By the time her consorts of the Dreadnought division had come up the German Battle Fleet was in full flight. The *Warspite* had beaten them off singlehanded and succoured the *Warrior.*

Just below, as a finishing touch, are some paragraphs headed,

More German Lies.

Let us now turn from this diverting account to the Admiralty communication through the Press Bureau, which states that the deployment was completed at 6.15 p.m.

As we now know 6.15 was the moment when the deployment was barely *commenced*, when the visibility was excellent from the Grand Fleet, and the First Battle Squadron was withdrawn from the action it desired and should have had. It is true that such firing as there was fell mainly to the rear squadron throughout the action, for the Battle of Jutland will ever be remembered as one in which the van of a line of 27 battleships, with a considerable advantage of speed, never got into action with the opposing line during nearly three hours of daylight except for solitary salvoes such as the one fired by *King George V.*

It will be remembered again as a battle in which the van, nay, the whole line, was taken out of action because the rear was threatened by a destroyer attack. The play which is made with the conditions of light in the official statements needs to be examined solely from the relative point of view as it affected the enemy and our own fleet. The whole truth is conveyed in Beatty's despatch:—

By 6.50 p.m. the battle-cruisers were clear of our leading Battle Squadron then bearing about N.N.W. 3 miles from *Lion*, and I ordered the Third Battle-Cruiser Squadron to prolong the line astern and reduced to 18 knots. The visibility at this time was very indifferent, not more than 4 miles, and the enemy's ships were temporarily lost sight of. *It is interesting to note that after 6 p.m. although the visibility became reduced, it was undoubtedly more favourable to us than to the enemy. At intervals their ships showed up clearly, enabling us to punish them very severely and establish a definite superiority over them.* From the reports of other ships and my own observation it was clear that the enemy suffered considerable damage, battle-cruisers and battleships alike. *The head of their line was crumpled up*, leaving battleships as targets for the majority of our battle-cruisers. *Before leaving us the Fifth Battle Squadron was also engaging battleships.* The report of Rear-Admiral Evan-Thomas shows that excellent results were obtained, and it can safely be said that this magnificent squadron wrought great execution.

The italicised parts show the condition of the enemy fleet which Lord Jellicoe surprised by his arrival at 6.15. The four *Barhams* and seven battle-cruisers were already engaged with the head of the enemy's line as Beatty has just related, so the head of the enemy's line was fully occupied and "crumpled up." Why, then, did not Lord Jellicoe deploy to starboard, to use his own words, "in order to bring the Fleet into action at the earliest possible moment"? His answer is that it involved both a torpedo and a gunnery disadvantage. "I assumed that the German destroyers were ahead of their battle fleet," and "it would be suicidal to place the battle fleet in a position where it might be open to attack by destroyers during such a deployment." The assumption that the German destroyers were ahead was a reasonable one, but affords no justification for their dictating the movements of a fleet so that both the chance of surprise and valuable time were lost.

Such golden moments should not have been missed especially as Beatty stated that the visibility was in our favour. The British destroyers were ahead of our fleet and ought to have been assembled in the most advantageous position to attack the enemy with such backing as could be given by our numerous cruisers which vastly preponderated over the enemy. Why could not our destroyers, which *were ahead* of the enemy fleet, have been used to throw the enemy into confusion during deployment. If he used his weakly armed destroyers in order to try and "counter" it would have been clear gain to our Fleet.

Had the fleet been deployed to starboard the Germans, practising their withdrawing tactics, would at once have turned to starboard, and our seven battle-cruisers and the four *Barhams* would have held on to the head of their line. As it was with the deployment to port the battle-cruisers had to think of forming to the head of a line over five miles further to the eastward. We have already discussed the course taken by Evan-Thomas when he took the *Barhams* away to port to form in rear of the line of battleships. All this dispersion from, instead of concentration on, the enemy, would have been avoided by the course which Lord Jellicoe describes as suicidal.

He evidently felt that the torpedo argument had to be reinforced, and he supplies us with a diagram from which he excludes the fire of the battle-cruisers and the four *Barhams*, to prove that at 6.22 the enemy battleships would be firing, in the case of our deployment to starboard, 9 broadsides to our 4½, and at 6.25, 13 to our 8½ broadsides. The calculation is incorrect, as can be seen from measurements of the diagram, and is based on equal speeds of 17-knots, whereas the *Barhams*, which must be added in, could have drawn ahead at 24 knots (they are reputed 25-knot ships and were so designed), and the *Marlborough's* division could have gone at 21 knots. It leaves out of account the better visibility from the British ships. Indeed, the visibility from the Grand Fleet was so good at the moment of deployment that the enemy's leading ships could be identified as battle-cruisers, then four *Königs*, of which the nearest was over 13,000 yards range, four of five *Kaisers* and four *Heligolands*, while beyond that nothing could be seen.

Even on Lord Jellicoe's estimates, when we take account of our seven battle-cruisers to only four (or possibly three) of the enemy; of the four *Barhams*; of the great superiority of the British 15-inch and 13½inch guns; and of the better visibility possessed by gunners; we see that we should have had a great gunnery advantage. The real points, however, are the psychological one that surprise means so much in obtaining decisive victory, and that every minute of daylight was precious in view of the pre-determined veto against fighting at night. As Nelson remarked to Keats his intention was to "surprise and confound" the enemy, and he also gave the caution that a day can be lost in manoeuvring. Lord Jellicoe threw away both time and surprise for purely defensive and theoretical reasons.

The fact that the battle-cruisers had, under the deployment to

BRITISH BATTLESHIP H.M.S. *KING GEORGE V*

port, to cross the front of the fleet and traverse a distance of nearly six miles to get ahead of the left-hand division led by *King George V.*, led to an immediate reduction of speed to 14 knots, and that, together with the big turn made by the *Barhams* to form astern of the *Marlborough's* division, caused a great bunching-up of ships in rear of the line exposed to the full view of the enemy, for in spite of his handicap as regards light he was firing at the *Marlborough's* division. Ships actually slowed down their engines to 10-knots, and in some cases stopped altogether to avoid collision.

They thus became ideal targets for torpedo attack. If the German torpedo flotilla were in the "assumed position," they certainly had a wonderful opportunity, whereas no attack was delivered until forty or forty-five minutes had passed, when the line was formed and in action, followed by a second one fifteen to twenty minutes later. Obviously, the sole motive in the minds of von Scheer and Hipper was escape from a death-trap, and the deployment would have offered that escape had it not been for the action of our battle-cruisers in forcing the fighting at the head of the line. Quoting once again from Beatty:

> The head of their line was crumpled up, leaving battleships as targets for the majority of our battle-cruisers.

The one absolute certainty was that the German Battle Fleet would not abandon its battle-cruisers, and would therefore follow them, and so far as it was able would keep them ahead, and that Beatty, with full information, was giving a lead, in fact a pivot, on which the battle fleet could work with the best advantage. His lead was ignored for considerations of caution based on the sort of indeterminate information which so often occurs in North Sea warfare when mist and battle smoke unite to mock at certainties. Had the combined information of the *Barham* that the German Fleet bore S.S.E. at 6.11 p.m., and of the *Lion* that it bore S.S.W. at 6.14 been true then, on the official plots made for the positions of the *Barham* and the *Lion* as given in the official diagram in Lord Jellicoe's book, at 6.14 the enemy van was only 8,000 yards from the *Marlborough*, which ship, *three minutes later*, opened fire at 13,000 yards with the enemy fleet in full view.

This, of course, makes the signalled S.S.W. bearing of the German Battle Fleet at 6.14 look ridiculous, for it is far to the westward of the plotted course of the German Fleet when drawn from the position given for the *Lion* at that time on the official chart in Lord Jellicoe's book. The real truth probably is that the bearing was approximately right for all practical purposes, but that the position indicated for the *Lion* is in error. The *Lion's* position is given as only 4,000 yards from the *Marlborough* at 6.15, whereas observations taken at 6.16 made her 6,000 yards off. It is quite probable that, having regard to the fact that she had been going full speed since 5.56, her distance was even greater. At 6.15 she had to alter course to eastward to avoid running down the *Defence*.

For a time, the *Defence* and *Warrior* interfered with the firing of the Battle-Cruiser Squadron, and afterwards Beatty had to follow the deployment to the eastward to take up his battle station ahead of the line. The exact positions of ships, at the time Lord Jellicoe commenced his deployment, will probably be a matter of controversy for some time. He mentions that immediately after turning, at 6.17, the *Marlborough* engaged:

> A ship stated to be of the *Kaiser* class at a range of 13,000 yards and on a bearing 20° abaft the starboard beam; this knowledge enables us to deduce the position of the van of the German Battle Fleet at this time.

Since four ships of the *König* class were leading, if this ship was a *Kaiser*, it would place the van at least two thousand yards further ahead, and then all the official diagrams in Lord Jellicoe's book are wrong. Assuming, as is probable, that the ship was the leading *König*, the diagrams are, still, obviously wrong in the fact that, on the bearing given, they plot the range of the *Marlborough's* target as 11,400 yards in one chart in Lord Jellicoe's book, and 12,000 yards in another, as can be seen by applying the scale, while given against the line of fire is the correct figure of 13,000 yards. This, of course, vitiates the whole plot of the course of the enemy, and renders nonsense of the much quoted and pretentiously accurate table of broadsides bearing at different moments, by which Lord Jellicoe sought to prove that a deployment to starboard would have been so foolish.

The position of the *Barhams* is also a matter of uncertainty. In the diagrams they are given as not having crossed the *Marlborough's* range to the enemy, though, if they were going full speed, they ought certainly to have done so, and as the *Marlborough* fired seven salvoes from 6.17 on, and other ships in her division started firing, while the *Barham* was forming astern of Beatty's division (see Jellicoe), and only realised that the deployment was to port at 6.19, it seems probable that she had passed clear of the range with the remaining three ships of her squadron.

This appears also to be borne out by Lord Jellicoe's words that:

> Evan-Thomas then determined *to make a large turn of his squadron* to port, in order to form astern of the Sixth Division, which by this time had also turned to port to form line of battle.

No large or difficult turn was necessary from the position shown in Lord Jellicoe's diagram, but would certainly be the case from the position following Beatty, which it may be conjectured was being taken up. This view is further confirmed by the accident to the *Warspite*

> Unfortunately, the helm of the *Warspite* jammed, and that ship, continuing her turn through sixteen points, came under a very heavy fire and received considerable injury.

To turn to port required starboard helm, whereas the helm jammed with port helm on, which was the helm required for turning into position ahead of the *Marlborough* and astern of our battle-cruisers. If then, these surmises are correct, the official diagrams are erroneous in a number of important particulars. The matter, however, does not end here, for the bearing taken by *Colossus* of the *Lion* at 6.5, which Lord Jellicoe does not mention, would place the *Lion*, as one would expect from her 26-knot speed, over a mile further eastward than in the diagram, and therefore in a still more favourable position for leading a deployment to starboard. Yet another discrepancy is the distance travelled in the diagram by the *Barham* in seven minutes (I refer to the large diagram, number 1, "Before and After Deployment"). A distance of over three and a half miles cannot be done by the *Barham* in seven minutes at the extreme limit of her speed.

Consideration of the whole matter shows how unpractical are all these theoretical considerations beside the one tangible fact that the safe pivot was the Battle-Cruiser Squadron already in action with the van of the enemy. To come into action rapidly with as many guns bearing as possible in comparison with the enemy, astern of that squadron, is what a commander-in-chief should bend all his energy to attain. The whole proceeding would have been simplified for every captain in the fleet if this had been understood. Hood, in the *Invincible*, came in ahead of Beatty. He showed both *coup d'oeil* and energy when he instantly turned his ships at 6.21 so as to prolong the line ahead, for that was the quickest way of getting into action.

If Lord Jellicoe had only prolonged the line astern, the *Invincible* might never have been lost, for so many more ships would have been in action distracting the attention of the enemy. As an example, when the armoured cruiser *Warrior* came under the fire of the enemy battleships through the fatal turn between the opposing lines which had already lost us the *Defence* at 6.16, the accident to the *Warspite's* steering gear brought the latter under the attention of the enemy and enabled the *Warrior* to get away from her predicament. By 6.30, or three minutes before the *Invincible* was sunk, all Lord Jellicoe's ships would have been in close action if he had followed in Beatty's wake. It is true that the deployment to port actually took twenty-two minutes on the lowest estimate to complete, but that was with twenty-seven ships, whereas a deployment to starboard would have been with twenty-four ships.

The deployment to port was done at 14 knots to allow the battle-cruisers to cover the extra six miles of front, whereas to starboard it could have been done for the most part at 20 knots. The truth is that an overreaching caution marred Lord Jellicoe's every action except in the one inexplicable act by which the Rosyth force had been 50 miles away without establishing visual contact. Even in this case, the fear of shedding a single destroyer, or using too much of its fuel supply, induced him to wait for a few destroyers searching vessels *en route*, so that his chances of establishing visual contact even as late as 2 p.m. on May 31 were lost.

The same passion for caution made him delay until eighteen minutes after sighting Beatty's battle-cruisers in action, or until 6.8 p.m., before ordering his destroyers to assemble in their battle positions from the spread-out screen which they occupied against submarines. The result was that they were neither in a position to attack the enemy nor to repel an attack when the time came, and the period of deployment itself was one of confusion when the greatest simplicity was most necessary. The rear end of the line, consisting of the *Marlborough's* division and the *Barhams*, as has been pointed out, was badly bunched up; ships actually slowed down to 10 knots or stopped altogether, and were therefore ideal targets for gun and torpedo attack.

Lord Jellicoe's large official chart gives the time of turning to port for the deployment as 6.14, and the time of the *Iron Duke* turning in the wake of the *King George V.* into single line as 6.21. The matter is of importance as applied to Diagram I. representing the "Plan of Jutland Before and After Deployment," which is calculated on the basis of the turns being at 6.16 and 6.23. If she turned at 6.21 on to the new S.E. course for the single line, she would have travelled on that course 4,667 yards at 14 knots by 6.31 when she sighted and opened fire on the leading *König.* This would bring the leading *König* about 1¼ miles further on than in Diagram I., and the *König's* guns would be bearing on the *Invincible*, which was sunk at 6.33.

It has already been said that Hood saw at once that his duty was instantly to reinforce the hard-pressed battle-cruisers under Beatty, and placed his three *Invincibles* ahead of Beatty's flagship, the *Lion*, and I have compared this with Lord Jellicoe's action in deploying away from the enemy. There is also a notable contrast in the use made of cruisers by the main force and this detached squadron.

Let us try to visualise Lord Jellicoe's situation. He had cruisers away on the starboard bow about one hour's steaming nearer to the enemy than his flagship the *Iron Duke*. He received reports of flashes of gunfire from that direction. The sound of heavy gun-fire was also heard from the South. The natural expectation was that he would at once detach his fastest cruisers to acquire the fullest information in the shortest time so as to guide him as to the best disposition of his Fleet; and this for the reasons which we have endeavoured to make plain in the chapter on the "Theory of Deployment." Lord Jellicoe on hearing guns ordered cruisers and destroyers to take station for action, instead of seeking further information.

Hood, on the contrary, sent the *Chester* immediately to investigate, though she had the bad luck to encounter three out of the eleven cruisers that came out with the High Seas Fleet. He observed flashes of gunfire to the south-westward at 5.30, while he was on a S. by E. course a good deal too far to the eastward for his objective. On *Chester* becoming engaged at 5.40 at about 6,000 yards, the three battle-cruisers turned to N. 30° W. to support. The enemy light cruisers turned to starboard, firing their torpedoes, and fled; but one of them was disabled and drifted into the battle area to be sunk by the British battleships, while another was on fire. Cruisers are satellites, never far in their orbit from their sun. At 6.10 Hood saw the advancing van, instantly drove into action, and by 6.21 turned up at the head of the line, fighting with his three ships at 8,000 yards against the enemy battle-cruisers.

The result of Lord Jellicoe not using his great cruiser preponderance to investigate was that the armoured cruisers on his right made contact at 5.50, not with Beatty, but with enemy cruisers, and the resulting fight served to confuse Lord Jellicoe, far to the rear, as to the position of the enemy's main force, for he now saw gun flashes ahead as well as on the starboard bow. Apparently, the first knowledge he had of the position of Beatty's force was at 5.50, when he sighted them on the starboard bow, bearing S.S.W., and steering E.S.E. The presumption in such a case is that the staff work is entirely at fault in the most important work of training and using cruisers.

CHAPTER 13

Eleven Destroyers Dismiss Twenty-Seven Battleships

We have seen that the deployment to port involved, besides the loss of the surprise, of time and of a range suited to the visibility, certain other disadvantages. The battle-cruisers had to turn as well, and in order to enable them to traverse the extra distance and form ahead, the whole battle fleet had to reduce speed, until 6.33, to 14 knots. The *Barhams*, instead of forming ahead, realised at 6.19 that they had to form astern, and there was a confused bunching of ships at the rear, in which some were going very slow and others had their engines stopped altogether. The fact that none of the ships incurred damage is good evidence that the enemy were in a state of panic at the appearance of the Grand Fleet, and had but the one object of escape.

At 6.24 the *King George V.* had to turn to port to enable the battle-cruisers, which had to traverse six extra miles, to pass ahead. At 6.33 Lord Jellicoe increased speed from 14 to 17 knots relieving the situation at the rear, and this speed was kept constant throughout the day and night. The sole reason given for not availing himself of his extra speed was the advantage of a reserve of speed in avoiding torpedoes. At 6.31 the *Iron Duke* opened fire at the leading *König* (12,000 yards), and that ship immediately turned sharply to starboard.

By 6.38 (some accounts place it later) the two fleets were in opposing lines, the British line heading S.E. instead of S.E. by E. as ordered, a difference of 11° 15' towards the enemy's line. The enemy had, however, turned to starboard the moment they were fired on, and when lost sight of at 6.40 bearing 20° abaft the *Iron Duke's* beam (the *Iron Duke* was the ninth ship in the line) they were steering almost in the line of their fire.

The important consideration to bear in mind is that the British line had such an overwhelming superiority that it could afford to shed ships unable to keep up. The other line was so weak that its aims were in the first place to shake off the British attack, and in the second to obtain sanctuary in its minefields and fortified harbours. If the Germans increased beyond 17 knots, then they lost the six pre-

Dreadnoughts of the *Pommern* class. Consequently, they held together and the initiative of bringing bis immense gunnery advantage to bear was entirely at the disposal of the British commander-in-chief.

What that gunnery advantage amounted to needs brief consideration. Making no allowance for losses or ships out of action, and assuming that all available German ships were present, the total weight of gunfire (not broadsides) of the heavy guns of the opposing battleships and battle-cruisers were:—

		Battleships. lb.	Battle-cruisers. lb.	Grand Total. lb.
British	..	341,800	78,800	420,600
German	..	190,098	35,976	226,074

This does not bring out fully the British advantages, since so much depends on the concentrated weight in guns of large calibre, a circumstance which had made a powerful impression on Mr. Churchill's mind when First Lord of the Admiralty. This survived; for when called on by Mr. Balfour, after the Battle of Jutland, to issue a statement from the Admiralty, he was betrayed into the exaggeration of ruling out all ships with guns less than 13½-inch calibre in the British Navy as no longer primary units. If he had reflected that this would rule out the whole German fleet at Jutland, he would have seen the absurdity of the statement which has a family resemblance to those officially issued when units like the *Formidable* and our battleships in the Dardanelles were lost and the public were asked to believe on authority that the ships were of no fighting value. Power is, of course, relative, but it is always useful in the right place.

The figures in the table assume that all available German units were present, and *are for battleships only*. This postulates that there were seventeen German Dreadnought battleships in the fight and not fifteen or sixteen, as generally stated. If the *Kaiser* class ship *König Albert* was absent, as stated in German accounts, then ten 12-inch guns will have to be deducted from the German figures as also 9,810lb. from the earlier table of weight of gunfire.

Of the guns tabulated for the battleships in the figures, the twenty-four battleships with Lord Jellicoe carried sixteen 15-inch, ten 14-inch, one hundred and ten 13½-inch, and one hundred and four 12-inch. The four *Barhams* accounted for thirty-two 15-inch. In the battle-cruisers we had in addition to the above table thirty-two 13½-inch and forty 12-inch to sixteen 12-inch and twenty-eight 11-inch in the five German battle-cruisers.

152

GERMAN BATTLESHIP S.M.S. *POMMERN*

		Calibre of Guns			
	15"	4"	13½"	12"	11"
Number of Guns :—					
BRITISH	48	10	110	92	Nil
GERMAN	Nil	Nil	Nil	138	72
Weight of each Projectile (lb.) :—					
BRITISH	1,950	1,600	1,400	850	—
GERMAN	—	—	—	981	760

[No discount has to be applied for broadsides to the table (owing to guns bearing on one side of the ship only) to the British ships carrying 15-inch, 14-inch, or 13½-inch guns, except for the *Erin* (13½-inch); but in the 12-inch and 11-inch category, more especially for the Germans, a considerable reduction has to be made, e.g., the four *Heligoland* class has to incur a penalty of four guns each, making a total reduction of sixteen 12-inch guns; and the four *Nassaus* a similar reduction in 11-inch guns, or sixteen in all. In his paper, "Naval Construction during the War," Sir Eustace D'Eyncourt stated that the superiority of the Grand Fleet to the High Seas Fleet at Jutland was 175 per cent. in weight of broadsides, or nearly as much as 3 to 1. Lord Jellicoe claims that tonnage is the only fair basis of comparison, and on this basis the force under his command aggregated about 1,139,000 tons as compared with 590,000 tons, or a far larger margin than had ever been contemplated for the whole Navy in comparison with a probable enemy.]

We had then exactly 200 guns of over 12-inch calibre superior to anything the Germans possessed. As at the Battle of the Bight, Coronel, the Falkland Islands and the Dogger Bank it was the gun which won the victory, so now at Jutland it was the gun which destroyed the *Indefatigable, Queen Mary*, and *Invincible*, in fact all the British ships which were sunk, except the destroyer *Shark*. While the torpedo may have lowered the speed of the *Lützow* and *Seydlitz*, there is reason to believe that the gun drove them out of the battle. Never in war had its crippling power been so great as at Jutland.

Such a table as the above conveys only a suggestion of the advantages of the British Fleet. Suppose we put the British advantage at 3 to 1 in any given broadside from the ships in action and take no account of the concentration that an advantage of speed gives. If the broadsides were delivered every minute, then in ten minutes the proportion would be 30 to 10, that is, a surplus of 20 as compared with 2 for a single range of salvoes. In addition, there comes the psychological factor in the concentrated horror and confusion to which the inferior fleet is subjected and which resulted in the earlier battle-cruiser action, in the falling-off of the enemy's accuracy of fire, to which Beatty called attention.

At no stage after the arrival of the Grand Fleet did the German gunnery inflict any injury on battleships or battle-cruisers in the line. This did not arise from the overwhelming superiority of the British gunfire, for, unfortunately, it was not brought to bear except in the case of the enemy's battle-cruisers which had been subjected to very drastic punishment; but it arose from *the fear of its use*. If the mere anticipation could bring about such results, what the actuality might have been it is not difficult to visualise.

It should be remembered in addition that it was never claimed for our heavy guns that they would sink ships with a few shell penetrating the water-line, because of the local sub-division of ships into water-tight compartments, but that the constant impact and explosion of heavy projectiles would strain and start the frames, bulkheads and armour backing so as to flood the ship in many directions, and ultimately make them an easy victim. It was precisely this sustained fire which the German Fleet never experienced except in the case of the battle-cruisers. The tactics of Lord Jellicoe therefore conceded to them all the advantages they could derive from their thick armour while pressing none of the advantages he possessed in his 13½-inch to 15-inch guns.

Lord Jellicoe's mind was unclouded by any thought of the fate of the *Queen Mary* and *Indefatigable*, for he did not hear that they were lost until the next day. He knew the enemy were practising their regular withdrawing tactics, for, at 6.35, he saw our battle-cruisers turning to starboard, and this he should have felt in every fibre of his body meant the annihilation of the enemy, as they would be cut off from their base, always provided that the advantage was pressed.

The reason for not allowing the fast ships to draw ahead was defensive, in that Lord Jellicoe was unwilling to sacrifice the order of his fleet though the battle was obviously a chase. He could still have preserved the order for the whole fleet at 20 knots, with the exception of the partially disabled *Marlborough*. This he was not prepared to do because of the defensive advantage to individual ships in avoiding torpedoes of being able to increase the speed at any given moment. The answer is that the advantage is trifling, and it is not to be balanced against what is conferred by speed in enabling guns and torpedoes to be concentrated in the most effective way.

The fact that the battle fleet never once steamed at a greater speed than 17-knots at Jutland is the more surprising in view of the statement in an earlier chapter of "The Grand Fleet, 1915-16," that in the war "the pre-Dreadnoughts were not a very important factor on

155

either side owing to the inferiority of speed." If we accept this, we also admit that Lord Jellicoe condemns his own action in bringing the speed of his fleet down to this inferior speed when the enemy was hampered by the presence of six pre-Dreadnoughts.

It is probable that the Germans made a bad tactical blunder in bringing these pre-Dreadnoughts with them, and this would have been proved as such but for the tactics of the British admiral. As confirming this estimate of their low tactical use, we now know that eighteen months later they were all broken up. Old ships are of the greatest use to a predominant naval power for the reason that behind the absolute protection which they obtain from the modern ships in the North Sea, they can fulfil many useful offices which otherwise would have to be left undone or be performed by modern ships. Chief among these uses was the defence of convoys which Lord Jellicoe resisted for so long. Convoys were proposed in order to save the situation created by the submarine war that broke out some months after the Battle of Jutland.

Let us now deal with comparisons of armour to which Lord Jellicoe directs our main attention. If we except the slight hit on the *Colossus*, the twenty-four Dreadnoughts which Lord Jellicoe brought with him to the Battle of Jutland were not hit at all, nor were the three *Barhams* after they joined his line. It is difficult, therefore, to see the point of the introduction of the armour question in regard to these ships in his chapters on the Battle of Jutland, except to claim the credit that:

> All German Dreadnoughts were provided with side armour to the upper deck . . . the *Orion* class of battleship, and the *Lion* class of battle-cruiser, designed during my service at the Admiralty as Controller, were the first of our Dreadnoughts armoured to the upper deck.

The statement is really immaterial as regards the British force, but as regards the German fleet it is incorrect. The four *Königs* were side armoured up to the upper deck, the five *Kaisers* were side armoured up to the upper deck for the greater part of the length but not aft, and the remaining eight German Dreadnoughts were only side armoured up to their main deck. This is confirmed by Lord Jellicoe's own table on a previous page. On the other hand, four of the German battle cruisers were side armoured up to the upper deck, and the fifth, the *Von der Tann*, was side armoured only to the main deck.

Of our ships that had to take punishment as well as give punishment at Jutland, there were nine battle-cruisers and four *Barhams*, eight of these were armoured up to the upper deck, and the remainder, consisting of the *New Zealand, Indefatigable* and three *Invincibles*, were only armoured up to the main deck. In every respect the German battle-cruisers were much better armoured than the British. Lord Jellicoe, for instance, compares the *Queen Mary* of 27,000 tons with the *Seydlitz* of 24,610 tons which took such a lot of hammering in the battle. The *Queen Mary* devoted 3,900 tons to armour and the *Seydlitz* 5,200 tons on her smaller displacement. The comparison would have been even more apt if made with the *Derfflinger*, completed in 1914, or the same year as the *Queen Mary*.

There was no such difference in the battleships. To obtain a difference Lord Jellicoe compares the *Orion* class of 22,500 tons with the *Kaiser* of 24,410 tons, and gives the weight of armour for the former as 4,560 tons and the latter 5,430 tons. The *Orion* class were completed in 1911-12, whereas the *Kaiser* class were completed in 1913, but the difference in weight of armour, allowing for the smaller displacement, is not great. The main improvement in the German designs on our own was in allowing about eight feet more beam, a situation which arose from the Board of Admiralty's decision that our docks should govern our designs instead of our designs governing our docks.

Since Lord Jellicoe has told us that during his period of service at the Admiralty he emphasised his view that tonnage is the true basis of comparisons as to fighting qualities, there is some point in the argument advanced by the German critic, Captain Persius, who is described by Lord Jellicoe as "a reputable and informed writer on naval matters." He points out that:

In August, 1914, we (the Germans) possessed vessels to the amount of somewhat over one million tons, against the British warships of 2.2 million tons. It was also a matter of widespread knowledge that the quality of our ship's material, apart from the quantity, was inferior to the British .. Our ships of the line, cruisers, and armoured cruisers, yes, even the destroyers were of less displacement than the British, were less strongly armed and of lower speed.

The latter statement is, of course, the precise opposite of the one put forward by Lord Jellicoe. The more important material points at issue we have dealt with, though none of them are of vital interest, for it is not here, but in the command and handling of the fleet that there was failure. It is to this factor that we now propose to return.

Before 6.40 (see diagram) it was noted from Lord Jellicoe's flagship, the *Iron Duke*, which was the ninth ship in the line, that the enemy had so turned to starboard as to steer almost in the line of their fire. At 6.40 they were lost sight of, bearing 20° abaft the beam. This was an observation taken of the leading enemy ships. And yet our van was still in the rigid line prolonged to the *King George V,* two miles ahead, and therefore steering away from the enemy. This course was persisted in until 6.55, by which time the battleships had run over three miles further on a divergent course.

Is this to go down as the naval interpretation of Napoleon's saying that in war, in every movement, our aim must be to secure a good position? That good position can only be secured when led from the van, and certainly the battle-cruisers endeavoured to lead the way. They were constrained in their movements by the need of the support of the heavy units, but within this limit they always sought the head of the enemy's line. At 6.50 the *Lion* was well inside towards the enemy three miles S.S.E. of the *King George V.*, but even so, the enemy was lost sight of as the visibility was only four miles. Contact with the British Battle Fleet had to be maintained, so Beatty reduced speed to 18 knots and shifted the *Inflexible* and *Indomitable* to the rear of his line. The order of the battle-cruisers became: *Lion, Princess Royal, Tiger, New Zealand, Indomitable*, and *Inflexible*. At 6.55 Lord Jellicoe altered course by divisions to south.

In view of the observations we have recorded from the *Iron Duke*, it does seem likely to mislead the casual reader for Lord Jellicoe to write:

> At 6.50 p.m., *as the range was apparently opening*, the course was altered by signal to south 'by divisions' in order to close the enemy.

The alteration of course had the desired effect though it resulted in some confusion through the old course having been needlessly persisted in. At least the change had brought the enemy in sight. At 7.5, course was further altered three points to starboard to close the range, making the course S.W. by S., but the original course of south was resumed at 7.10 on the sighting of enemy destroyers and a report of a submarine on the port bow.

Lord Jellicoe states that between 7 p.m. and 7.30 p.m. our battle

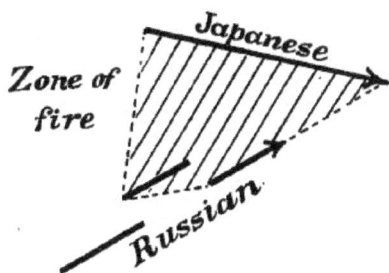

II

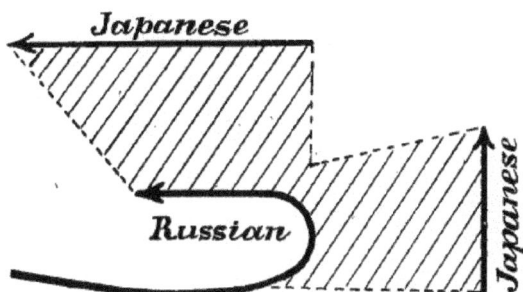

Two examples of Tsushima. In both cases Togo leading holds on to the
van and uses his superior speed to concentrate on the van.

fleet was again in action with enemy battleships and battle-cruisers.
If we leave out the battle-cruisers, I cannot find any record of firing
from individual battleships earlier than 7.10 or later than 7.26.

One has the impression from Lord Jellicoe's account of a regular
fleet action for half-an-hour. There are paragraphs such as:—

> At 7.17 p.m. the *King George V.* opened fire on a vessel, taken
> to be the leading ship of the enemy's line, at a range of about
> 13,000 yards.

It would have been fairer to the reader to state that a single salvo
was fired, and no more, if this was the case. Lord Jellicoe mentions
nine ships out of twenty-seven as firing. The Admiralty were asked, on
July 24th, 1919, "the total number of salvoes fired by each capital ship
at the Battle of Jutland." It is characteristic of the circumlocution of
the bureaucrat that Mr. Long should decline to give the information,
over three years after the event, on the ground that the Admiralty will
issue a book in due course. However, one can gather, that in the main,
firing was in the rear as Lord Jellicoe states, that the range varied from

as much as 15,000 yards at the van to as little as 8,500 yards in the rear, a condition of affairs which was obviously brought about by the enemy turning away and the failure of the van to hug the enemy. Let us, to illustrate what this hugging means, hark back exactly twelve years before Jutland to the Battle of Tsushima and take notice of the intense zone of fire which Togo brought to bear on the van of the Russian Fleet at two stages of the battle.

During the Battle of Jutland, the course, which started at southeast by east at six o'clock moved through an arc of 148°, or over one-third of the whole circle, the Germans, of course, moving on the inner arc, as was expected from their invariable withdrawing tactics. To this should have been opposed the superior speed of the fast ships, and the van turning with the enemy and not long after. But above all things the obvious desire of the enemy to avoid action should have made us resolute, in the conditions of low visibility, to give him close action. By using speed, and turning towards him, the bearings could, have been kept constant.

The whole Grand Fleet had an advantage of 3-knots, or 100 yards a minute over the enemy; but by taking the 24-knot to 25-knot *Barhams*, and the majority of ships which could draw ahead at 21 or 22 knots, the advantage could have been much improved in concentrating on the van. An enemy that avoids battle, an enemy which concedes the initiative to its opponent, is an enemy with whom one can take great liberty. It was also necessary to force the pace in order to make the enemy shed his lame ducks, which the armoured cruisers and the *Marlborough*, whose speed was reduced to 17-knots by the torpedo which hit her at 6.54, could very well have taken care of. The *Warspite* also appears to have continued at sea.

The armoured cruisers only impeded the line with their smoke in the van. But it was not a liberty that was taken. On the contrary, great liberty was conceded, so great indeed that, as far as the British battleships were concerned, the German reports alleged that they steamed north after turning away from the destroyer attack, and that the fleet seen by the Zeppelin to the south the next morning was our Channel Fleet, which never on any occasion came into the North Sea. If this was their belief it speaks volumes for the hammering their fleet had received, the absolute need for getting them back to port, and the scattered state of the fleet that, in the circumstances of this Zeppelin report, they did not dare divert any ships to risk an encounter with ships they believed to be pre-Dreadnoughts.

In his despatch mentioning that the Germans knew by 4 o'clock the next morning from a Zeppelin his exact position, Lord Jellicoe says, "the enemy made no sign." Did he really think it conceivable that a panic-stricken fleet, which had been avoiding action and had successfully shaken the Grand Fleet off, was going to direct its energies towards searching for its enemy?

Let us now revert to the position at 7.10, when contact had been established with the enemy. It had at all costs to be maintained while the guns did their work. Before nine o'clock darkness would be setting in. It was essential that the range should be closed so that all ships could be fighting instead of letting off a few salvoes among which were some that were by no means in the class of probable hits owing

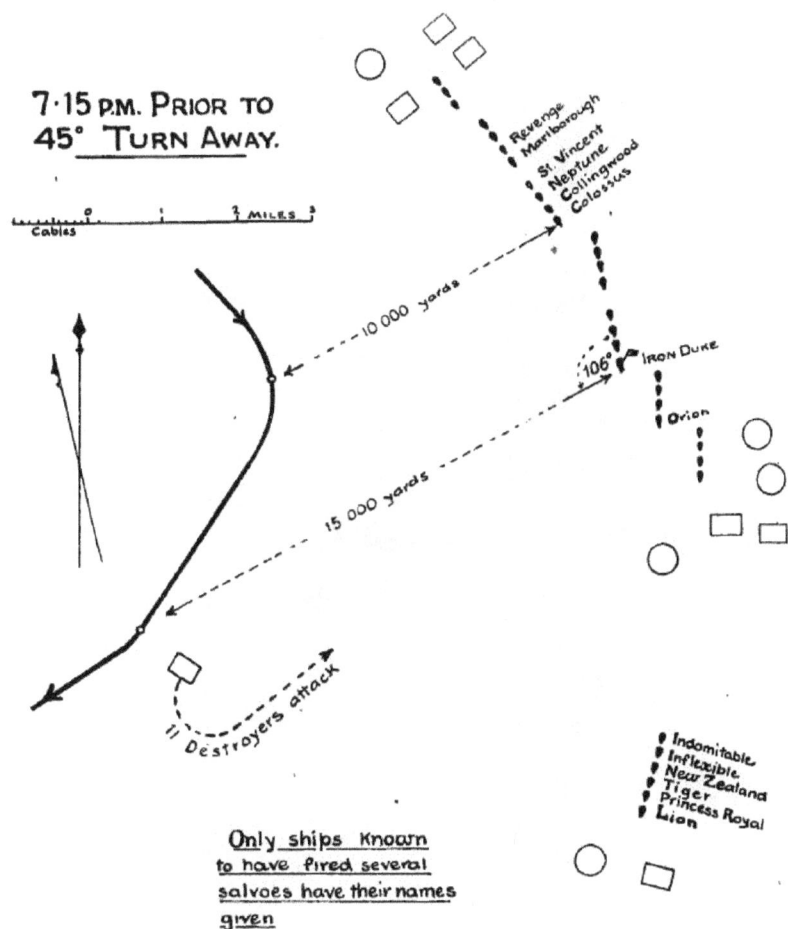

7·15 P.M. PRIOR TO
45° TURN AWAY.

Cables

3 MILES

10 000 yards

15 000 yards

Revenge
Marlborough
St. Vincent
Neptune
Collingwood
Colossus

106°   IRON DUKE

Orion

Destroyers attack

Only ships known
to have fired several
salvoes have their names
given

Indomitable
Inflexible
New Zealand
Tiger
Princess Royal
Lion

161

H.M.S. *Tiger* and other British battle-cruisers

to the difficulties of sighting.

This was the position of affairs when Lord Jellicoe turned the whole fleet away at 7.10 because:

A flotilla of enemy destroyers supported by a cruiser was observed approaching on a bearing S. 50° W. from *Iron Duke.*

It was to avoid this attack of eleven destroyers that twenty-seven battleships turned away at 7.21, 22½° and finally 45°, while in the rear—where ships had enjoyed a closer view of the enemy, owing to the rear enemy ships not turning with, but after, the van—ships actually turned away as much as 90°. The enemy at the same time turned away under smoke clouds, and contact, so far as the battleships were concerned, was never really regained. It is impossible to imagine a more definite break from the whole spirit of naval tradition, or from the practice, suited to modern invention, of the golden rule that once an enemy is sighted, he must be cut off, closely engaged and annihilated. Our cruisers and destroyers who could have pressed home their own attacks on the enemy line were by this time in the van.

Our ships had their great secondary armaments of 6-inch and 4-inch guns to attack the enemy destroyers, and the admirals of different battle squadrons if threatened—and only the rear appears to have been threatened—could have turned 45° *towards* the destroyers, which would present very little target indeed. The matter is discussed in the chapter on the torpedo. It suffices here to remark that no turn ought to have presented itself to the mind of a British admiral but the turn towards the enemy. The actual turn away, as we have shown elsewhere, did not avoid the attack. In fact, it presented a larger target; and towards the end of the line, single ships, trying to avoid torpedoes, caused considerable confusion.

From about 7.21 to 7.33 while this turn away was in progress, Beatty steered well to the west towards the enemy and engaged them. At 7.32 he reported his course as S.W., speed 18-knots. He made one desperate effort to save the situation by a signal, taken in by the whole fleet, imploring the van of the battle fleet, led by the *King George V* (Admiral Jerram), to follow him, cut off and surround the enemy. But the rigid line could not be broken! The signal from the *Iron Duke* was a thing that must be obeyed, and the Grand Fleet went out of action. Lord Jellicoe makes no mention of this vitally important signal in his account of the Battle of Jutland, but it is a matter of common knowledge throughout the navy that a signal of this nature was made and logged. It will require an examination of the logs to ascertain if Admiral Jerram asked permission to follow Beatty, and if so, whether any response was made. The chronology in the Appendix shows that it was not until 8.10 p.m. that a signal was made to the *King George V* to follow the battle-cruisers, but then they had passed out of sight.

Nor does Lord Jellicoe sufficiently bring out the great work of the battle-cruisers. He refers to the better visibility at the head of the line through freedom from interference of funnel and cordite smoke. The inference is that Lord Jellicoe did not consider it possible for the head of his line to keep touch and engage the enemy at close range in a similar way, otherwise it is difficult to conjecture why the remark is made. Yet Beatty, using no higher speed than that of which the battle-ships were capable, was able to make his opportunities by continually working to the westward whilst the main battle fleet kept to the eastward and ultimately turned away altogether.

Much of the smoke which interfered with the vision from *King George V.* came from the armoured cruisers which were stationed at the head of the line where use could only be made of them to keep touch with the battle-cruisers, a task which could be better done by fast light cruisers. If, however, the physical vision on board the *Lion* was better, and in our judgment there can be no question about the mental and moral vision, it was a powerful argument for basing the whole of the movements of the fleet, as they should have been when the Grand Fleet first deployed, on the lead given by the *Lion*. So clearly was this lesson of leadership in a fast unit impressed upon Beatty that when he, in after months, succeeded to the command, he shifted his flag from the 21-knot *Iron Duke* to the *Queen Elizabeth* of 25 knots.

In battle one never knows how much the enemy may be suffering, what unseen opportunities he is offering, and the only safe rule is to hammer all one knows. Beatty, at 7.14, found the visibility improved, and had two battle-cruisers and two battleships under fire, while about nine miles astern of him four of our battleships were firing at more battle-cruisers—a fact which is eloquent of the scattered state of the enemy fleet. What really was in progress behind the smoke screens with which the enemy absorbed Lord Jellicoe's attention while he dictated his movements with a destroyer attack, was firstly, the determined attempt of the enemy to escape from the toils; and, secondly, the German admiral of the Battle-Cruiser Squadron was shifting his flag, having boarded a destroyer to go from the disabled *Lützow* to the *Moltke*. This wonderful opportunity was missed because we did not force the fighting.

Lord Jellicoe's method of explaining the circumstances in which touch was lost with the enemy is interesting. It involves three pleas:—

(1) The torpedo attacks "did not produce any great effect." To this the answer is they drove our 27 battleships out of action both at this stage and a later one after 8 o'clock.

(2) The British turn-away only opened the range some 1,750 yards; so that the turn was not responsible for losing the enemy. The only comment necessary on this is that the object of the enemy was to get free, and he succeeded by a combination of (2) and (3). As the same method would have been repeated, he would have got free every time so long as he had destroyers in position to attack. It should be added that in the misty light 1,750 yards may make a considerable difference.

(3) The enemy's "very large turn to the westward," was the determining cause of the loss of touch in the case of both the British Battle Fleet and Battle-Cruiser Squadron.

> Neither our battle-cruisers ahead of our van (which did not turn away at the time, as it was not necessary in their case) nor the battle fleet were able to regain touch until 8.20 p.m. because of the retirement of the enemy.

Number 3 affords a striking example of Lord Jellicoe's method of dealing with the facts in regard to the obvious contrast which suggests itself between the handling of his own force and that of the battle-cruisers. Because of the German destroyer flotilla moving out to attack Lord Jellicoe executed his first turn to south at 7.10, and then turned away gradually, four points at and after 7.23. At 7.26 Beatty's battle-cruisers were engaging the enemy as closely as 14,000 yards to 8,000 yards, and it should be remarked that more torpedoes were fired at the battle-cruisers in proportion to their numbers than at the battleships, *but this did not cause Beatty to let go at any period for that reason.*

At 7.40 he reported the bearing of the leading enemy battleship. Only then did Lord Jellicoe, concluding, from a report stating that enemy battleships were to the west, that their fleet was divided, steer west for the enemy. He sighted them for a few minutes to the north-westward at 7.55, only to be driven off at 8.22, before he had fired a shot, by another destroyer attack, which was apparently a very half-hearted one, on his cruisers, which his cruisers and destroyers tackled and mastered. The First Flotilla, in the van, proceeded to attack enemy

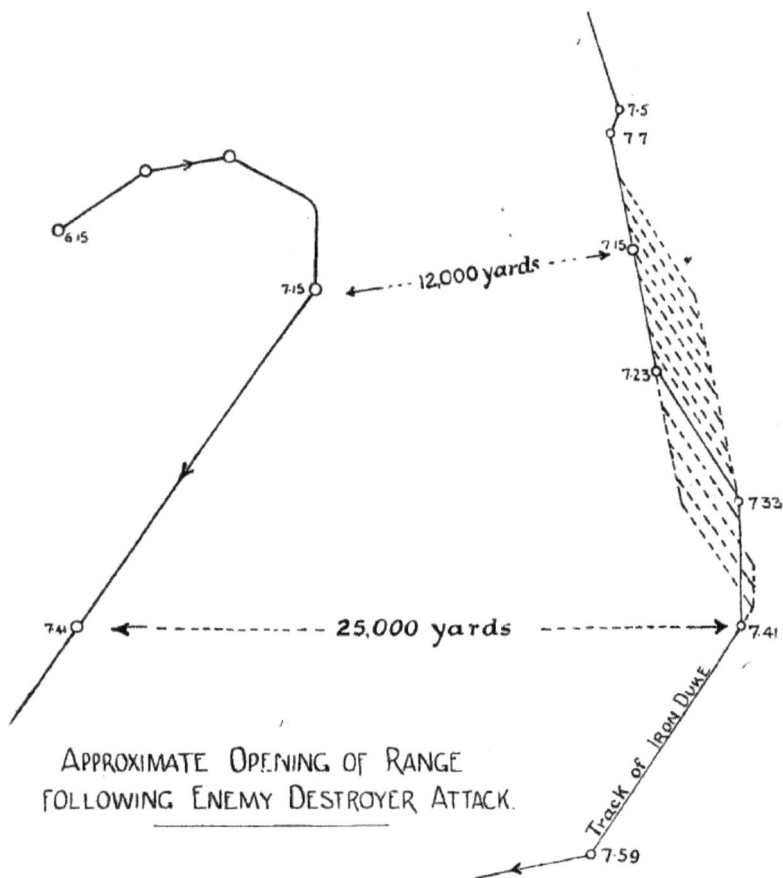

12,000 yards

25,000 yards

Approximate Opening of Range
Following Enemy Destroyer Attack.

battleships, but was recalled.

It was only at 7.45 that Beatty lost sight of the enemy in a smoke cloud; that is to say, some thirty minutes of fighting on the part of the battle-cruisers with the enemy had gone on since Lord Jellicoe made his first turn to the south because of the threatened destroyer attack. At 7.58 Beatty ordered both his cruiser squadrons to sweep west and locate the head of the enemy line, and once again got into action from 8.22 to 8.28, when they turned away. The head of the enemy's scattered line was again brought to action at 8.30 by Beatty, until, being unsupported by the battle fleet, he was driven off by enemy battleships. Lord Jellicoe's fleet was out of sight of even the linking armoured cruisers. This brief recital shows how baseless is the attempt to make it appear that the battle-cruiser position, in losing the enemy, was similar to that of the battle fleet.

It will thus be seen that, for Lord Jellicoe, the battle resolves itself into three distinct nibbles at intervals of one hour, and each time he withdraws because of something suspicious which he does not like. He comes into action at 6.14, but does not like the outlook, so he deploys to port. He again comes into action at 7.10, and a destroyer attack drives him off. An hour later the same thing occurs. The excuse that the enemy turned away is too puerile, for that is what he was certain to do. Enemies never ought to do exactly what you want them to do, though in this respect Lord Jellicoe was most obliging, for the one thing von Scheer wanted him to do was to turn away. The turn was most important, and lost us the action, for Lord Jellicoe ought to have turned towards the enemy.

Thus, the first of Lord Jellicoe's pleas that "The German attacks at Jutland did not produce any great effect, and their importance should not be exaggerated," falls to the ground. So stupendous a result from so trivial a cause has not been seen since Troy. Indeed, Mr. Archibald Hurd, a most wholehearted admirer of Lord Jellicoe, has felt the necessity of magnifying the cause, so he has announced in the sober pages of the *Fortnightly Review*, that at the Battle of Jutland the Germans endeavoured to torpedo the British Empire! We deal with this idea in the chapter on the torpedo at Jutland.

What great plea of justification is there to be found for an absolutely unscratched fleet steering away from a much weaker one which is obviously on the run and losing it in spite of a superiority in cruisers and destroyers? At the same time, the weakly-armoured battle-cruisers, which had been in action for nearly four hours and had sustained heavy losses, forced the fighting while the distance between them and their heavy supports in the battle fleet increased from four or five miles, at 7.17, to eight or nine miles. Beatty closed the range from 14,000 yards to 7,800 yards, and continued firing until a smoke screen concealed the enemy at 7.45. He then spread his cruisers in order to sweep for the enemy and found two battle-cruisers by 8.22, when he resumed firing at 10,000 yards range.

The enemy battle-cruisers were lost for a few minutes, resighted at 8.30, and closely engaged. Their battleships came to the rescue, and Beatty learning from the *Minotaur* that the Grand Fleet was not in sight hauled off. It is all too extraordinary, and it needs investigation to find out how it came about. Only at 8.10 was a signal made to the *King George V.* to follow the battle-cruisers, but the *King George V.* signalled back that they were not in sight. Well may one wonder why that great array of cruisers and destroyers were put ahead of the fleet unless to help in matters of this kind by keeping touch between the battle fleet and battle-cruisers; by attacking the enemy with torpedoes; and by helping to punish the temerity of those German destroyers who made such an attack as drove the Grand Fleet out of action.

Beatty's allotted post was five miles ahead of the *King George V.*, slightly on the engaged bow. The battle-orders provided that, if the battle-cruisers stretched ahead, the armoured cruisers should push on or keep touch between them and the battle fleet. This would have been easy enough if the Grand Fleet stayed in action, or put on speed to get into action; but it did not. So, Beatty stretched the touch, so much so as to pass out of sight, in order to keep hold of the enemy, and the armoured cruisers also lost touch with the battle fleet.

There was reason for his so doing, for victory was imperative, and our own observations and other indications showed the Germans to be so disordered that it was within our grasp. The figures of steaming are suggestive of how Beatty endeavoured to keep touch with the battle fleet after Lord Jellicoe's arrival. Before that arrival, he steamed 64 miles in 149 minutes, and afterwards 57 miles in 163 minutes while the battle lasted. In the earlier period he was fighting nearly all the time: in the latter, he was conditioned by the ultra-cautious tactics of his chief.

And yet there must have been three clear pieces of evidence upon which chief could act, if, he gave any such consideration to the enemy's position as he obviously did to a hypothetical situation in regard to his own fleet. This evidence was at his disposal in spite of his failure to probe into the enemy's position. Each piece was powerful in itself, but taken together they presented a convincing picture that the German formation and fighting spirit were broken.

(1) The enemy continued to fire but had ceased to hit.

(2) The enemy was on the run.

(3) The enemy was using smoke screens to escape. Two of his battle cruisers had drifted down the line but this information was not passed to *Iron Duke*.

In other words, the appearance of the Grand Fleet alone had established a moral ascendency in spite of all that had happened.

The sequence of events can be studied in the chronology. At 7.33, or twelve minutes after the turn, the battle fleet's course was altered to S. by W., while Beatty was on a S.W. course, continuing the firing he had commenced at 7.26 and closing the range from 14,000 to 8,000 yards on an enemy bearing N.W. by W. At 7.40 Beatty's report of the enemy bearing N.W. by W. from *Lion* was received by *Iron Duke*. As Beatty held the enemy under fire at 7 to 4 miles range, there is a good deal of ambiguity about Lord Jellicoe's statement that:

> At about 7.40 I received a report from Sir David Beatty stating that the enemy bore N.W. by W. from the *Lion*, distant 10 to 11 miles, and that the *Lion's* course was S.W.... I assumed the *Lion* to be 5 or 6 miles ahead of the battle fleet, but it appeared later from a report received in reply to directions signalled by me at 8.10 p.m. to the *King George V.* to follow the battle-cruisers, that they were not in sight from that ship either.

At 7.40 a turn was once more made to a course a little more to the westward, but still at the same speed of 17 knots. Considering how much the range had been opened by the two fleets turning away from each other, as can be seen by the diagram, there was reason for expedition. At 7.59 a large alteration of the course was made to West on the cruisers sighting enemy N.W. from *Iron Duke*. On this course the *Iron Duke* crossed a point at 8.7 which, according to the official chart, the *Lion* had passed over twenty-two minutes before. Beatty had lost the enemy at 7.45 and his cruisers at this time were sweeping to the west to locate the head of the line.

At 8.20 he altered course to west to attack. In twenty-two minutes, the enemy would have covered six miles, so as Beatty had engaged their van, the battleships going 17 knots, were only likely to come up with the rear of the enemy's line or a detached squadron.

Lord Jellicoe does not seem to have made quite as full use of his cruisers, which far outnumbered those at the disposal of the enemy. They ought to have swept for the enemy and kept touch with the battle-cruisers. An enemy battleship was seen by *Orion* at 8.3 bearing N.W. by W. One minute later Lord Jellicoe saw a line of battleships on his starboard bow, or about N.W., but made no increase of speed. The enemy turned away and sent out a destroyer attack, which resulted in the battle fleet altering course four points away from the enemy. The enemy destroyers were met by one of our destroyer flotillas, and the 4th Light Cruiser Squadron which included the *Calliope*.

The attack was in fact directed at our cruisers and not at the battleships. The *Calliope* was heavily fired on, but got so close to the enemy line as to fire a torpedo at 6,500 yards, and an explosion was heard.

The battle fleet's alteration of course was from West to South-West, or once again four points. The battle was then definitely abandoned by the battle fleet being reformed in a cruising formation and steaming south. Lord Jellicoe's last mention of any daylight fighting in connection with his own fleet is of this action with the enemy destroyers. He does not mention that he had then the opportunity of action with the enemy battleships. He does not say that he turned away four points because of a destroyer attack which was countered by his own small craft, but states that—

> The ships sighted turned away, and touch could not be regained, although sounds of gunfire could be heard from ahead at 8.25 p.m., probably from our battle-cruisers which obtained touch with and engaged some of the enemy's ships very effectively between 8.22 and 8.28 p.m. The *Falmouth* was the last ship of the battle-cruisers fleet to be in touch with the enemy, at 8.38 p.m.; the ships then in sight turned eight points together away from the *Falmouth*. At 8.30 p.m. the light was failing, and the fleet was turned by 'divisions' to a S.W. course, thus reforming single line again.

We have seen that after Beatty had regained touch, and opened fire at 8.22 on a S.W. course at leading enemy ship before the beam, bearing N.W. by W., 8,000 yards range, the enemy turned away again at 8.28.

The *Inflexible* is stated to have been as close as 6,000 yards in this six minutes' action, in which our battle-cruisers were fighting battleships as well as the two enemy battle-cruisers. A few minutes later he had enemy battle-cruisers again in sight under fire, then battleships came to their assistance and our battle-cruisers hauled off to port, while the enemy escaped in the mist. The armoured cruiser *Minotaur* on the port quarter had reported that there was no support from Grand Fleet, so in accordance with orders Beatty altered course to south at 17 knots, in the belief that it was the full intention of his commander-in-chief to intercept the enemy at dawn.

Our intact fleet occupied the interior positions between the enemy and the Heligoland Bight while the enemy had been driven so far westward as to be unable to reach the Horn Reef Channel before 3.30 the next morning. The Grand Fleet turned south at 9.15 and the battle-cruisers at 9.30. Beatty held that it was not necessary to fight a night action, as we were in a good strategic position for bringing the enemy to decisive action in the morning.

CHAPTER 14

The Torpedo at Jutland

The 21½-inch torpedo which Germany was introducing into her fleet in 1914 was said to have an effective range of 7,700 yards when set for 29 knots speed. While it is certain that some of the German destroyers at Jutland were armed with this weapon, the majority would carry the older 19½-inch torpedo, and some of them a still older type. People are inclined to think in terms of the very latest torpedo, whereas such a torpedo is generally to be found only in the very latest ship. There is no reason to believe that the German torpedo was more destructive than our own; and it was, from all the evidence, not such an effective one.

The fact that all the modern German battleships and battle-cruisers survived the torpedo both at Jutland and elsewhere, such as in certain fine attacks carried out by submarines, was due to armoured bulkheads running the whole length of the ship a few feet inside the inner skin on each side of the ship, to a well thought-out subdivision of the ships and to general attention to stability in the design. It would not have been difficult to discover this secret of German construction from the fact that the beam of the German ships was so much greater than in our own Dreadnoughts.

Since the most extravagant claims are being made for the torpedo as the reason for Lord Jellicoe's withdrawals at Jutland, it may be just as well to discuss the matter somewhat more fully. Let us clearly grasp the fact that the Grand Fleet was built largely under Lord Jellicoe's auspices, firstly, as Director of Ordnance, secondly, as Controller responsible for shipbuilding, and, finally, as a member of various Boards of Admiralty to carry out the very definite policy of the British people that it should fight and destroy the German Fleet. To make doubly sure, throughout 1915 and 1916, every other requirement had to yield to the demands of the Grand Fleet.

It was the predominant partner both before and during the war. Setting aside, then, the smaller issue, such as any supposed advantage which the Germans had in regard to torpedoes—and this they undoubtedly had in the number of torpedo-tubes on board their destroyers which came about through ignorance of the offensive role of destroyers on the part of Boards of Admiralty of which Lord Jellicoe was a member—nothing but the most overwhelming reason could excuse the failure of Lord Jellicoe to bring the German Fleet to decisive action with his great preponderance of force. We say this with the more reason because so much about the torpedo is the merest mental mirage.

Actually, we know only of some sixty torpedoes fired by the Germans in the battle at all sorts of targets, or no target at all, such as chance shots; and we do know of eighty-five torpedoes fired by the whole Grand Fleet in a similar way so that the argument in regard to the extra tubes and torpedoes carried by the German destroyers had little application at the Battle of Jutland. In addition, it was Lord Jellicoe's own fault that the British destroyers, other than those with the battle-cruisers, made no daylight attacks. There were 47 destroyers with Lord Jellicoe and 31 with the battle-cruisers, so that this consideration applied to over half our destroyers.

Now let us say in the first place that the test of experience and practice is against Lord Jellicoe and his apologists. At the Battle of Jutland, Beatty did not lose the enemy because of the torpedoes. With his weak battle-cruiser force he did all that man could do to keep contact. When he succeeded to the command of the Grand Fleet, the battleships were more and more practised at turning towards the torpedoes for the paramount reason that thereby you do not lose your enemy; and, for the secondary reason that you have better command of your ships while exposing the small target of the twenty-nine yards beam of the ship.

As to what really happened at Jutland, Lord Jellicoe tells us that:—

> As a result of this attack and another that followed immediately, some twenty or more torpedoes were observed to cross the track of the battle fleet in spite of our turn (a turn of four points, or 45°), the large majority of them passing the ships of the First and Fifth Battle Squadrons at the rear of the line. They were all avoided by the very skilful handling of the ships by their captains. . . . I doubt, however, whether the skill shown would have saved several ships from being torpedoed had the range been less, and the torpedoes consequently running at higher speed.

In the first attack which was not seen only individual ships turned to avoid the tracks of torpedoes. In the second the whole line of 27 ships turned away and 11 tracks of torpedoes were seen. In a later attack, which was again on the rear of the line, 11 more tracks were reported. Lord Jellicoe quotes from the actual reports of captains but obviously two ships will both report the same torpedo passing between them, and, it is better to give the actual facts as he does when he mentions "twenty or more torpedoes" in the two attacks. It must not be assumed that every torpedo reported, any more than every submarine reported, or "ship seen to sink," is an authentic case. The disturbed water in the wake of a destroyer is enough to create the impression of a torpedo.

Now the range of the German torpedo was under 8,000 yards. Lord Jellicoe allows that, in the second attack from which he turned, the destroyers' torpedoes were fired at ranges from 10,000 to 6,500 yards and only at the latter range did the destroyers turn and pass to the rear of the line under a heavy smoke screen. It may be confidently predicted then that most of the torpedoes were fired at or near the shorter range, and since, even with the turn away, the Grand Fleet course was still approaching the course of the torpedoes, it seems likely that they all had under 8,000 yards to run to cross the track of the rear squadron. Only one torpedo is mentioned as running short. The inference is that no more torpedoes would have been encountered had the fleet turned towards the destroyers.

Had this been done the enemy destroyers would certainly have encountered a far heavier gunfire, and, what is much more important, the German Fleet would have been defeated in its object of escaping the devastating salvoes of twenty-seven battleships.

There were about sixty cases throughout the whole of the battle on May 31 of torpedoes being reported, and only one battleship (the *Marlborough*) and one destroyer (the *Shark*) were hit. We can leave out the destroyer fights, and such attacks as were not made on a line of ships. This reduces the number to about fifty torpedoes fired on May 31, of which eight in ten were at a line which did not turn away from its enemy.

Only one hit, on the *Marlborough*, was secured, or a result of a little over two *per cent*. The belief was general in the Grand Fleet that the *Marlborough's* hit was the result of a submarine, but the Germans deny that any submarines were present, though periscopes were several times reported. The belief rests largely on the fact that the ship following the *Marlborough* turned to port, felt the shock of a collision and oil was seen. The presumption in that case was that the submarine after firing a torpedo dived under the line and then came up nearer the surface. The *Marlborough* remained in action and kept up 17 knots

173

until late at night. What, then is there in this solitary case to justify Lord Jellicoe for having failed to grasp what was possibly the greatest opportunity which was ever given to a sailor during the war?

Let us suppose that any aimed shot could only affect three ships, that is the margin of error in the destroyer is such that a torpedo aimed at one ship might hit either the ship ahead or astern. These three ships occupy a space in line of 1,200 yards, of which the maximum target is, say, 600 yards and the minimum is, say, 84 yards, according to the length and beam of the ships. The next factor to bear in mind is that, throughout the war, it has been possible to see the tracks of torpedoes. Steering end-on, then, one has full control of the helm, and it is possible the better to dodge them, the torpedo not being like a projectile which travels some 7,000 yards in ten seconds, but only covers less than 200 yards in ten seconds. In the same ten seconds the ship at a speed of 20-knots, which was the speed of Lord Jellicoe's ships, could cover 113 yards or nearly four times the minimum target she affords.

Now, from the nature of the case, the German destroyers chose to fire at long range, for there was no rescue for them from the flying battleships of their own side. In addition, their gun armament was far inferior to that of the British destroyers which they did not care to fight. The advantage therefore, which attached to a British destroyer attack which could be pressed home to short range as compared with a German destroyer attack at long range is very obvious. The German position was further complicated by the fixed direction which their ships must endeavour to steer, having but one objective, the home port; and, therefore, any turn they made to defend themselves against British destroyers was detrimental to the supreme necessity of steering for their protected waters.

On the other hand, there was only one fatal turn which the British battleships could make, and that was away from the enemy. To get the most efficient team work to enable the battle-cruisers, cruisers, destroyers and aircraft to achieve much better results than they can hope for when they work alone, it is absolutely essential that the heavies, or the battleships, shall stay in action. They should be pounding for all they are worth from the swift opening of the surprise, which is the best gift that the subsidiaries can bring to the battle fleet when they work in front of it before the opening of the main battle, to the decisive completion of the victory.

It seemed to the writer worthwhile to make these brief remarks in order to emphasise the fact that we had every reason to induce us to make torpedo attacks as the Germans did. That we did not make them was due to the fact that our doctrine was to use destroyers defensively, and the failure to keep the British battleships in close action was in any case detrimental to the offensive use of the destroyers.

The Germans made seven attacks on our ships, all of which were during daylight. The following is a brief summary:—

Two were on the Battle-cruisers Squadron at 3.45 and on, and at 5.45 and on.

One on the rear of battle fleet 6.45, but it is uncertain where the torpedoes were fired from.

One on the rear of the battle line by a destroyer flotilla at 7.21, when the British line turned away.

Two were on our cruisers at the head of the line at 6.40 and 7.30, apparently from enemy line.

One on our cruisers and destroyers at 8.22 by destroyers, when the British battle line again turned away though it was obvious the enemy was divided, for Beatty was fighting battleships many miles ahead.

There were also isolated torpedo attacks by one of two destroyers on a cruiser, and again on a destroyer during the night.

The contrasting failure to use the Grand Fleet destroyers in the daylight action needs a close inquiry. The idea of keeping the small cruisers and destroyers in reserve to fight their own types is a blind following of the precedent of former wars when frigates never attacked line-of-battleships. The possession of the torpedo capable of inflicting great injury on large units has changed the situation, much as the fireship created new conditions in former times. As has been pointed out elsewhere, the whole submarine campaign, and, in fact, the results of the war, depended on the continued existence of the German large units.

The time taken to replace them is shown by the fact that the large battleships laid down towards the end of 1913, and the battle-cruiser *Hindenburg* laid down in the summer of 1913, were not ready in time to take part in the Battle of Jutland on May 31, 1916. In addition, it should not be lost sight of that to attack the German battle line with destroyers was a course calculated to force the Germans to use their own destroyers with inferior armaments, in defence, instead of attack.

We, on the other hand, made only four destroyer attacks by day, and all from the Battle-Cruiser Fleet. They were as follows:—

One on the German battle-cruisers before they turned north.

One on their battle-cruisers after they turned north.

One on their battle fleet when advancing north (this was an overflow by two destroyers from the first-mentioned attack).

One by a few destroyers on the head of the German line as the *Invincibles* came into action.

At night our attacks were as follows:—

May 31, p.m. 9.50 to 10.50. Destroyers attacked cruisers.

10.21. The *Southampton* fired at vessel using searchlights.

11.10 to 11.45. Fourth Flotilla fired eleven torpedoes at vessels believed to be light cruisers, but accompanying battleships. There were three torpedo explosions. The battleship *Malaya* was able to watch this and the next attack. The first one was abaft her starboard beam. By the light of the explosion the leading enemy ship was distinctly seen as apparently one of the *Westfalen* class.

11.30 to 12.30. Five torpedoes were fired at battleships. Attack was some way astern of Malaya but explosions could be seen from her.

June 1 a.m.

2.0 to 2.30. Seventeen torpedoes were fired at a group of battleships or battle-cruisers, and eight hits were claimed.

2.37. The *Moresby* attacked four *Deutschland* class and claimed a hit on third ship of line.

All the attacks by night were made at under 4,000 yards range, and the majority were under 1,500 yards.

We have, of course, no final information as to the behaviour of our own torpedoes. Though explosions register hits, the same hit is often claimed by more than one boat. As regards the German torpedoes, at long range, several are reported to have run under the ships, and at short range several ran along the surface, where if a hit had been registered much of the force of the explosion would have been dissipated upwards. The inference is that the torpedo track was more visible at the beginning of the run than at the end, which, if this is correct, would be an additional subsidiary reason for turning towards the enemy.

Any discussion on the torpedo at the Battle of Jutland will start from a fundamental error if it assumes that the question is one of battleships *versus* torpedo craft—instead of fleets *versus* fleets. Fleets derive their inherent strength from the qualities of the chief command and

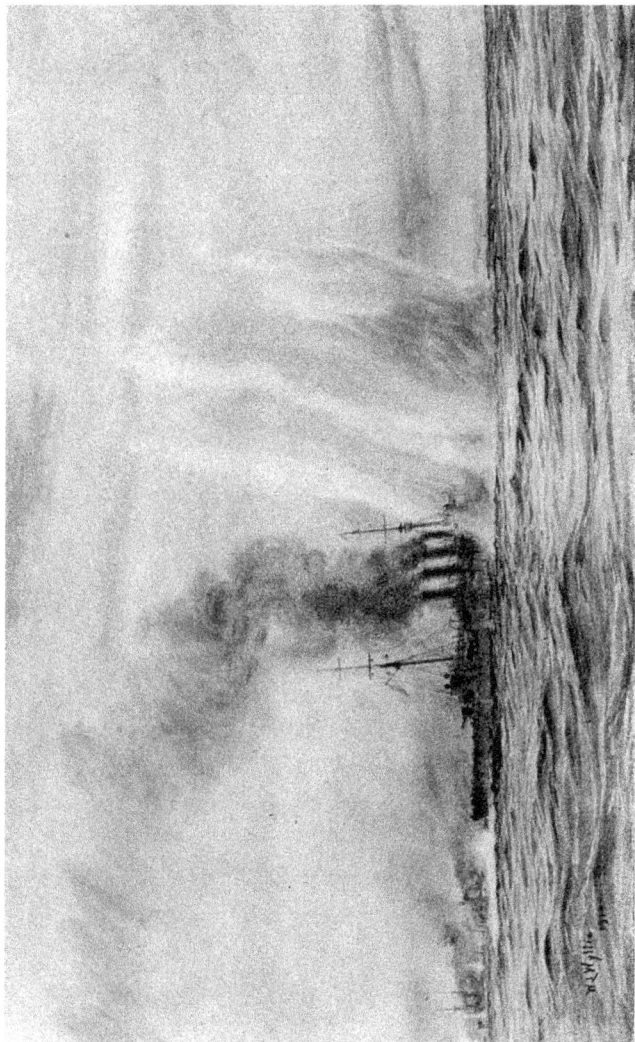

BRITISH LIGHT CRUISER H.M.S. *SOUTHAMPTON*

the training of the personnel; and we must bear in mind that, they consist of various bodies, even as an army consists of infantry, cavalry, artillery, tanks, air forces, etc. It is necessary to emphasise the qualities of the chief command; for the fleet which forces the fighting dictates the moves. For example, the destroyers are held to have an offensive and a defensive role. We have already expressed a sceptical view as to the counter being efficacious in preventing the enemy from developing an attack.

Still it may well be that if the British destroyers are attacking, their action keeps the enemy's light cruisers and destroyers so busy that they are unable to attack themselves. To argue, as the late Admiral Colomb did, that the battleship is degraded from its proud supremacy because it leans on other craft, like cruisers and destroyers, is to misconceive war, and one might as well argue that man yielded his supremacy when, instead of depending on his hands, feet and teeth, he took to using tools and weapons. The different classes of fighting craft are complementary to each other and the small fry sally out on the offensive with the more assurance because they look to the battleships as a great protecting base on which they can always retreat if necessary, to do so. The disabled, whether surface craft or hydroplanes, know that the sea is theirs if they belong to the stronger fleet, while those of the retreating force know no other protection but fortifications and mined waters.

On January 11, 1917, Lord Jellicoe, in a speech delivered shortly after exchanging his post of Commander-in-Chief of the Grand Fleet for that of First Sea Lord of the Board of Admiralty, said:—

> The torpedo, as fired from surface vessels, is effective certainly up to 10,000 yards range; and this requires that a ship shall keep beyond that distance to fight his guns.

The logical conclusion is that, in misty weather, such as characterises the North Sea, a ship cannot fight her guns at all, for she must not go inside 10,000 yards. In the Battle of Jutland, though ships were struck by torpedoes, the only ships known to have been sunk by this weapon were the pre-Dreadnought *Pommern*, the light cruiser *Rostock* and one British destroyer, the *Shark*. On the other hand, seven big ships were sunk by the gun, and probably five others were put out of action; while all the smaller ships which were sunk on the British side, with the exception of the destroyer *Shark*, were victims of the gun.

Everyone would see the absurdity of arguing that ships, therefore, should not be ventured inside 18,000 yards range because of the gun. Why, then, should we have this sloppiness of thought in regard to the torpedo? The only British big ship hit by a torpedo at Jutland, the *Marlborough*, kept her station at 17 knots all day, and the greater part of the night, and fired fourteen salvoes subsequently to being hit, in the brief interval before the fleet turned away from the 7.21 p.m. destroyer attack.

The argument takes on itself the character attributable to dwelling too much on conjectured results rather than on probabilities, or what Napoleon condemned as "making pictures," so that

Imagination frames events unknown,
In wild fantastic shapes of hideous ruin;
And what it fears, creates.

The mere fact that the torpedo shots are "browning" shots at the long line of a fleet seemed to create a condition bordering on panic in some minds. The Germans played on this fact, just as in times past it was a favourite gibe of a continental monarch that "the English will stampede like wild horses before their own imaginations." The great minds trained in war are too perspicacious to become the victims of phantasmagoria; but the mind steeped in mere material knowledge is peculiarly apt to do so.

Through neutral sources, judicious stories were floated that the Germans possessed torpedoes which showed no indications on the surface of the direction in which they were running. How the bubbles which follow in the wake can be completely got rid of was not explained. The story was not true, but it seems to have left its impression. The watching of the tracks is useful for avoiding torpedoes, though frequently the wakes of destroyers are mistaken for their surface indications, and their number is apt to be exaggerated by false alarms.

Following Lord Jellicoe's lead about not getting inside 10,000 yards range because of the tubes on board the German battleships, the apologists for Jutland seem to say:

We grant you that Jellicoe had at Jutland a fleet with exactly 200 guns of 13½-inch, 14-inch and 15-inch calibre, superior to anything the Germans possessed; we grant you that before the war we demonstrated in print the overwhelming superiority of the British 13½inch gun to the German 12-inch and still more of the British 15-inch, but we forgot the terrible German torpedoes, and they had more tubes!

179

As Mr. Archibald Hurd puts it in the *Fortnightly Review*, April, 1919, in the opening words of his article:

Lord Jellicoe's book contains only one arresting revelation regarding the naval war, and that is that on the evening of May 31st, 1916, the Germans, after long training and many rehearsals, tried to torpedo the British Empire. As the Battle of Jutland was drawing to its close, liberal civilisation was in greater danger than at any period since Magna Charta was signed.

Certainly, this is as arresting as lightning and has a distinct tendency to create an atmosphere such as the Fat Boy in *Pickwick* was skilled in producing. Then we are told that *hundreds of torpedoes* were fired at the enormous target of a seven mile line. Then comes the conclusion:—

That the British Empire was saved and the world rescued from passing under the control of Prussian autocracy, with its vast naval and military machines, was due to the instant decision, and prompt action of the commander-in-chief of the Grand Fleet, supported by the admirals commanding divisions and the captains of the heavy ships which the enemy attacked. If that attempt, made with large forces and audacity, had not been frustrated, that Grand Fleet might have been so weakened that the command of the sea would have passed from us.

The time referred to is 7.23, when a division of eleven destroyers attacked the rear of the battle-line in an endeavour to shake us off while the German fleet turned to the westward, an endeavour in which the German admiral was entirely successful, for Lord Jellicoe turned away the whole battle-line of 27 ships. Altogether eleven torpedoes were believed to have been fired!

The reader may be tempted to wonder why the torpedo should be so potent in the hands of a German, and so impotent in the hands of a British sailor. Mr. Hurd says that the German Battle Fleet:

Though less heavily gunned, so far as battle guns were concerned, than the British, possessed at least 25 *per cent*, more torpedo tubes, besides a considerable superiority in destroyers.

The official estimate is that we had 78 destroyers to the German 77, and a calculation giving the Germans the best of their destroyers shows that we had a 30 *per cent*, superiority in displacement. In regard to the torpedo tubes, those that mattered in the battleships, with which we are dealing, were the German tubes that bore to port and the British tubes to starboard.

The 28 British ships would muster 38 tubes on the broadside to the German 42, or with the battle-cruisers 50 to the German 52. Mr. Hurd's arguments as to great German superiority thus fall to the ground both in regard to ships and destroyers. The writer has no predilection for depreciating the torpedo, for in 1913, on the ground that the war was drawing near, he openly advocated fitting pre-Dreadnoughts with large numbers of torpedo-tubes for use in battle. He does, however, object to exaggerated language, and still more to panicky action, because of a well-understood risk for which Lord Jellicoe was provided with an ample margin of safety.

There is no escape from the fact that whenever our fleet began to get into action the Germans would launch a destroyer attack so long as they had flotillas in a position to attack, and therefore turning away was tantamount to a determination not to fight. Torpedoes were reported throughout the early stages of the battle and then, after the eleven torpedoes reported in the turnaway from 7.21 to 7.33, they were reported again at 7.35, 7.43, 8.0, and 8.25 by various battleships. Before 7.21 was the only time our twenty-seven battleships were in action. They then turned away because of a destroyer attack from a flotilla from which eleven torpedoes are said to have been fired. They had an opportunity of again attacking a portion of the enemy's line at 8.20 p.m., in spite of the one hour of daylight that was thrown away, but on the mere threat of a destroyer attack they were again turned away without firing a shot.

So far, we have only had pictures from our own side which suggest a somewhat disordered psychology. Though Lord Jellicoe's book does reveal loyalty and comradeship to all who have served with him, if we can consider it as such when all are praised alike, whether they did well or not, the book hardly seems to recognise the existence of psychology in war. It is only as an unconscious revelation of his own temperament that it has its value in this respect. The strange German deterioration is not brought out, and no mention is made of the fact that the *Inflexible* and *Indomitable* were fighting at 6,000 yards range at 8.26 and came out unscathed. Yet this has an important bearing on the fighting spirit of the German Fleet at the time. To find out what happened on the other side we must have recourse to what has been revealed by Germans since the armistice.

In the *Times*, January 14, 1918, "A Member of the Allied Naval Commission in German Waters" had an informing article on German opinion about Jutland. He gave the results of a number of conversations with a Zeppelin officer who was gunnery lieutenant of the *Deutschland* in the battle. This gunnery officer revealed to us a German fleet that thought only of flight from the moment the Grand Fleet was sighted. He speaks of their situation as that of a fleet absolutely crushed. He states that their destroyers could not stand up against the better armed and more speedy British destroyers, and that as a result "torpedo attack in the daylight was almost hopeless." The truth of his first statement has been proved in every destroyer fight in the war. The inference that torpedo attack was almost hopeless is simply an illustration of the psychological effect of the first truth, for the British destroyers could not prevent them from launching their attack but could make them pay for their temerity.

The picture has all the appearance of truth. Such a nearly panic-stricken fleet is one that a resolute leader quick to seize his opportunities, like Beatty, had he been in full command, could have done almost anything with. The interesting paragraph about the German destroyers must make all wonder that these same German destroyers should have dictated our deployment, our two subsequent turns away which lost us all contact with the German fleet, and have turned us south rather than risk night action.

The next morning, at dawn, it was the thought of torpedo attack that deterred the admiral from going in the direction of the Horn Reef lightvessel to intercept the demoralised enemy on his return. He had lost contact with his own destroyers, and let us parenthetically remark that the only way to keep contact, all with all, is for all to force the fighting from beginning to end. It was a remarkable end to the setting out from Scapa Flow when the whole Great Fleet was delayed to save the fuel of a few destroyers carrying out searches of fishing vessels met *en route*, rather than let them overtake the fleet which was advancing at only 14-knots on its course, allowing for zigzagging, that in the end all of them should have been lost to the fleet on June 1, until 9 a.m. that forenoon.

There were altogether 151 ships in Lord Jellicoe's fleet at Jutland as opposed to 115 under von Scheer: that is to say, there were 151 torpedo platforms opposed to 115. We had 78 destroyers to 77, and 36 cruisers to 11 for the enemy. The gun armaments of the British destroyers were much superior to the German, and there was this vast preponderance of individually more powerful cruisers, numbering 3½ to 1, to counter any efforts of the enemy and to back up our own destroyer attacks. No admiral ever had less cause to complain of the force at his disposal.

The only really genuine cause of complaint was the number of tubes per destroyer, and the inadequate allowance of only four torpedoes per destroyer, compared to the German six. There were a few instances of waste which ought never to have been allowed in the teaching of destroyer tactics in fleet action so long as the allowance was only four per boat. I refer to occasions when our destroyers, with their superior gun armaments, made use of torpedoes in firing them at destroyers at long range. Even so, though individual destroyers fired all their torpedoes, nothing like all the torpedoes were fired, for the total number used from the 151 torpedo platforms only exceeded by a very small figure the number of destroyers we had at Jutland.

Therefore, allowing for torpedoes fired from larger ships, we may say that an average of not more than one torpedo per destroyer was fired. It is certain that this would have been exceeded had there been more tubes to fire from, which only goes to prove that we had not thought out the offensive role of the destroyer which ought to be called by its proper name of a torpedo boat.

CHAPTER 15

The Night Action

We have now come to the end of the daylight battle with its final example of the vicious circle of failure which is inevitably started when the big units, on which all else is based, go out of action. The battle-cruisers forced the fighting, but the heavy enemy battleships were too much for them. The armoured cruisers, which were the connecting links to the battle fleet, reported that there was no Grand Fleet in sight, so Beatty was obliged to lose the enemy. It is the working of the vicious circle. Lord Jellicoe having regained touch, a destroyer attack threatened; and though it threatened only the cruisers ahead, the Fleet was once more turned away.

The destroyer attack was dealt with by our cruisers and destroyers, and the *Calliope*, when within 6,500 yards of the enemy battleships, fired a torpedo; but cruisers and all must go when the Grand Fleet goes, especially when they have not got the protective cloak of night. So enemy battleships, separated from the force ahead, were permitted to pass on, nobody recking as to where they went.

Von Scheer would naturally argue that if a destroyer movement in the direction of the British Fleet can always drive twenty-seven battle-ships away by daylight, what can they not achieve by night? It is said that a German cruiser came and observed the fleet turn south, and that a wireless message was sent out after 9 o'clock to the German ships to steer south-east at 16 knots. There was only one other episode as the light failed and the ships were turned south. At 9.5 the cruisers *Caroline* and *Royalist* fired five torpedoes at ships stated to be *Deutschland* class at 7,600 yards. As our battle-cruisers came into view a few minutes later somewhat in the same direction, it seems possible that the torpedoes were fired at them. If so, it is fortunate that the torpedo so often misses. Lord Jellicoe makes no mention of the episode, but says that the last seen of the enemy was by the cruiser *Falmouth* at 8.38.

At 9 p.m. Lord Jellicoe had made his dispositions for the night and formed the fleet on a southerly course with his destroyers acting as a protecting screen five miles astern. He tells us plainly that his object was to avoid night action, and that he considered the enemy to be better equipped for such a contingency. Here, as elsewhere, the moral factor is not discussed. It is always material, and on this occasion no explanation of defective material is forthcoming. The politician who has served as whipping boy in the book can hardly be so used because the German searchlights were better than our own, and the Germans had star-shells and we had not.

It is not worth the worry of inquiring why Lord Jellicoe had not applied to the army for the loan of a few star-shells. The point was that he had as many destroyers and three and a half times as many cruisers as the Germans. His cruisers and destroyers were of greater tonnage, and possessed heavier gun armaments. Our capacity for re-placing them was shown in the case of the 30-knot cruiser *Caroline*, which was laid down January 28, 1914, and was delivered after trials on December 17, 1914. For the sake of victory, he could use all his forces together, but he was determined not to fight a night action. The decision could only be justified if he was resolute and was taking steps to bring the enemy to action in the morning. Beatty gave the true estimate of this governing factor, he wrote:

> In view of the gathering darkness, and of the fact that our stra-tegical position was such as to make it appear certain that we should locate the enemy at daylight under most favourable cir-cumstances, I did not consider it desirable or proper to close the enemy battle fleet during the dark hours.

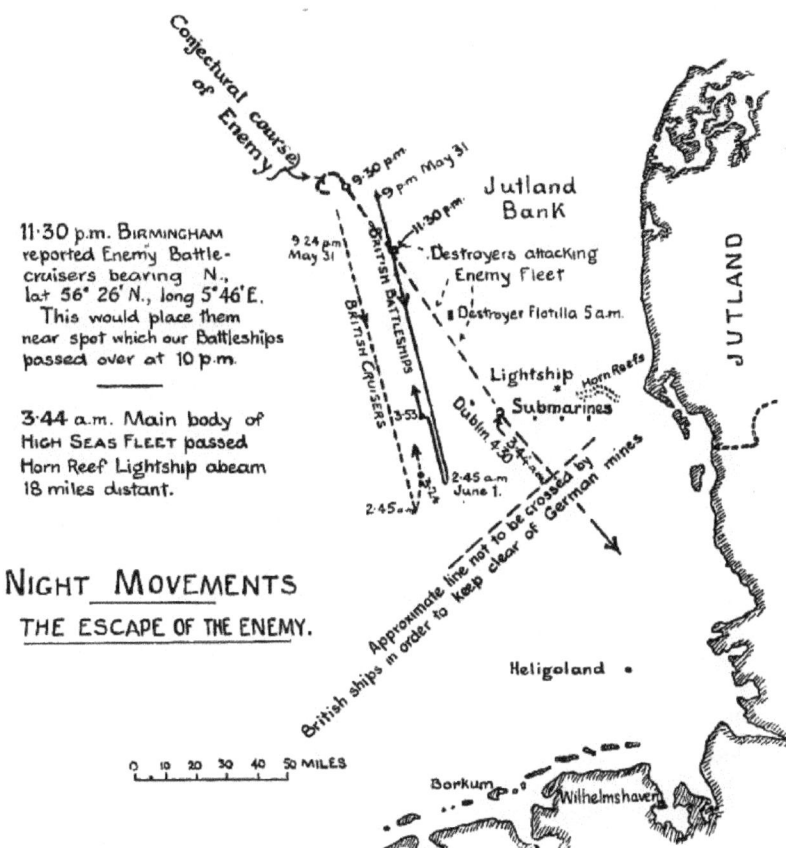

Conjectural course of Enemy

9·30 p.m. May 31

9 p.m. May 31

11·30 p.m.

Jutland Bank

9 24 p.m May 31

Destroyers attacking Enemy Fleet

Destroyer Flotilla 5 a.m.

Lightship Horn Reefs

Submarines

Dublin 4.25

2·45 a.m June 1.

2·45 a.m.

Approximate line not to be crossed by German mines

Approximate line not to be crossed in order to keep clear of German mines

British ships

Heligoland •

Borkum

Wilhelmshaven

JUTLAND

BRITISH BATTLESHIPS

BRITISH CRUISERS

11·30 p.m. BIRMINGHAM reported Enemy Battle-cruisers bearing N., lat 56° 26′ N., long 5°46′E.
This would place them near spot which our Battleships passed over at 10 p.m.

3·44 a.m. Main body of HIGH SEAS FLEET passed Horn Reef Lightship abeam 18 miles distant.

NIGHT MOVEMENTS

THE ESCAPE OF THE ENEMY.

0   10   20   30   40   50 MILES

What Lord Jellicoe actually did with his fleet was to steer 97 miles to the south, and then, at 2.45, or after dawn, when he was about 44 miles S.W. from the Horn Reef lightvessel, he turned north and went back for about fifteen miles by exactly the same lane which had brought him south. At 4.25 a.m. the *Dublin* reported that she had sighted an enemy cruiser and two destroyers steaming fast, and lost sight of them in lat. 55° 28′, N. and long. 6° 32′ E. Shortly before 4 a.m. the leading German ships appear to have passed the Horn Reef lightvessel abeam at a distance of eighteen miles.

It therefore appears that if the Grand Fleet had turned up to the Horn Reef lightvessel at 2 a.m. (which is very near dawn at the beginning of June), his cruisers would have been less than forty miles from the Horn Reef lightvessel at that time, and less than eighteen miles from the spot passed over by the High Seas Fleet. By 2.45 his cruisers could have been there, and his battleships at 20 knots soon after

185

3 o'clock, thus completely bearing out his subordinate's forecast, and enabling him to dispose his fleet right across the path of the High Seas Fleet which was not due there for another half-hour.

The general situation, as it must have presented itself to Lord Jellicoe, was that the enemy was to the westward, and had, by the persistence of the battle-cruisers, been driven sufficiently far to the westward to make it certain that he could be intercepted at daylight by the Horn Reef lightvessel. This conviction would be confirmed if we succeeded in decoding any of the German wireless messages when they made their turn to the S.E. at 9 o'clock, a course which would bring von Scheer abeam of the Horn Reef lightvessel an hour after daylight. There was every reason why von Scheer would not adopt the alternative route by the channel skirting the Dutch coast. Wireless messages had passed to England, and he believed that the latter route would bring him into the vicinity of our Channel and Harwich forces which he would certainly expect to be rushed up. He would have been arguing on the soundest lines of probability, but history tells us that psychology has a way of exalting possibilities far above probabilities. At any rate, Lord Jellicoe relates that:

> The Harwich force, under Commodore Tyrwhitt, had been kept in port by Admiralty Orders on May 31, and was dispatched to sea on the morning of June 1, when I was informed that it was being sent out to join me and to replace vessels requiring fuel.

It would require Dean Swift to do justice to Admiralty strategy, and to write a companion for the lines:—

> *Behold a proof of Irish sense,*
> *Here Irish wit is seen:*
> *When nothing's left that's worth defence*
> *We build a magazine.*

> They (the Harwich force) would have been of great use at daylight on June 1, had they been on the scene at that time, and it is needless to add how much I should have welcomed the participation of the Harwich force in the action had circumstances admitted of this.

That is the gentle chiding with which Lord Jellicoe admonishes the Admiralty. It is possible that a Select Committee of the House of Commons would put it differently. It is certain that Lord Fisher would give us the concise common sense in language both Biblical and profane. It must have been present to the minds of what was called "the War Staff" of the Admiralty that small cruisers and flotillas which had been steaming hard since the previous night; which had, some of them, been fighting since 3.30 the previous afternoon; which had, in fact, been operating in the presence of the enemy for twelve to fifteen hours, and so might reasonably be expected to have fired away their small allowance of four torpedoes per destroyer, were not in so favourable a position to attack their flying and scattered enemy as would be the Harwich flotilla. We have here one more instance of the vicious circle which has befogged all our naval failures from the *Goeben* onwards, in that the Admiralty was so seriously involved as to cause the Board to save itself by whitewashing everybody else.

Another consideration which would weigh with the Germans in the selection of their route was the fortified and mined havens from Heligoland to near Esbjerg, where, even if refuge could not be obtained owing to considerations of depth, their vessels could be run aground on the sand dunes to the west of the North Frisian Islands. In a scattering some could make for the Baltic. On the southern route, similar sanctuary could only be obtained for a much shorter distance.

During the night, our light cruisers and the destroyer flotillas came into action from 10.4 to 2.0 a.m. from west to east, showing that the enemy were on a course for the Horn Reef Channel.

p.m.

10.4 Destroyers fighting enemy light cruisers. (11th Flotilla).

10.20 Cruisers fighting enemy light cruisers.

11.30 Destroyers fighting enemy light cruisers. (4th Flotilla, *Tipperary*).

12.00 *Do.* fighting enemy 2nd Battle Squadron. (*Pommern* sunk.)

a.m.

0.10 *Do.* fighting enemy battleships.

0.30 *Do.* do. do.

2.00 Destroyers *do. do.* (12th Flotilla).

2.25 *Moenad* of 12th Flotilla *do.*

2.37 *Moresby* fighting enemy battleships.

The attacks were carried out with great gallantry, mostly inside 3,000 yards range, and at least 38 torpedoes were fired. A number of hits were claimed, but the Germans only lost the *Pommern* and the light cruiser *Rostock*. The observations of explosions, however, render it certain that other ships were hit. Lord Jellicoe says:

> Information received after the action made it certain that at least four battleships of the *Dreadnought* type were hit by torpedoes, in addition to the pre-Dreadnought battleship *Pommern*, which was admitted to have been sunk by a torpedo as was the light cruiser *Rostock*.

Some of these explosions were seen from the Grand Fleet, for the destroyers were only from five to fifteen miles behind. The certainty that these torpedoed ships would be greatly hampered in making the Horn Reef Channel and possibly disabled from further fighting would, in any enterprising mind, be an imperative argument for cutting them off as soon after dawn as possible. Some of the injured ships must have had their upper decks level with the water and could not fight their guns.

The circumstances in which the Fourth Flotilla was fighting enemy cruisers at 11.80, and the enemy's Second Battle Squadron at midnight needs explanation. After the first attack the flotilla altered course to eastward (that is, to port of the enemy's line of advance). It then turned south-east and came in contact at midnight with vessels of the *Deutschland* class. A vessel was hit, and was observed to list over considerably. She has since been identified as the pre-Dreadnought *Pommern*, which sank. The flotilla was driven north.

The Twelfth Flotilla, following the *Marlborough's* Squadron—the *Marlborough* was now falling below 17-knots owing to the damage by torpedo—was astern of position, and while the Fourth Flotilla was steering S.E., this flotilla, to avoid it, got into a position about five miles to the eastward and ten miles to the northward of the First Battle Squadron instead of being in its station five miles astern, or to the north, to protect the First Squadron. It thereby came across, at 1.45, six enemy battleships, of which four were *Kaisers*, steering S.E. With great promptitude, the flotilla steered at 25 knots to attack, and a message was sent to the Grand Fleet, at 1.52 by wireless, as follows:—

> Enemy battleships steering S.E. approximate bearing S.W. My position ten miles astern of First Battle Squadron.

Altogether, seventeen torpedoes were, fired about 2 o'clock, and a number of hits were claimed. The flotilla was forced to the north by the enemy cruisers. The *Moenad*, of the same flotilla, made a later attack at 2.25, and the *Moresby* at 2.37, and both claimed hits.

The destroyers with Beatty and Hood were the only destroyers which had been given an opportunity of firing torpedoes at the enemy during daylight. A destroyer flotilla had on one occasion moved out to attack during the daylight action, but was recalled. We may be sure that they welcomed the opportunities given to them of attacking during the night.

Whether the message reporting the course and position of the German Fleet at 1.52 was taken in by the Grand Fleet can only be settled by an examination of the signal logs; and in particular the *Iron Duke's* wireless log should be produced. It is a circumstance illustrating the carelessness with which important papers are kept, and records mislaid, that this important log was lost for a long period, and the obvious conclusion is that the further we recede from events the less available will the evidence become.

As we jammed or tapped the enemy messages, so they jammed our own to the best of their ability, and it is important to ascertain if this message to which we have referred was jammed. We know from Lord Jellicoe that it was not brought to his notice. The enemy messages indicated the scattered state of von Scheer's ships. With the exception of the destroyers, which had been carried northward and eastward by their attacks, our fleet was concentrated. As Lord Jellicoe speaks in terms of great admiration for our wireless service it seems hardly conceivable that the 1.52 message, to which all other signals should have given precedence, from a few miles away was not taken in by a single ship.

The difficulty of providing an explanation may possibly be responsible for the allegation that it was logged in the *Iron Duke's* wireless log. In any case the log must have come under the examination of high Admiralty officials and they ought to be made to disclose whether this signal was logged as well as the one in which Beatty asked the leading battle squadron, as it was turning away from the enemy in obedience to Lord Jellicoe's order, to follow him and cut off the enemy. Lord Fisher, the *Times*, September 13, 1919, recalled a cynical utterance of Mr. McKenna, who was First Lord of the Admiralty and at whose hands we learned its application. It was:

Never fight a public department. You cannot win. It marshals facts which are incontestable.

The records of the Battle of Jutland have now come to the bar of public opinion and it is for the people to say whether they will continue to allow the facts to be drilled by a public department.

We have now seen that the failure to destroy the enemy was due neither to lack of information nor to any other cause such as low visibility or mist, but to the deliberate steps taken by Lord Jellicoe, all of which had as their one controlling thought the preservation of his own ships.

A curious feature of so many of the naval actions of the war is that the North Sea mists are so often blamed as the cause of failure. Strategically and tactically, the mist may enable an enemy to escape altogether, but so long as there is contact one is at a loss to understand why it is a positive advantage to one side and a disadvantage to the other. If one side is on the defensive and the other on the offensive, one can easily understand that the conditions of low and variable visibility are a disadvantage to the defensive because surprises are constantly coming out of the mist.

Again, if one side has an advantage of speed, or, still more, if it is so strong that it can shed ships so that the speed of the fleet is the speed of its fastest divisions while that of the enemy is the speed of the slowest ship, one can well understand that it is in a better position to gain the bearing which best conforms to gunnery advantages according to the state of the sea, the direction of the sun and wind—in fact, all that is due to the variable visibility in different directions. This advantage becomes the more pronounced from the certainty that the enemy has a "one course" mind, namely, the shortest and quickest way home. Hence, we are more than a little puzzled by all these communications such as the one from the Admiralty that the German fleet escaped owing to "low visibility and mist." It had not the merit of a single grain of truth, but it had become an obsession with the Admiralty to blame the weather.

There was a similar attempt to mislead when the three *Cressys* were lost, by the statement that the weather was too bad for destroyers. The ships never had been screened by destroyers, and every midshipman called them the "live bait" squadron because they were bound to be torpedoed. The Dardanelles—it was the weather again. After Scarborough the Germans escaped because of the mist. Does it never occur to the mechanical school, which wants war to be all certainties, that the sea belongs to the most skilful and ardent wooer who adapts himself to its variable moods?

Villeneuve summed up his fleet for all time in the words, "They were not drilled in storms." It is all a matter of a trained war judgment. How Nelson looked upon it may be seen in a letter he wrote in 1796 from the Mediterranean:—

This country is the most favourable possible for skill with an inferior fleet; for the winds are so variable that at some one time in 24 hours you must be able to attack a part of a large fleet and the other will be becalmed or have a contrary wind.

No, the new teaching is all wrong. The ever-blamed mist is at once the veil of timidity and the screen of skill.

The only positive disadvantage to one side or the other about the weather conditions was that they robbed the Germans of the use of their Zeppelins, so that both a battle and a surprise were possible for the Grand Fleet. But even to his own Fleet, Lord Jellicoe on June 4 issued a memorandum saying that:

Weather conditions of a highly unfavourable nature robbed the Fleet of that complete victory which I know was expected by all ranks.

It would be interesting to have heard the comments of the officers and men in the battle-cruisers and the *Barhams* on this statement when it appeared.

It was pointed out with emphasis in the House of Commons thirteen years ago, in the discussions on the Dreadnought's design, that the normal condition of the North Sea is one of low visibility, and that the Germans would choose those conditions. In fact, the Dogger Bank fight has been the only one in really clear weather, and then the Admiralty invented a minefield, about 90 miles from Heligoland, to account for Admiral Moore having turned away. To the bureaucrat it was the weather which blew the first British minefield on to the European coast almost immediately after it was laid. Only an "Alice in Wonderland" court-martial might dare to say that the natural resting-place of this minefield was on the beach because the Admiralty of peace and economy had limited the cost of the British mine to one-fourth of the cost of the German.

It was not the weather, or the visibility logged at 6,000 yards, which deterred Lord Jellicoe from going to the Horn Reef Channel at dawn on June 1 to intercept the enemy, but the old reason of the torpedo. It had helped to dictate the deployment; it had been responsible for both turns away from the enemy; it had determined the mind of Lord Jellicoe against a fleet action by night, and now, by reason of his protecting destroyers not being with him, he was not prepared to go to the Horn Reef Channel. Considering the trend of night actions, he would probably have found his destroyers on the way. We have already commented on how remarkable was this end to the setting out from Scapa, when a great fleet was delayed to save the fuel of a few destroyers, that in the end all of them should have been lost to the fleet on June 1 until 9 a.m.

Again, we must reiterate that the best way to keep contact, all with all, is for all to force the fighting from the beginning to the end. The net result was that though, as Beatty stated, "our strategical position was such as to make it appear certain that we should locate the enemy at daylight under most favourable circumstances".. we lost him all the same! For Lord Jellicoe would neither fight a night action, nor did he feel himself to be in a position to accept the other and better alternative of going round to the Horn Reef Channel to achieve the dearest objects of his country.

CHAPTER 16

Losses at and from Jutland

Lord Jellicoe only mentions Nelson's name once in his book. The reference is where he contrasts his own position with that of Nelson prior to Trafalgar. He maintains that he could not take the risks that Nelson took because beyond Nelson's force of twenty-six battleships were twenty-six more under Cornwallis, ten under Keith and eleven refitting, while he had no such reserve. The argument has no force unless it can be shown that Cornwallis and Keith had units they could spare from the vital duties the ships were performing. Lord Jellicoe evades this point by not mentioning the strength of the commissioned French and Spanish fleets that Nelson, Cornwallis and Keith had to face.

The different writers who defend Lord Jellicoe advance the same argument, that as Nelson only commanded a portion of the British Battle Fleets in war, he could take risks, a course which was not open to Lord Jellicoe, who commanded a fleet embracing all our modern battleships. The argument, even if the premise were true, is puerile. Lord Jellicoe had Germany's *all* at his disposal. If he fought a decisive action with his great preponderance of force, he wiped out all the risk of the future in losses from submarines and mining craft, since the operations of these vessels depended on the protection of the German High Seas Fleet.

Those risks are very fully put forward in Lord Jellicoe's book. Thus, we are told that:

In a really dense fog there was great risk in attempting to leave Scapa with a large fleet, owing to the strong tides in the Pentland Firth, and nothing but the gravest emergency would have justified the attempt being made.

The anxieties of the approaches to the Firth of Forth in thick weather are also mentioned and: "These approaches would have been mined by the enemy with great ease by surface ships had they been sufficiently enterprising, and it was a standing wonder to me that the attempt was never made."

In fog on April 22, 1916, we lost for a time the services of the battle-cruisers *Australia* and *New Zealand*, the battleship *Neptune* and three destroyers through collisions. These are examples of the waste of the waiting period, a favourite subject of my pen during the time before hostilities when I was begging my countrymen to provide the margin of safety for the coming war. The risks of any action, or what is ignorantly called luck or chance, in battle where our force had an adequate margin of safety are small indeed compared to the wasting, or attrition, of a long waiting period. In accepting the risks of a battle, one kills in a single hour a thousand ever present risks in the long-drawn months when attrition is at work.

When Lord Jellicoe tells us in the prominence of italics that there was present in his mind that "our Fleet was the one and only factor that was vital to the existence of the Empire," I can assure him it is a very old discovery; but his methods at the Battle of Jutland were directed not so much to the preservation of that fleet, but unconsciously towards the preservation of the High Seas Fleet. *All risks would have been wiped out, including the submarine menace and the overthrow of the Russian Army as well, had he realised his opportunities at Jutland.*

It is just as well to recall what this submarine threat which followed the indecisive battle of Jutland really meant. On July 30, 1918, the First Lord of the Admiralty said in the House of Commons:—

> A year ago we were faced with a situation which up to that time was considered by many almost inconceivable and insoluble. Our available mercantile marine power was being sunk at a rate which would soon have brought us to the point of inability to continue the war, and we were without tried and recognised means of combating it.

The advantage of a decision on May 31 and June 1, 1916, does not end with the fact that it would have wiped out the submarine menace

British battleships H.M.S. *Valiant* and *Malaya* in the Firth of the Forth

and preserved millions of tons of shipping. It would have made possible a thorough blockade, a great reinforcement through the opening up of the Baltic, the release of the Russian Baltic Fleet, and the revival of the spirit of the Russian people.

Lord Jellicoe had a great margin of superiority in the fleet actually present; and it should never be forgotten that when one's force is twice as strong as that of the enemy, the latter must inflict twice as great a loss before he begins to score. Nor is it true that we had no reserve. Germany had no reserve except in ships building, but we had six Dreadnoughts all but ready or refitting, namely, *Ramillies, Resolution, Queen Elizabeth, Emperor of India, Royal Sovereign*, and *Dreadnought*, one battle-cruiser, the *Australia*, refitting, two *Lord Nelsons* and a number of pre-Dreadnoughts. If we balance the stronger Italian fleet against the Austrian, and two of the French *Dantons*, each with four 12-inch and twelve 9.4-inch guns against the *Goeben*, and so leave them out of the calculation, there were in all still available as a reserve 13 Dreadnoughts, 1 Battle-cruiser, 3 *Dantons* belonging to the Dreadnought era, two *Lord Nelsons* and 5 *Patries*.

Ultimately, allowing for distance, there were the Japanese Dreadnoughts as well; and to these must be added the result of our great building efforts which, during the whole war, added seven battleships and five battle-cruisers to our navy. The battle-cruisers *Renown* and *Repulse* joined up a few months after Jutland. It should also be remembered that the damaged ships of a flying foe—in the case of the German fleet at Jutland, the enemy was cut off from his bases—ought to be lost ships, whereas that is not the case with the victorious side.

Many ships were badly damaged on the German side, and it is extraordinary that we permitted all of them to be saved. Even the battle-cruiser *Seydlitz* was saved after beaching, and subsequently repaired, though the hammering she received is evidenced by the fact that 168 of her crew were killed. She had been hit by twenty-eight shells and was torpedoed on the starboard side when Hood's squadron made its brilliant dash in at 6.10. She kept her place in the line until after 7 o'clock, and if the battleships had been kept in action, instead of turning away at 7.21, they could have finished her.

The *König* was another example. This battleship, of the most powerful German type present at the battle, was hit fifteen times by heavy shell. Her forecastle was only 6½ feet above the water, and a few more salvoes would have finished her. The result of permitting the escape of these badly-damaged vessels is to be seen, first, in the fact that the

German Fleet was out again in strength on August 19, 1916, or eleven weeks after the battle and, secondly, in the relative loss of personnel in the battle, a matter of some consideration in view of the importance of the manning question in the subsequent submarine campaign.

	British.	German.
Officers killed, drowned or missing	343	172
Officers wounded	51	41
Men killed, drowned or missing	6,104	2,414
Men wounded	513	449

The high proportion of British dead was due to the six large ships which were sunk.

Now in considering the argument of Lord Jellicoe about an alleged absence of reserves, if we apply the above considerations to the Battle of Jutland, and disregard the reinforcement from ships building, let us assume that of the 21 German Dreadnoughts and battle-cruisers they had lost 15, leaving them 6 escaped. Let us make the large assumption that the stronger side, the British force, out of its original strength of 37 Dreadnoughts and battle-cruisers lost 25, or 10 more than the Germans. The result would leave us 12 surviving ships which had fought and got battered, as compared with 6 battered Germans; but, in addition, we should have had 6 Dreadnoughts and 1 battle-cruiser which had never fought at all, and which had been away completing or refitting.

To these would have to be added 7 splendid French Dreadnoughts, 3 *Dantons*, 2 *Lord Nelsons*, 5 *Patries* (similar to *Lord Nelsons*), and all our pre-Dreadnoughts. In fact, the result of a battle in which we suffered far greater losses than the enemy would have been to produce a preponderance of force of about six to one, and, in addition, to free the Russian Baltic Squadron.

I am, of course, merely for purposes of argument, making an extravagant estimate of possible British losses. They could not have been caused by shell fire, for so demoralised had become the shooting of the German Fleet in face of the odds, that they had ceased to hit; and the one shot that hit the *Colossus* out of the whole twenty-seven battleships was at 7.10 p.m., or nearly an hour after the arrival of the Grand Fleet. The losses could only have been caused by the torpedo. In the case of the first turn-away, at 7.23, eleven torpedoes were reported. In the second turn-away, after 8 o'clock, which was a peculiarly bad example of the evasion tactics, since we did not even engage the divided enemy, and turned away from west to south-west on sighting the enemy destroyers, two torpedoes were reported between 8 o'clock and 8.30. They were not attributable to this attack, for it was delivered against our cruisers and destroyers.

We have therefore the facts that only eleven torpedoes had to be evaded in turning towards the enemy, and that the risks to the enemy destroyers would be increased by such a turn bringing into play all the secondary armaments of 6-inch and 4-inch guns. What then was the probability of hitting? At a very liberal estimate we might concede three ships, of which one, possibly, would drop out of action. And yet we have shown that if we had lost twenty-five ships, we should have scored a decisive victory, and changed the whole course of the war. Lord Jellicoe himself never claims that there would have been such great losses as here conceded, if I interpret correctly the view, expressed where he says:—

> I doubt, however, whether the skill shown would have saved several ships from being torpedoed had the range been less and the torpedoes consequently running at a higher speed.

Therefore, it is a matter of pure conjecture that several ships might have been torpedoed; and for that we sacrificed our overwhelming preponderance in gunnery and lost the enemy. This then in sober language is the correct proportion of the dummy which Mr. Archibald Hurd has decked out in the *Fortnightly Review* when we were informed in the passage quoted that Lord Jellicoe had saved the British Empire from being torpedoed and from the greatest danger that was threatened us since Magna Charta.

Lord Jellicoe claims for the night actions of our destroyers, as:

> Certain that at least four battleships of the *Dreadnought* type were hit by torpedoes in addition to the pre-Dreadnought battleship *Pommern*, which was admitted to have been sunk by a torpedo, as was the light cruiser *Rostock*.

What then can he claim for the Grand Fleet battleships? The battle-cruiser *Lützow* certainly perished at the hands of the Rosyth force, and the *Wiesbaden* was sent disabled down the lines by the cruiser or battle-cruiser action, though the *coup-de-grâce* was probably given by the battleships. At the best, this leaves only a few destroyers to the credit of the battleships, and a certain amount of damage, but no losses.

Lord Jellicoe in his account complains that the Germans in their official statement omitted to mention that:

> The *Seydlitz* had to be beached to prevent her sinking, thereby slurring over the point that the *Seydlitz* would undoubtedly have gone to the bottom as our *Warrior* did, had the action been fought as far from the German bases as it was from British bases. They also said nothing of at least four German battleships being torpedoed, and of several battleships and all their battle-cruisers being so severely damaged by gunfire as to be incapable of further fighting for several months. The case was very different with the British ships, as has already been stated.

"The case was very different," for only one of the 24 Dreadnoughts that Lord Jellicoe had brought into battle, the *Colossus*, had been hit by gunfire without any resulting damage, and the *Marlborough*, hit by a torpedo, continued in action. Yet this battered German fleet, with ships steering for the Horn Reef Channel with their upper decks awash, was permitted to escape from one greatly superior, which had a three to eight knot or even nine knot advantage of speed: for, owing to the presence of the six slow pre-Dreadnoughts, the speed of the German fleet Was only 17 knots, and apparently by 9 p.m. only 16 knots. This statement is based on the fact that the speed of a pursuing fleet is not that of its slowest unit, but of its powerful fast divisions.

Thus, it came about that the ultimate loss of German big ships was only one battle-cruiser, the *Lützow*, and the pre-Dreadnought *Pommern*, as compared with our own three battle-cruisers and three large armoured cruisers. It escaped after the skilful tactics of the fast division under Beatty had completely cut off its retreat. It is necessary to accentuate the fact that Lord Jellicoe had the advantage of position from the first, and a three to eight knot advantage of speed. It is necessary because a former First Lord of the Admiralty, Lord Selborne, on June 9, 1916, tried to explain matters by saying that:

> So precipitate was the enemy's flight when the British Battle Fleet appeared, that on all Sir John Jellicoe's ships only three men were wounded and none fired longer than six minutes.

Another ex-First Lord of the Admiralty, Mr. Churchill, who was responsible for the selection of Lord Jellicoe, rushed in after the battle to reassure us. The opening words of the statement he issued through the Press Bureau, at the request of the First Lord, Mr. Balfour, were:—

> I have had an opportunity of examining the reports of the ad-

mirals and of considering the information in the possession of the Admiralty. The following facts seem to me to be established:

1. The naval supremacy of the British Fleet in capital ships depends upon the super-Dreadnoughts armed with the 13.5-inch and 15-inch guns, and these are sufficient by themselves to maintain control of the seas. Of these vital units of the first rank we have only lost one—the *Queen Mary*.

This, coupled with his subsequent declaration that the 12-inch gun-armed *Invincible* and *Indefatigable*, which we had lost, had ceased to be primary units, was tantamount to saying that Germany, having no ships with guns of over 12-inch calibre at the battle, had therefore no primary units! It shows the absurdities to which people who consider war from the point of view of mere material factors may be led; but allowing his argument, it deepens the mystery why a fleet having so many primary units with 13½-inch, 14-inch and 15-inch guns accomplished so little. It only ceases to be a mystery when we examine the mental upbringing and psychology of the British commander-in-chief.

In regard to the big ships, Lord Jellicoe says that the Germans exaggerated our losses by one battleship and one armoured cruiser, but he omits to comment on his own list of German losses. He accompanied his despatch with a statement which he said was compiled "after a most careful examination of the evidence on June 18, 1916 . . . gives the minimum in regard to numbers."

The document was as follows:—

List of Enemy Vessels considered to be sunk May 31-June 1, 1916.

Certain:
2 Battleships *Dreadnought* type
1 Battleship *Deutschland* type

Probable:
1 Battleship or Battle-cruiser
1 Battleship *Dreadnought* type

In the earlier memorandum of June 7, 1916, Lord Jellicoe stated that the three battleships were actually seen to sink. Here was exaggeration indeed, given, of course, in good faith. Still it is the exaggeration natural to one who builds pictures rather than concentrates all his energies on obtaining decisive results which brook no contention, as Nelson and Hawke were wont to do. The former, indeed, brooded with dissatisfaction if a single ship escaped that might have been captured.

As a matter of fact, during the whole war Germany lost in big ships only one battleship and one battle-cruiser, both at Jutland. We lost thirteen battleships and three battle-cruisers. The thirteen battleships were none of them lost in the fights of fleets *versus* fleets, but in the attrition of war, which shows the overwhelming importance of gaining decisive results when the one opportunity came.

Our allies lost in a similar way eight battleships, and Austria three by attrition. Togo's advantages just twelve years before, on May 27 and 28, at Tsushima were certainly not greater than Lord Jellicoe's at Jutland, but of the eleven Russian battleships, he sunk seven and captured four, and of thirty-eight ships only two escaped. Behind Togo's ships there was nothing, and the Japanese army in Manchuria depended on them for communications. The knowledge that Japan risked all, led to no indecisive action, but to a battle offensively waged, a series of staggering blows, and the annihilation of Russian sea-power.

It was Nelson's object on all occasions to tempt the French fleet to put to sea. The most unhappy result of the indecisive battle of Jutland was that it taught the enemy how fortunate had been his escape from utter disaster, and so led to a much-strengthened determination that there should be no next time. Captain Persius, after the armistice, wrote that:

> On June 1, 1916, it was clear to every thinking person that this battle must, and would be, the last one. Authoritative quarters said so openly.

It is characteristic of Lord Jellicoe that he should quote this as proof of victory. It was, on the contrary, our greatest loss. We had taught the enemy the part of wisdom; henceforward the war could not be ended by the navy but by the operations of the allied armies, to which our blockade contributed. But those very armies were to be seriously hampered by Lord Jellicoe's failure, not merely through the growing submarine menace, but through the defection of Russia following on her Baltic position. As Sir Douglas Haig says in his final despatch, published April 11, 1919:

> The military strength of Russia broke down at a critical period, when, had she been able to carry out her military engagements, the war might have been shortened by a year.

This defection was preceded, as we all know, by the combined expedition under the protection of the High Seas Fleet against Riga, and the terrible attrition of Russian troops was due to the failure to get munition supplies in.

It should be remembered that throughout 1916 and a part of 1917 there were three very sinister factors:—

(1) Russia was being bled of men through want of supplies.

(2) Our army lacked munitions; but, if the naval menace were removed, industry could be freed to a large extent for military supplies instead of naval.

(3) The submarine menace.

Had Jutland been a decisive action, Russia would have been saved and our army more quickly rescued from its terrible handicap. When munitions did arrive in sufficient quantities, we had the three separate offensives of April, June and August, 1916, and the indications pointed to the enemy being sufficiently worn down to secure a decision. Relief came to him with the collapse of Russia.

The greatest suffering, we incurred through the Jutland failure was one which nearly lost us the war. As Sir David Beatty said at Liverpool on March 29, 1919:—

The German High Seas Fleet was the bulwark behind which the submarine menace grew. Assailed by wasps we could not take their nests. German strategy, science and brain-power evolved a system of land defences, and the High Seas Fleet supplemented them, and the menace went further afield. If the Grand Fleet could have maintained a position close to the nests, we could have throttled the submarines and the menace would have ceased to exist. That was not possible. Had the High Seas Fleet been destroyed the menace would have disappeared.

Our opportunities of destroying the High Seas Fleet are known to everybody. One opportunity was given of short duration.

The merchant shipping losses of the Allies and neutrals remained practically stationary at a little over 500,000 tons a quarter up to the Battle of Jutland. Then came a big rise to over 1,100,000 tons in the fourth quarter of 1916: over 1,600,000 tons in the first quarter of 1917, and over 2,200,000 in the second quarter of 1917. If the convoy system, which the Board of Admiralty of 1917, consisting of Lord Jellicoe and the subordinates of his own choice, most strongly opposed for so long, had not then been adopted we should have lost the war. With the convoy system we had also the heroic remedy of about 10,000 armed vessels for all the Allies to fight the operations of less than thirty submarines at sea at any one time.

In the single month of September 1918 in home waters, our surface craft covered 7,000,000 miles and our aircraft 170,000 miles hunting for twenty submarines. Such were the losses and such the effort to which extreme caution during brief opportunity condemned us for two and a half years to come, not to mention a Grand Fleet under continuous watch and steam. We continued to enforce a blockade, which America contended was not effective since Germany was supreme in the Baltic.

But for the High Seas Fleet Germany could have been threatened on her coasts both in the North Sea and Baltic, and a great diversion of troops would have taken place for the sedentary task of defending her coasts. The deepest discouragement would have fallen on the German people, and the whole basis of finance would have crumbled. As it happened, Germany was flooded with celebrations of victory, and £600,000,000 was at once obtained from the Reichstag for the war.

Lord Jellicoe's first claim was that Germany had lost at Jutland six capital ships and fifteen other vessels, or in all 158,520 tons, as compared with three capital ships and eleven other vessels for Great Britain, or in all 112,350 tons. We were also led to believe that other vessels might be lost, so that a Press report which gave the above added without interference from the Press Bureau, that "Sir John Jellicoe's statement of German losses does not include heavy damage undoubtedly inflicted on ships which were most probably lost." The actual German tonnage lost was 60,720 tons. The names of the ships were:—

BRITISH.		GERMAN.
Queen Mary.	*Defence.*	*Lützow.*
Indefatigable.	*Black Prince.*	*Pommern.**
Invincible.	*Warrior.*	*Wiesbaden.*
		Frauenlob.
Tipperary.		*Elbing.*
		*Rostock.**
Ardent.	*Nestor.*	
Fortune.	*Nomad.*	*5 destroyers.*
Shark.	*Turbulent.*	
Sparrowhawk.		

*Lost to torpedo attacks. The remainder lost to the gun.

Lord Jellicoe quotes Captain Persius, "a reputable and informed writer on naval matters," as saying in the *Berliner Tageblatt* on November 18, 1918, that "our fleet's losses were severe." So they were, considering how small a portion of the British Fleet had fought. But what the same paper, inspired by Captain Persius, said just after the battle was that:

> On the British side the losses were exceedingly heavy; on our side exceedingly small, and in proportion to the results obtained, extraordinarily small.

I accept Captain Persius as a conscientious and courageous critic, though not as a very profound student of naval war; but since Lord Jellicoe brings him forward as "a reputable and informed writer on naval matters," in which description I concur, it seems right that his summing up of the Battle of Jutland should be quoted as far as it affects us:—

> Off the Skagerrack our fleet was preserved from disaster through the clever leadership of Admiral Scheer and the unskilful handling of the British Fleet under Admiral Jellicoe, bad visibility working in our favour also. Had visibility been good, and had there been a resolute chief on the side of the enemy, the result would, according to all human calculation, have been disastrous for us. The British guns, with their much greater range, would have completely annihilated our less powerfully armed ships. The losses sustained by our fleet were enormous, in spite of the fact that luck was on our side, and on June 1st, 1916, it was clear to all intelligence that this fight would and must be the only one to take place. Those in authority have often openly admitted this!

Russia was most profoundly discouraged by our failure at the battle, and throughout the world, more especially in Japan, British naval prestige was lowered. It was not the navy, but one man, who failed; but the battle had this clear gain, that it revealed the great merit of the admiral who a few months later succeeded to the command of the Grand Fleet. As Admiral Mathews's failure at Toulon brought out Hawke, so Lord Jellicoe's failure at Jutland brought out Beatty. The latter had fought with badly-armoured ships against heavy odds. His own ship had been struck by twenty-five times as many heavy shells as the whole great line of twenty-seven heavily-armoured ships which

Lord Jellicoe was able to form on entry into battle. His losses had been incurred through structural defects in the designs of ships, for which he had no responsibility and by which he nearly lost his own flagship when the roof of a turret was blown off.

In face of it all he held on, his own ship firing with six guns instead of eight, the first in action and the last out, using his small force with the skill of one who plays a stronger foe into a position where a much more powerful ally is enabled to give the *coup de grâce*. Such was the indomitable fighting spirit of the man whose earlier career at Tien-Tsin had foreshadowed it in the brief words of the Royal Navy List "although twice wounded he still led his men to the attack."

Nothing in Lord Jellicoe's despatch of June 17, 1916, gave indication of anything but a very closely contested action in which the gravest losses were inflicted on the enemy. No suggestion was given of withdrawals in face of destroyer attacks or the unfortunate loss of the advantage of surprise by the method of deployment. We were told:—

> The action between the battle fleets lasted intermittently from 6.17 p.m. to 8.20 p.m. at ranges between 9,000 and 12,000 yards, during which time the British Fleet made alterations of course from S.E. by E. to W. in the endeavour to close. The enemy constantly turned away and opened the range under cover of destroyer attacks and smoke screens as the effect of the British fire was felt, and the alterations of course had the effect of bringing the British Fleet (which commenced the action in a position of advantage on the bow of the enemy) to a quarterly bearing from the enemy battle-line but at the same time placed us between the enemy and his bases."

No mention was made of the uniform speed of only 17 knots. The only possible reference to his own action in losing touch with the enemy by turning away from destroyer attacks was conveyed in the somewhat cryptic sentence:—

> The menace of effective torpedo attack on a long line, however, in weather conditions which were ideal for the purpose, contributed to the difficulty of keeping within effective gun range of the enemy. Two separate destroyer attacks were made by the enemy.

That eleven destroyers approaching to about 6,500 yards in the first attack, and about 10,000 yards in the second, of an overwhelming

British force, should make the whole line of twenty-seven battleships turn away and lose an enemy who was completely at its mercy, is a circumstance so inexplicable and unparalleled that atonement must be sought for its omission from the despatches at the time by some reiteration and examination today. During this time, the hit on the *Colossus* at 7.12 p.m., from which she suffered the most trifling damage, was the only gunnery hit on the ships Lord Jellicoe brought into battle.

Thus, out of about 30,000 men in his battleships only four were wounded. To talk of such an action as lasting intermittently from 6.17 p.m. to 8.20 p.m., in reference to his battleships, is to play with words. The salvoes fired by each ship will give some indication of the extent he engaged the enemy's line, but even here caution will be necessary in view of the way heavy guns like 15-inch were blazed away at the eleven destroyers that attacked at 7.21. Taking a ship at random, the *Conqueror* let fly no less than five turret salvoes from her 13-inch guns at these destroyers! Numbers of salvoes, in addition, were fired at the two cruisers which the advanced forces had disabled and sent drifting down the line (*see* Chronology). For instance, the *St. Vincent* fired three and the *Iron Duke* several salvoes at these cruisers. Such salvoes, though doubtless necessary, are not part of the fight with the enemy's line.

At daybreak on June 1 Lord Jellicoe still had the opportunity of inflicting a disastrous defeat, for he could intercept the German Fleet off the Horn Reef lightvessel, where its ships would arrive, many of them, as I have pointed out, with their upper decks awash, incapable of fighting. To inflict losses nowadays is even more imperative than when Boscawen gave us a classic example. The pursuit is everything, for dockyards work miracles. If a vessel once reaches sanctuary, she lives to fight another day. In this battle there was no pursuit. With the door at our command, we left it flung wide open.

(Note.—The following details are given under reserve.)

The High Seas Fleet under Admiral von Scheer consisted of:—
16 Dreadnoughts.
6 Pre-Dreadnoughts classed by Lord Jellicoe as obsolescent and reducing the speed of the fleet to 17 knots as compared with 20 for the Grand Fleet.
5 Battle-cruisers under Rear-Admiral Hipper.
11 Light-cruisers.
7 Destroyer flotillas of 11 boats each or 77 in all.

★★★★★★

It is widely stated that only 21 battleships were present, but in the House of Commons the Admiralty, in July, 1919, or over three years after the event, declined to give any information, saying it would be published in due course.

★★★★★★

The names of the 16 Dreadnoughts were:—

Tons and knots.	
25,890 23 knots 10 guns on broadside.	*König.* *Markgraf,* hit with torpedo. *Grosser Kurfürst,* hit with torpedo. *Kronprinz Wilhelm.*
22,435 Trial speed 20 knots. 8 guns on broadside.	*Helgoland.* *Thüringen.* *Oldenburg.* *Ostfriesland,* struck on mine and was towed into port.
24,410 over 21 knots. 8–10 guns on broadside (two units in échelon).	*Kaiser.* *Friedrich der Grosse.* *Kaiserin.* *Prinzregent Luitpold.*
18,200. 20 knots 8 guns on broadside.	*Nassau.* *Westfalen.* *Rheinland.* *Posen.*

(The *König Albert* of the *Kaiser* class is not included as she does not appear in the German lists. If she was present then there were 17 Dreadnought battleships at Jutland.)

The names of the five battle-cruisers were:—

Tons.	Knots.	
26,180	28	*Lützow,** sunk (flag of Admiral Hipper).
26,180	28	*Derfflinger,* seriously damaged.
24,610	26½	*Seydlitz,* seriously damaged, beached and salved.
22,640	27	*Moltke* (Admiral Hipper shifted his flag to *Moltke*), seriously damaged.
19,100	26	*Von der Tann,* seriously damaged.

*The *Lützow* was hit by at least 15 heavy shells and early in the action was believed to have been hit by a torpedo, but continued fighting. She was unable to remain inline, and Admiral Hipper boarded a destroyer and transferred his flag to the *Moltke*. This took place when the Grand Fleet turned away because of a destroyer attack.

The names of the six pre-Dreadnoughts were:—

The whole of Germany's pre-Dreadnoughts were broken up at the beginning of 1918.	*Deutschland.* *Schlesien.* *Hessen.* *Hannover* *Schleswig-Holstein.* *Pommern,* sunk after being torpedoed.

The lost light-cruisers *Rostock, Wiesbaden, Elbing and Frauenlob* are believed all to have been hit by torpedoes, but the Germans state that the *Pommern* and the light-cruiser *Rostock* were their only losses due to torpedoes. The *Wiesbaden* was in all probability sunk by the gun, and it is known that she was lost in the daylight action. The Germans state that the *Elbing* was rammed by a German battleship and was subsequently blown up to prevent her falling into our hands. The *Rostock* was torpedoed. One German destroyer was blown up by a mine and the other losses of destroyers were due to gun fire.

CHAPTER 17

The War Staff

Though Colbert had laid down the division between the Sword and the Pen in the seventeenth century, it required the disaster of Jena, in 1806, to teach the Germans that men concerned in preparing for and conducting war must be separate from, and require a far higher order of brain than, those who obey their direction by fulfilling the demands of supply and routine, and who deal with all its technicalities. Even so, the chief of the General Staff was not freed from the administrative chief until 1821; then gradually the intellectual side asserted its supremacy, so that twice as many men were employed on the planning and thinking work as were to be found in the departments of administration.

The Staff mind in the British Navy has always to fight against the opposition of men who are only professional seamen, and the civilians who, in their ambition to run the navy, have no desire that brains should exist at the Admiralty which by patient investigation may put on record conclusive arguments against their policy.

Nothing better illustrates the harm that can be done by working without a staff than the bungling and waste of the South African War, which had been prepared for by an Intelligence Division of the War Office equipped with seventeen officers costing £11,000 for their services, such as they were, in studying military affairs over the whole wide world. The result of methods such as these is mere accumulation of pigeon-holed and undigested matter which is subordinated to no principles of action.

It is inevitable that in similar conditions in the Admiralty, the future, involving investigation, research, and plans, is thrust out of view by current work. Overworked officers are only too glad to ignore the fact that, if a War Staff is ever to be built up and permeate the navy with its doctrine, the training of the navy must come under its general direction. The painstaking attention to details in orders which characterises the administrative mind is really a sign of inefficiency, as will be seen by the failure in land war of armies so conducted, as compared with the brevity of the war orders of successful armies. A similar contrast will be found in the Russian and Japanese fleets which fought at Tsushima.

Lord Jellicoe's line of battleships at Jutland extended over about six miles, while the visibility was occasionally as low as two miles. There is infinitely more reason for decentralisation when proceeding at speeds equal to that of ordinary railway trains, in such circumstances, than there is in the operations of land wars, and yet one must insist again that decentralisation is only possible when admirals and captains are inspired by a common doctrine of war in which victory is the predetermined goal. Thus, the signalling, a fruitful source of hesitation, delay and confusion, is reduced to a minimum, and judgment, initiative and courage are given their fullest scope.

It is only fair to Lord Jellicoe to say that the Grand Fleet was not a weapon he had forged during peace, nor even was the weapon forged for him. There was a great deal of technical study of material, but there was no doctrine of war. The whole tendency he brought with him was towards defensive tactics, the accentuation of material worship, and a marked leaning towards the administrative side. Like Lord Jellicoe himself, his chief of the Staff, Admiral Madden, and the other real Staff officers, as distinguished from those only technically called Staff officers, arrived unexpectedly to their duties after war had broken out. The system thus described is one which can produce captains of the Fleet who deal with the administrative side, but it is not capable of giving to the Fleets the efficient Staffs that they require.

At the same time, however, Lord Jellicoe's mental outlook was opposed to the staff idea with its consequent organisation and decentralisation of work. He did nothing to encourage its development before the war. During his command of the Grand Fleet he made no serious attempt to separate operations from administration. His own time was largely devoted to all kinds of minor administrative matters to the corresponding neglect of large questions of policy and tactics.

When he left the Grand Fleet a very different staff system was built up, and eventually after four years of war, sound tactical doctrines permeated the Grand Fleet because it was commanded by a man who knew how to inspire and utilise a staff. This work was done in a manner and under conditions which entitle Earl Beatty and his staff to the gratitude of the nation. It should be remembered that the feat was accomplished under a great handicap. When ships like the *Queen Elizabeth* were building, the necessity for War Staffs was not foreseen by the material school. So just as we found that our ships were designed not wholly to suit fighting requirements but to fit existing docks, so now we have to relate that this brain of the fleet had to be compressed as best we could to fit into ships which were not designed to carry a War Staff!

The Admiralty on the other hand had not even succeeded during nearly four years of war in creating the right kind of atmosphere for efficient staff work. Various staff divisions with high-sounding titles were introduced, but their efforts were never co-ordinated and directed towards a common end, because there was no authority with sufficient character or knowledge to forge the rough material into an effective weapon. The young staff has had two deadly enemies to contend with. On the one hand there were senior officers who, being ignorant of modern war direction, attempted to do everything themselves.

On the other hand, there were those who had neither the knowledge nor the character to come to vital decisions, without which the best staff in the world cannot be expected to function. There is also a tradition of mediocrity at the Admiralty which has militated against the appointment of the right kind of personnel to the staff. The fates of certain officers who questioned either Lord Fisher's system of entering officers for the Royal Navy and Royal Marines or his cruiser policy, of others who gave evidence before the Cabinet Committee inquiring into the late Lord Beresford's charges in 1909, were warnings to every officer in the Admiralty to devote attention solely to minor questions of routine and administration.

During the greater part of the war, officers who were known to have made some study of war and to be capable of that type of analytical criticism which is the obverse of the constructive faculty, were excluded from the Admiralty Staff. Even when this policy was to some extent abandoned under the stress of the submarine campaign, the men who were introduced had several sharp reminders that the necessity of beating the enemy was not always sufficient reason for initiating proposals which might not be approved by the higher authorities because they involved some degree of risk.

There is only one solution to the whole question and that is the appointment of a First Sea Lord who understands and believes in the necessity of staff training and staff organisation, and who has the strength of character and determination to enforce them against the opposition of many senior officers. Otherwise we shall go through a dreary repetition of the history of the last ten years, (as at 1919). The country will remember that as the result of setting up a Cabinet investigation into the late Lord Beresford's charges we had "the Navy War Council," in 1909, which handed over War Plans and Strategy to the Naval Mobilisation Department! The business of the latter was the rapid manning and readiness for sea of our fleets.

In January, 1912, we had another official announcement that "the Lords Commissioners of the Admiralty having determined on the immediate formation of a Naval War Staff, etc." The results we have set out in the earlier chapters. It is only necessary to state that the announcement in the Press on January 8, 1912, was accompanied by a memorandum from the First Lord which is an interesting document. We have no space to deal with it, but as bearing on some of the revelations of our earlier chapters we may select this extract:

> The problems of transport and supply; the infinite peculiarities of topography which are the increasing study of the general staffs of Europe, do not affect the naval service except in an occasional and limited degree.

Hence storage was not provided for a drop of oil for the navy along the east coast from one end of Great Britain to the other, and so on! In 1916-17 there were fresh attempts to form a War Staff, followed by Sir Eric Geddes' effort in 1918.

The truth driven into our minds by all this experience is that the inspiration of the chief is all-important. He must both believe in and have proved himself as an exponent of the War Doctrine it is desired to infuse into the navy as a whole. In addition, he must be a man of large sympathies so that he spurns the spirit of aloofness which makes the Admiralty wander apart from other departments with which it is bound to co-operate, for its strategy involves the Foreign Office, the War Office, the Air Board and the Board of Trade. If we fail to place the power in the hands of such a man, we shall go on muddling the two functions of a War Staff.

(a) Preparation during peace.

(b) Direction during war.

If we find the man and give him the power then all the rest comes to us in time. He selects the best men, deeply versed in the principles of war, to work with him in considering the strategy to be employed, the operations such strategy will involve, and the type of personnel and material necessary. He takes particular care that they are kept free from current work so that they can devote their minds to planning for the future. Beyond them he forms his Operations Division which has the business of working out and preparing the operations, and his Intelligence Division for the collection and sifting of information.

All these men must, in order to know what is required, be conversant with the principles of war. Hence to produce such men, to enlarge the field of selection, and to spread the knowledge of what war requires, so that while the plans are good their execution will not fail, we must look upon training as a part of the War Staff's functions. Only in this way can a great chief provide that his successor will reap where he has sown, where he prepared the ground which was so maltreated by those who came before him.

It is the work of years through the Staff direction of our educational system to infuse the War Doctrine through the whole service. Hitherto naval education has been subject to many changes because there was no clear vision as to the end to be attained and its direction was under a Professor of Engineering who was preceded by a Professor of Mathematics! It has been at the beck and call of the specialists so that a multiplicity of technical subjects has been taught, none of them thoroughly and none directed towards war except in the most limited way.

Until a real War Staff has been at work for some time, and a mass of officers passed through it and into the various fleets, the importance of decentralisation in command will not be generally recognised; for then, and then only, will the personnel of the navy be possessed of a common doctrine of war which enables the subordinate to anticipate the wishes of his chief. Failing that, all look to the flagship. The spirit is to conform in all circumstances to the movements of the commander-in-chief, and to await his orders. Such a system is impossible in a battle area which spreads itself over several hundred square miles, and where movements are at a speed of from 20 knots upwards on the sea, and from 100 knots upwards in the air, and where, in a sea so misty as the North Sea, the larger portion of his own fleet, as well as the enemy, may be out of sight of the flagship.

The truth is that the navy has always been in constant danger of mistaking mere seamanship and technical knowledge as complete equipment for war. Because Blake understood the principles of war and their application, he was able to go to sea at the age of fifty, and do better than men educated on mistaken lines. There is every reason to believe that the self-same erroneous standards would have lost us Nelson, but for the irrefragable proof of victory; for, as we have seen, two such typical sailors as St. Vincent and Codrington had condemned him on those standards, the former saying his ship was always in bad order, and the latter that he was no seaman.

Similarly, Foch, Pétain and Joffre were what the material school would describe as "paper men," capable as they were of expressing their ideas on paper and having taught in the war colleges. If the Admiralty will give the public the document issued by the "practical" men at the Board in the Battle Orders to the Mediterranean under which the *Goeben* escaped, the Press might well, as a bitter lesson, publish it side by side with Joffre's famous order of the day at the Battle of the Marne:

You must be prepared to die rather than yield ground.

If Foch had been educated in our Admiralty system, where everything is noted on authority of almost Euclidean proportions, he would never have saved the liberties of the world. Had the clever young gunnery officer, Lieutenant Jellicoe, escaped that system, and had his mind been wisely directed to the study of how to wage war, then with mind broadened, with heart enthused, and steeped in the will to conquer, he, too, when the day of trial came, might have won a victory which would have profoundly modified the history of the world.

The navy, the army and the air force are parts of a machine fashioned for the purpose of waging war, and the supreme function of those at the head is to conduct war. This is no more an administrative task than it is in the case of a great general in the field. The working of the material supplies and the administrative details of the personnel constitute an absorbing occupation, involving a special kind of brain with a genius for details. Its importance and its special prominence in peace time should not be allowed to blind us to the fact that it must be subordinate to the instructions received from the men who conduct war. In the armies this imperative distinction has been fairly well understood. In the British Navy it was completely lost sight of. The Board of Admiralty was supposed to conduct war. The board, presided over by a civilian, consisted of other civilians and admirals.

The First Sea Lord concerned himself with each of the administrative departments; the Second Sea Lord with personnel, but though his work was administrative, he was required to take on the duties of the First Sea Lord when the latter was away from his post; the Third Sea Lord with material and the Fourth Sea Lord with supplies. A summary of the work of the Second and Third Sea Lords would fill two or three of these pages with items of purely administrative detail. Now it takes thirty to forty years to form a great War Staff, with its traditions and body of doctrine derived from the study of the past so as to apply principles of war to the present and future.

Yet these four admirals, in the intervals they could spare from their duties, were expected to conduct war, to fashion the navy which would wage war, and decide how best co-operation could be effected with the air and land forces. The permanent character of the civilian force which peopled the Admiralty, and knew and fashioned the intricate administrative ropes, while admirals came and went at intervals of from one to two years, had helped during the long period of peace to give a purely administrative atmosphere to the Admiralty. Treasury sanction was required for the addition of any naval officer to the Staff, and when the "War Staff" was formed on January 1, 1912, the Board of Admiralty issued an official note giving the savings on other votes to pay for its extra cost.

The system was bound to fail, and to prove an almost fatal handicap to the navy. It is due to the writer to say that this is no new criticism which he did not make before the war. The issue was repeatedly raised, and in 1908 was brought by letter before the prime minister in a request for an inquiry in which it was pointed out that it was better to inquire before the coming war rather than after, as the French did in 1871, and it was stated that there was then time to set our navy in order before the German preparations for war would reach fruition. The letter received the usual promise of consideration, but it evidently never fructified in that super-consideration which, "like an angel, came and whipped the offending Adam out of him." Consideration on the tongue of a minister is too often the tune played by the old man from which the old cow died

So, he took down his fiddle
And played her this tune,
Consider, good cow, consider,
This is not the time for grass to grow

Consider, good cow, consider.

That is why the Greeks and the Romans spoke of politicians as fiddlers, because they were always considering when they ought to be acting.

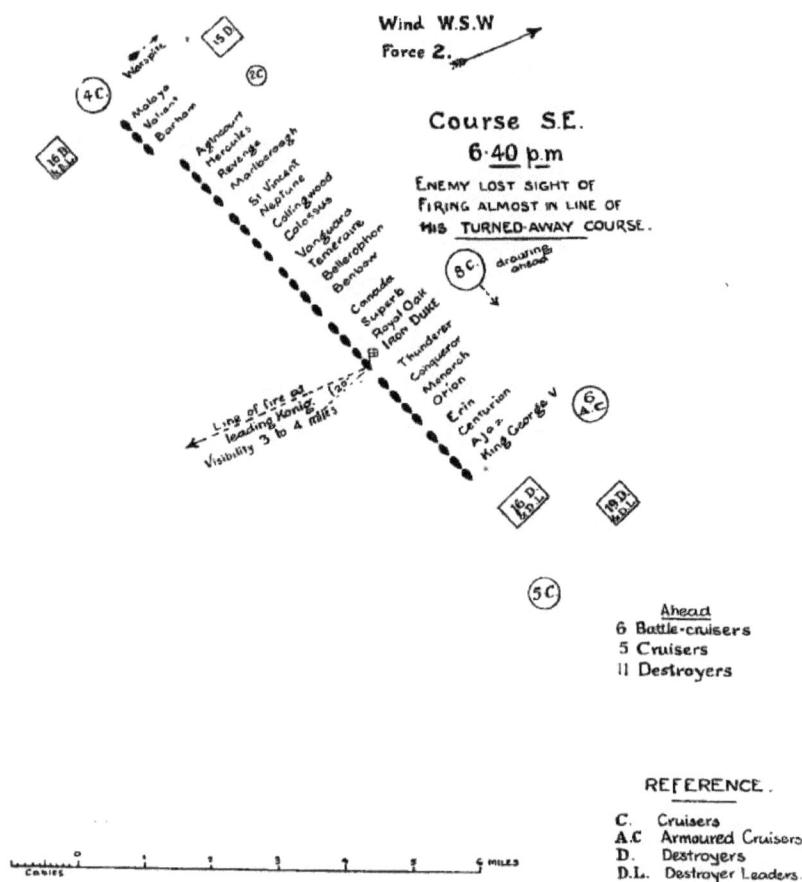

Wind W.S.W
Force 2.

Course S.E.
6·40 p.m

ENEMY LOST SIGHT OF
FIRING ALMOST IN LINE OF
HIS TURNED-AWAY COURSE.

(4C)
Warspite (15 D)
(2C)
Malaya
Valiant
Barham
(16 D)
Agincourt
Hercules
Revenge
Marlborough
St Vincent
Neptune
Collingwood
Colossus
Vanguard
Temeraire
Bellerophon
Benbow
Canada
Superb
Royal Oak
Iron Duke
Thunderer
Conqueror
Monarch
Orion
Erin
Centurion
Ajax
King George V

(8C) drawing ahead

(6 A.C)

Line of fire at ─ 130°
leading König
Visibility 3 to 4 miles

(16 D)
(13 D)

(5C)

Ahead
6 Battle-cruisers
5 Cruisers
11 Destroyers

0 .... 6 MILES
Cables

REFERENCE.

C.   Cruisers
A.C   Armoured Cruisers
D.   Destroyers
D.L. Destroyer Leaders.

In the course of these pages the writer has found it a necessity to criticise individuals, but that should not obscure the fact that these individuals are the results of a system which fashions them or directs their energies into wrong channels. The training system of the navy is made a matter of purely administrative routine. Yet a proper training system is essentially a War Staff matter, to be framed on the best lines, to give us the men of genius who, as the War Staff, will gradually permeate both Admiralty and navy with a good doctrine of war. The weapons, whether aircraft, battleships, cruisers, destroyers, submarines, "scooters," mines, hydrophones, guns, torpedoes, etc., are still being made a matter of administrative routine.

Yet these things are entirely subordinate to the principles of war, and any proper War Staff work would have resulted in orders as to rigid airships, skimming motorboats, or "scooters," the best elevation to be given to guns, the kind of mine required, the provision of boom and gun defences, adequate horizontal armour, range-finding and listening devices, wireless apparatus for submarines, etc., which it required several years of war to force on the material school. With a proper War Staff, it is almost inconceivable that we should have made such mistakes as our earlier motor-launches and blockade mines, the "hush-hush" ships without armour, and submarines carrying very heavy guns for which the entire Admiralty was unable to find any fit employment. The German War Staff work on this side was good. It anticipated all these things so far as it could use them, except a good listening device, which is more necessary to the hunter than to the hunted, just as most inventions, when properly understood, are of more use to the strong than to the weak.

The German doctrine of war on the sea, however, lacked enterprise. It lacked the offensive spirit without which no amount of knowledge will avail. If the Germans had interpreted aright and at once the true moral of the escape of the *Goeben*, they would have struck hard and at once with all their force before the utter lack of War Staff direction in the British Navy, and its consequences, could be in some measure rectified. They did not do so because they thought that they would gain relatively on the material side by waiting. We gave them a great opportunity with the transfer of the expeditionary force across the Channel, and it was missed.

The German system was one which was by no means perfect. The personal rule of the *Kaiser*, making him the authority on all questions, was bad, though it had some good points in stimulating the exertions and enterprise of the senior officers. The German War Staff, like our own, was merely advisory. It was not well coordinated with the army, though the appearance of *liaison* work was there in the presence of two military officers on the Naval War Staff and two naval officers on the General Staff. It did not conduct war, but it studied war, and prepared plans for war, and was therefore in a better position to judge of weapons it wanted for war than our own War Staff. In neither Service was the education and training of officers in the hands of the Staff, which is an indispensable factor of a successful War Staff. The War Staff did, however, advise the *Kaiser* on naval training, so that his personal intervention could be exercised, and in this way, it had some power, whereas our own War Staff had none in this direction.

On the other hand, the Secretary of State for the Navy, the Chief of the War Staff, and the Chief of the Emperor's Naval Office were all independent of each other, and had direct access to the *Kaiser*. The result depended on the idiosyncrasies of the *Kaiser*. In details such as training and material it was very good, but in the broader aspects of policy the results left much to be desired. This arose partly from the mixing of the conduct of war with administration, which the standard work of the German Army characterises as:

> A terrible mistake for the reason given, that it would be impossible that a man would be found who . . . was equally master of the art of military administration and of handling armies.

As regards the British Navy the Hartington Commission, over a generation before the war, had endeavoured to separate the two functions, but bowed to the unanimous opinion of the sailors that:

> They could not, with advantage, be separated from some at least of the administrative duties which now devolve upon the First Naval Lord, which keep him in constant communication with the officers of the navy, and secure that he is fully informed of the opinions, requirements and condition of the service.

It may be laid down, almost like a law of motion, that the moment a First Sea Lord meddles with administration, he will muddle his strategy. Under Lord Fisher, the evil grew to huge dimensions. He was chairman of a committee on the personnel, of the Estimates Committee, of the Designs Committee, and of the Dockyards Committee, and there were no War Plans. a German general said, *after dinner*, about this period in London:

> We have discovered the secrets of every War Department in Europe, but your Admiralty is wonderful. We have never been able to find out their war plans!

Lord Haldane, when he formed the General Staff of the War Office, observed very truly that:

> If they got out of touch with the army, or if they exercised their authority by interfering in the details of administrative business for which others are responsible, the failure of the present at-

tempt to form a General Staff is certain ... if, on the other hand, they show themselves capable of mastering the sciences of war, of fully understanding war organisation in all its branches, and of imparting their own knowledge to the army at large, the influence of the General Staff in this country will become as far-reaching as in Germany or Japan.

There are those who see in the last sentence the danger of government by generals, such as was very real in the case of Germany. There is no such risk in the case in a country with such constitutional safeguards as we possess. The government lays down policy. All that is claimed is that the military method of carrying out that policy and the determination of the force required is a matter for the War Staff. If this direction is over-ridden then Parliament should be cognisant of the fact. We write in absolute agreement with the maxim of Chatham, that the civil power prescribes the ends to be attained, but the commander of a force should enjoy perfect freedom as to the ways and means by which it is attained.

The real danger is that the civil power will choose subservient men of weak character; and it is in this direction that the public "should watch closely the acts of the Cabinet. In the days when the personal rule of the sovereign tended in a similar direction it was the public which demanded that Chatham should be entrusted with the direction of affairs.

BEATTY'S WAR STAFF
|
CHIEF OF STAFF
|

| GENERAL DIRECTION |

FLAG CAPTAIN.   CAPTAIN OF THE FLEET

| WAR STAFF SECTION | SIGNAL SECTION | ARMAMENT SECTION | MAINTENANCE - SUPPLY - PERSONNEL |

CHAPTER 18

Conclusion

In war there must be concentration on the decisive point, and that is the business of the sailor in command of the fleet. In peace there must be concentration on the decisive period; and that is the business of the statesman in command of the Ship of State. We failed both in the preparations of peace and the use of the fleet in battle. The fight, however, took place twenty months after the war broke out, so that ample time had been given to remedy the defects of preparation. The Grand Fleet went into battle, at six o'clock, with an overwhelming superiority except for defects of construction in the battle-cruisers. In the times to come, Jutland will be looked upon by our people as a day of tremendous opportunity and monumental failure; and it is essential that we should be fearlessly frank with ourselves in regard to this battle if out of it we are to draw and apply the rich lessons which it gives us.

One cannot but observe that the men who were so busy in thwarting all attempts to bring about the increase of the navy; who were content merely to support the Admiralty programme against the insignificant section led by the late Sir John Brunner who would have placed us at the mercy of our enemies, that these men have during the war been loudest in acclaiming the tactics of Lord Jellicoe on the ground that the risks to the Grand Fleet of a decisive action were too great. If this were true, it would be the strongest condemnation of their former conduct. Much of the harm for which the bad guidance they had given to public opinion was responsible had, however, as I have said, been obliterated by twenty months of feverish effort during war.

In reading Lord Jellicoe's book, one feels as though in the presence of a man intent on building up a case for caution, which is really an honest revelation of a temperament impervious to Nelson's doctrine that:

> The boldest measures are the safest: nothing great can be achieved without risk.

He loads all the dice against his fleet. He still asserts that he had only 78 destroyers at Jutland against at least 88 with the German Fleet, whereas it is well known and officially stated that the Germans had seven flotillas of eleven boats each.

The line could not be obtained in its perfection to the eye except by deploying away from the enemy. The precise way the fast *Barhams* should join was regulated by paper rules to suit the rigid line, and not left to the judgment of the man already in action. At a later stage its rear was threatened by a few destroyers, so the whole line was turned away and the enemy lost. Once again, the whole fleet turned away on sighting the enemy, after 8 o'clock, because a destroyer attack again threatened. Under such leadership men become creatures of routine, deficient in initiative, and no response was made by the Admiral of the

Second Battle Squadron to Beatty's imploring signal at 7.20 p.m. to follow him and cut off the enemy.

In all probability he signalled for permission to follow Beatty and got no answer, or a refusal. Only an investigation of the logs can settle the question; but if he did, it shows a severe limitation on his discretion in spite of the claim advanced that the Battle Orders provided for decentralisation.

Do not admirals say to themselves "How would Nelson act?" Nelson wrote to his First Lord, in 1798:

> Much as I approve of strict obedience to orders—even to a court-martial to *inquire* whether the object justified the measure—yet to say that an officer is never for any object to alter his orders is what I cannot comprehend. The great object of this war is 'Down, *down with the French!* To accomplish this every nerve and by both services ought to be strained.'

Again, he writes of the destruction of French naval power as the Great Order:

> And if it can be proved that a breach of the lesser order is a more strict compliance with the former then there can be no doubt of the duty of the breach of the lesser orders.

The enemy escaped. What matter! Routine! discipline! the rigid line! In half an hour Lord Jellicoe signalled the *King George V.* to follow the battle-cruisers, but they were out of sight, for they had followed the enemy. We had lost the enemy but the inexorable "*imponderabilia*" of rules were satisfied, as they had been satisfied by past indecisive actions which add to the lessons but not to the laurels of the British Navy. We remained in command of the sea, with communications still safe. Therefore, we had won a victory! In less than twelve months the communications were tottering to the onslaught of the submarine, showing that the preservation of one's ships is not a substitute for the destruction of the enemy.

The truth is, Lord Jellicoe saw too many details instead of vital things, and it is a habit of mind inseparable from a long apprenticeship in administrative work. The vital thing was the enemy's fleet. He spoiled his knowledge of its position by delays over such details of conservation of force, as the oil supply of a few destroyers that happened to dash off to search one or more trawlers met *en route*. He could delay his own entry into action by fifteen minutes and throw away all the advantages of surprise because he assumed that the enemy destroyers would attack from ahead of the enemy's battle fleet, and he had worked out by some process that he might at the onset, if he deployed towards the enemy, be at a risk of gunnery disadvantage. It is the habit of such minds to estimate the situation at its worst, never to push the business to a finality, and to be wedded to rigid methods.

There is little hope for the navy of the future unless we are going to think with resolution and clearness concerning this battle. On May 30, 1919, Lord Selborne spoke to the students of King's College, who are making a speciality of naval research, and said:

> No one who had any opportunity of studying naval history or anything of the problems involved, could have had the slightest doubt from the first moment that the battle was a decisive victory—not an overwhelming victory in the sense that Trafalgar was, but decisive in this sense, that that side is decisively beaten which avoids the fight and flies into port.

It is a shock to find an ex-First Lord of the Admiralty, just three years after the battle, appealing to history to prove it to be a decisive victory. If so, we must look upon the battle of Toulon, for which Mathews was cashiered, as a decisive victory for the reason that both the French and Spanish squadrons fled to harbour and did not put to sea again during the war. Clearly Lord Selborne would have made Mathews a viscount. As for Byng, who was shot by order of a court-martial, he, too, won a "decisive victory" at Minorca. Byng said:

> There appeared to me, no further possibility of bringing the enemy to action, as they declined it, without I had a sufficient superior force and superiority to make the general signal to chase.

Calder was severely reprimanded by a court-martial in 1805, though he captured two battleships and the superior Franco-Spanish Fleet ran away, and therefore he scored, according to Lord Selborne, a "decisive victory." And so, we could go on rewriting our history according to Lord Selborne. The truth is that the really decisive victory of Trafalgar followed a few months after Calder fought and showed the meaning of the word, and the same thing would have happened if the High Seas Fleet had come out and fought Beatty. They came out in August, 1916, and again in April, 1918, when the *Moltke* was torpedoed on the return journey near the Horn Reef; but they were very careful not to give the Grand Fleet a second opportunity of bringing them to action. Jutland impressed on them the cautious tactics which it was to our interest they should not practise, and it left them in numbers, both of personnel and material, stronger than they were before; but the morale was broken in the sense that they realised that a real battle meant their annihilation.

So, they inflicted on us a sustained agony which is prolonging its effects into the years of peace. The High Seas Fleet remained the great controlling factor behind a two years' submarine campaign which nearly lost us the war. Its existence completely deterred us from action in the Baltic, and was therefore a great factor in the downfall of Russia. For two and a half years after Jutland it forced us to maintain the Grand Fleet under continuous steam with all the immense diversion of personnel and material urgently needed for the anti-submarine campaign. It kept up the menace of a German invasion, which, rightly or wrongly, so impressed our government that a great army was maintained in this country until Gough's army was defeated through the lack of these men, who were then sent.

Surely in an affair of such magnitude there ought to be an inquiry upon oath. The public is being fooled with statements about hundreds of torpedoes being fired at the Grand Fleet by the destroyer attack which made Lord Jellicoe twice turn his fleet four to eight points from the enemy, and so go out of the fight. Actually, it is known that only eleven torpedo tracks were seen on the first occasion and about two on the second. The tactics taught by Beatty to the Grand Fleet, when he took command, were the tactics he held to with his battle-cruisers at Jutland. *The enemy must be held.*

Indeed, the conceptions on which battles should be fought were very different with the new leader for the simple reason that decisive victory became the supreme goal. It was not the least of the evils of Jutland that it taught the enemy too much. It taught the high command of the German Navy that, however it might be with some men, Beatty would never let go. The claim of decisive victory, indeed, really originates from the consciousness that it ought to have been won in view of the immense gunnery preponderance. The attempt to find a makeweight in the torpedo armaments is simply countered by the fact that there were 151 ships in the Grand Fleet to 115 under von Scheer, and each of these ships can be regarded as a torpedo platform. We had 78 destroyers better armed than the 77 destroyers under von Scheer, and 36 cruisers to his 11, which were decidedly inferior in armament.

With the exception of the protective armour in his battle-cruisers, no admiral ever had less cause to complain of the force at his disposal; and it was these same battle-cruisers, together with the night work of the destroyers, which will enable the future historian to say that, had the battleships and cruisers been used with as great enterprise, Jutland might indeed have been the most decisive naval battle in history. Otherwise the record would stand like this:

Jutland was a battle which did not resemble former victories, for at St. Vincent we pitted 15 battleships against 27 of the enemy, and at Trafalgar 27 against 37 battleships. At Jutland when 27 Dreadnoughts stood in line against 16, in spite of a preponderance in cruisers and destroyers, they allowed 11 destroyers to drive the whole 27 Dreadnoughts out of action so that they never fought again.

The future historian will examine this extraordinary occurrence from the German point of view in the light of utterances such as that of the gunnery lieutenant of the *Deutschland* that:

Torpedo attack in the daytime was almost hopeless, because the English destroyers averaged faster than ours, and I do not need to tell you that their guns were very much heavier.

Again, Lord Jellicoe tells us that:

The Grand Fleet Battle Orders provided for considerable decentralisation of command, and great stress was laid on this point in the general instructions for 'Battle Tactics.' The opening paragraphs of this section of the Battle Orders emphasised this strongly. It was pointed out that whilst the commander-in-chief would control the movements of the whole battle fleet before and on deployment, he could not be certain of doing so after deployment, when funnel and other smoke made both vision and communication difficult. The necessity for wide decentralisation of command was then pointed out, combined with a close watch on the movements of the commander-in-chief, with which flag officers should generally conform."

The Battle Orders must be read as a whole before we can pronounce judgment. The latter quoted paragraph of itself would prevent the van under Admiral Jerram, which was not threatened by any German destroyer attack, responding to Beatty's signal to follow him and cut off the enemy.

It is the spirit and not the letter which matters. The spirit of the command under Lord Jellicoe was a narrow conformity to formal defensive tactics which could never achieve victory and which failed to do so at Jutland.

It is also clear that after Jutland the Battle Orders had to be modified in the direction of decentralisation. Lord Jellicoe writes that:

> The principal changes that were made in the Battle Orders were in the direction of laying still greater emphasis on the discretionary power which was vested in flag officers commanding squadrons, owing to the difficulty, always clearly recognised, and confirmed at Jutland, which the commander-in-chief would experience in controlling the movements of the whole fleet in the heat of action: also in defining still further the different movements that might be adopted to deal with torpedo attacks whether the torpedoes were fired from battleships or from destroyers.

It is difficult to reconcile this with the earlier statement that the Battle Orders prior to Jutland "provided for considerable decentralisation of command." Decentralisation is a great word which can be made to mean almost anything, as the word liberty does in the hands of various governments. It is the interpretation in practice that matters in regard to battle, and that interpretation is the outcome of the commander-in-chief's orders, practice and relations with subordinates taken as a whole.

Similar contradictions in conduct are afforded by what is said in the Battle Orders and what was done at Jutland. Thus, Lord Jellicoe says:

> The instructions for destroyers laid emphasis on the fact that they should carry out an early attack on the enemy's battle fleet, commencing their attacks in clear weather, as soon as the battle fleets were engaged. Under conditions of low visibility, they were instructed to attack without waiting for the battle fleets to be engaged.

Why, then, were the destroyers painted black, which is not the best colour for fighting by daylight? *After* Jutland they were painted grey. The test of practice is to ascertain whether the destroyers had been trained to attack in the manner quoted above. It is only in this way we can judge, after studying the Battle Orders in full, why Lord Jellicoe's destroyers, though favourably placed, never once attacked the enemy fleet during the daylight action; and when one flotilla attempted, after repelling the enemy destroyers, to follow up and attack the High Seas Fleet, it was recalled. Its role, apparently, was purely defensive.

It is one thing to write volumes of instructions as to what officers are to do; it is quite another to create in the officers the habit of acting in accordance with the spirit of the instructions. As a matter of fact, *they had not been so trained*, and, consequently, in the favourable conditions of low visibility not one flotilla with Lord Jellicoe put into practice the instructions which he tells us were so emphatically laid down. These Battle Orders were apparently adumbrated during the war, and we had to wait for the war itself for a statement which should form one of the principles of training during peace as is the case with all military services.

It is hopeless to suppose that new habits of thought can suddenly be grafted upon men. Decentralisation formed no part of the doctrine of naval tactics before 1914, because the training of officers was not conducted by a staff whose minds were steeped in the preparation for war. Officers were instructed in technical matters; but they were not trained to fight. Therein lies the difference between administrative and staff control of training.

We have now completed our survey, and it is open to the reader to pass judgment on Lord Jellicoe's own estimate in his telegram to the Admiralty the day after the battle that:

The battle fleet took the fullest advantage of the few opportunities of engaging which the weather conditions, the short amount of daylight, and the enemy's tactics afforded.

If that had been done, the Battle of Jutland would have corresponded with Trafalgar and Tsushima in its decisive character. The intensive submarine campaign would never have taken place. Russia would not have fallen but would have been immeasurably strengthened. The war would have been very considerably shortened, and the legacy of misery and disaffection which comes in the train of an unduly prolonged war would not be afflicting us today.

The indictment then is:—

(1) That our preparations for war were defective because they were not thoroughly thought out owing to the absence of a properly constituted War Staff. The Admiralty had no doctrine of war. So far as

Treasury control is concerned, the Treasury could not have held out against an unanswerable case. In other words, the Admiralty Boards, of which Lord Jellicoe was a member, were at fault.

(2) We escaped grave dangers through the German naval doctrine of war not being inspired by the offensive spirit.

(3) The Admiralty failed to develop a high standard and doctrine of war by their determination to hold no courts-martial on superior officers.

(4) Lord Jellicoe failed through his own arrangements to establish visual touch with the Rosyth force under Beatty, so that the information sent by that force as to the enemy's position was not based on the reckoning as to latitude and longitude of the *Iron Duke*. Lord Jellicoe therefore met the German Fleet earlier and to the westward of the anticipated point.

(5) Lord Jellicoe's deployment to port lost the advantage of the surprise, delayed his entry into action, and contributed to the loss of the *Invincible*.

(6) The visibility conditions necessitated closer action, and this was not sought owing to fear of torpedoes.

(7) The British destroyer flotillas attached to the battle fleet made no attack upon the enemy by daylight because they had not been trained to attack by day.

(8) The turning away on two occasions of the whole fleet of twenty-seven battleships from the enemy, because of a destroyer flotilla attack, was a grave error of judgment. On both occasions it took the Grand Fleet out of action altogether when it had the enemy fleet, or a portion of the enemy fleet, at its mercy, and it left only the battle-cruisers and small craft to continue the action. Beatty asked for support by a signal taken in by the whole fleet as the Grand Fleet was turning away at 7.21, but it is evident that decentralisation was not effective, for none was given him.

(9) The arrangements for information as to the whereabouts of the German Fleet were again so ineffective during the night, that, though our cruisers and destroyers were fighting them astern of the Grand Fleet from 10 p.m. to 2.30 a.m. while their ships were steering to South-eastward towards the Horn Reef Channel, the enemy escaped with his battered ships, so that his total loss was considerably less than our own, involving in armoured ships only the battle-cruiser *Lützow*

and the pre-Dreadnought *Pommern* as compared with our own loss of three battle-cruisers and three large armoured cruisers.

(10) We did not seek the enemy after dawn at the spot where we could certainly intercept him, off the Horn Reef lightvessel, because Lord Jellicoe claims that it would have been dangerous on account of torpedo craft, his own destroyers not having been assembled after the night action. It is a matter for inquiry whether if he had steered for the Horn Reef lightvessel, he would not have found them at once. The organisation, habitual practices and battle orders must be studied to see where the blame lies.

(11) The Admiralty, with full knowledge of the naval battle in progress, failed to send out the Harwich force; but ordered it to remain in harbour, until after the German Fleet had successfully escaped. They endorsed all Lord Jellicoe's actions. As soon as we have full particulars of the extent to which ships were engaged, we shall be able to judge their *bonâ fides* in regard to the distribution of honours for the Battle of Jutland. If it is found that in some cases captains of ships received C.B.'s whose ships had practically never seen the enemy, and that D.S.O.'s were given to officers who never came under enemy fire, or that rewards were given for particular services which had never been rendered, then it will be evident that these things were done in accordance with the general idea of persuading the public that a great victory had been won. The game of pretence has gone on ever since the battle, with the connivance of the government as though it were some necessity of State, lest

> *Some evil chance*
> *Should make the smouldering scandal break and blaze*
> *Before the people.*

The public admission of failure in battle in regard to our cherished navy is too great a strain, and so the cry is:

> Tell it not in Gath, publish it not in the streets of Askalon lest the daughters of the Philistine rejoice.

The first hint given of the truth at last is that Beatty, who was the subordinate, becomes an earl and gets £100,000; and Lord Jellicoe remains a viscount and gets £50,000.

(12) The consequences of Lord Jellicoe's failure to achieve a victory when the work of the battle-cruisers had cut the enemy off from their base, and when he had an advantage of 3 to 8 knots speed and an

immense preponderance of force, were world-wide, and profoundly affected Russia. The submarine menace depended on the support of the High Seas Fleet; and it grew to dimensions that nearly lost us the war through the immense toll it took from British and Allied shipping and trade during over two years. It required a stupendous effort on the part of British industry to keep it in check. The Grand Fleet itself had to be kept in constant readiness for the next naval battle. As the Admiralty would not assume responsibility for the defence of the United Kingdom against invasion a great army was retained in England, the lack of which in France contributed to the terrible losses of March–April, 1918. *After* these losses a quarter of a million men were sent to France.

This is the general indictment. It is the arraignment of a system and not of a man, for the man is the victim of the system which produced him. At this very moment the mechanical side of naval training is being accentuated. I can only say that it is the road along which Lord Jellicoe travelled, and it leads to certain disaster.

From his earliest days Lord Jellicoe had been a gunnery specialist. As a captain he devoted himself to gunnery problems. He held the post of Director of Naval Ordnance, and later, Third Sea Lord at the Admiralty, both positions dealing only with material. During his period of command at sea he devoted himself chiefly to gunnery problems, and when he became Second Sea Lord, he still dealt with material matters in addition to the purely administrative work in connection with the naval personnel. So immersed was he in the material side of the naval profession, being a most hard-working man who himself attended to every detail, leaving little or nothing to subordinates, that the higher side of naval war was practically excluded from his outlook.

It is known that when Mr. Churchill proposed the foundation of a Naval War Staff in 1912 and the special training of officers to fit them for command in war, Lord Jellicoe had no sympathy with the idea, and when he went to the Admiralty as Second Sea Lord he did much to kill the possibility of such a War Staff ever being a reality. He could not conceive that training for war, based on history, was required. In his opinion, the men to command were those who had received their entire training in the specialist schools, and had spent their time at sea on specialist problems. His own ideas of a staff were bounded entirely by material considerations; and on his staff in the *Iron Duke* predominance was given to material.

It would have been the grandest thing that could ever have happened if Beatty, with the Sixth Battle Squadron of American ships under Admiral Rodman, could have fought a last great sea fight against the High Seas Fleet as the culmination of that splendid and harmonious co-operation which had gone on for eighteen months. But rather than face and fight the fleet which, under Beatty, would never let go one single ship that could, within the bounds of human possibility, be brought to action, the High Seas Fleet mutinied. Not a gun was heard, not a man died except when German killed German, not even a sight of British or American ships was on the horizon but just the fear of Fate five hundred miles away.

They would not face it, so they fought their own officers. The High Seas Fleet had ceased to exist as a fleet. Its soul had gone out, and it was therefore unhesitatingly given up in the armistice terms to save the German Army from utter overthrow by Foch and the armies under his command. So, it came about that the Grand Fleet shepherded to Scapa a mass of iron manned by what once were men. The Grand Fleet dispersed after a record of four years of arduous and monotonous blockade, for which splendid services the crews can never be sufficiently rewarded.

The Sixth Battle Squadron went back from the old home to the new home, or the new home to the old home, put it which way you will, carrying with it the thousands who could proudly recall that they had stood in the place of Franklin, as ambassadors of America. Their hopes were our hopes, and our dreams were their dreams, of things which will be accomplished, which were born in the Sea of Mists, tempered in the furnace of war, and which are the expression of

.... *the prophetic soul of the great world*
Dreaming on things to come.

These are the hopes, and these are the dreams which are stronger than navies and armies.

There was room for a tragic misunderstanding in the days when not a single Member of Parliament had ever visited America, and only one of the signers of the Declaration of Independence had been in England, days when the ocean closed up like a wall behind those who went forth on Great Britain's ventures to found new Britains beyond the seas. The Sixth Battle Squadron, the *Australia*, the *New Zealand* and the *Malaya* crossed the oceans and were, in the truest sense of the words, hand-clasps across the sea, pledges that whatever may happen between the Mother of Parliaments and her families in other capitals, the old and the young navies of the British Empire and America will never fight except against a common foe. Then let us serve together now in peace in the Atlantic and the Pacific, inspired by a common doctrine of war which will never be satisfied with results if more can be achieved.

Appendix

May 30th.	*Battle Fleet* (JELLICOE).
9.30 p.m.	Battle Fleet (24 battleships) three battle-cruisers (*Invincibles*) and cruisers left Scapa and proceeded eastwards.

	Rosyth Force (BEATTY).
10.15	Six Battle-cruisers and four battleships (*Barhams*) left Rosyth.

May 31st.	JELLICOE AND BEATTY.
2.00 p.m.	*Iron Duke*, lat. 57° 58' N., long. 3° 45' E. Battle Fleet speed of advance 14 knots, zig zagging and steering S. 50° E. Rosyth Force 56° 46' N., long. 4° 40' E.

	BEATTY.
2.20	*Galatea* reported two enemy cruisers in sight bearing E.S.E. Course shaped for Horn Reef to cut off the enemy. Lat. 56° 52' N., long. 5° 22' E.

	BEATTY.
2.25	*Galatea* reported large amount of smoke " as from a fleet " bearing E.N.E.

	HOOD.
2.30	*Invincibles* ordered to steer to cut off enemy from escape into the Baltic. *Invincibles* had been stationed 20 miles ahead of Battle Fleet and were accompanied by two cruisers and four destroyers.

	BEATTY.
2.35	*Galatea* reported seven ships accompanied by destroyers steering N. These proved to be battle-cruisers of the German High Seas Fleet accompanied by two light cruisers and a number of destroyers. Beatty shaped course to bring enemy to action.

2.40 Battle Fleet stopped zigzagging. Steam ordered for full speed.

3.00 Grand Fleet's course S.E. by S., 18 knots.

3.20 Grand Fleet going 19 knots.

3.25 Beatty sighted and reported five enemy battle-cruisers and a number of destroyers bearing N.E. Both squadrons steering E.S.E. Range 23,000 yards. Beatty's ships in following order : *Lion, Princess Royal, Queen Mary, Tiger, New Zealand,* and *Indefatigable. Lion's* position 56° 53' N., 5° 18' E. bore Speed 25 knots. At this time Fifth Battle Squadron N.N.W. five miles from *Lion.*

3.47 Beatty reported engaging enemy who bore N.N.E., range 18,000 yards, steering E.S.E. on parallel course.

3.52 First hit on *Tiger.*

3.55 Hits on two of *Tiger's* turrets.

3.56 First hit on *Princess Royal* forward.

4.00 Battle Fleet's speed 20 knots.

4.00 Roof of one of *Lion's* turrets blown off and two guns put out of action.

4.04 *Indefatigable* blew up, having been hit simultaneously by three shell " at the outer edge of the upper deck level in line with the after turret." Magazine was exploded by shell fire.

4.05 Fifth Battle Squadron (*Barhams*) opened fire on rear enemy battle-cruiser at 20,000 yards. Enemy's fire seemed to slacken from now on.

Hood.

Third Battle-cruiser Squadron's 2.30 instructions cancelled and Hood now ordered to join Beatty sixty miles to southward, 56° 53′ N., 5° 33½′ E., enemy's course being given as S. 55° E. at 3.50 p.m. This squadron was then well to the eastward, having been sent to intercept conjectured escape of enemy cruisers to Baltic.

Beatty.

4.16   *Barhams* shifted fire to second ship from rear. Twelve British destroyers ordered out to attack enemy.

Beatty.

4.18   Third enemy battle-cruiser on fire. Enemy's gunnery depreciating considerably in accuracy and rapidity.

Beatty.

4.20   Enemy destroyers accompanied by a cruiser moved out to attack our battle-cruisers.

Beatty.

4.23   *Barham* received her first hit.

4.26   *New Zealand* hit (she was only hit once by heavy shell). *Queen Mary's* magazine exploded by shell fire.

4.38 Enemy's fifteen destroyers were repelled by our own
to   destroyers, who then attacked enemy's battle-cruisers
5.10 *Nestor* fired three of her four torpedoes at enemy battle-cruisers. Captain¹ Bingham, who commanded in the *Nestor*, states that members of the German crew of *Lützow* admitted to some of the *Nestor's* men, who were taken prisoners, that one torpedo hit her and reduced her speed (see 5.10 p.m. enemy battle-cruisers quitted line). The reduced speed would have brought her under gun fire of the *Barhams* (see also 5.00 p.m.). Eight torpedoes fired before German battle-cruisers turned north.

Several destroyers subsequently attacked enemy's battleships. In the destroyer fight the Germans acknowledged that they lost two destroyers and crippled the *Nestor* and *Nomad* and later destroyed them by the guns of the Battle Fleet. The *Nestor* and *Nomad* were the only losses, and at 4.50 the German destroyers retreated and the *Nestor* before sinking fired her last torpedo at the German High Seas Fleet about 5.25 p.m.

4.38	The 2nd L.C.S. ahead of Beatty reported the enemy Battle Fleet in sight bearing S.E., and standing to the northward to join their battle-cruisers. At this time the British Battle Fleet was about 50 miles to the N.N.W. of the scene of action, steering S.E. by S. at 20 knots.

Beatty states that the enemy ships were heavily hit and reduced in speed, but none quitted the line. Range about 16,000 to 18,000 yards.

The light was in favour of the enemy. Evan-Thomas states that he could only lay on and fire at the enemy's gun flashes.

4.42	Beatty sighted enemy Battle Fleet, bearing S.S.E., and altered course to north. Fifth Battle Squadron formed astern of Beatty's battle-cruisers a few minutes later. Visibility very bad to the eastward and very good to the westward, 12 miles.

4.45	Beatty reported enemy Battle Fleet consisting of 26 to 30 ships bearing S.S.E. Enemy's battle-cruisers reduced in speed and fire. Third ship in flames. Beatty altering course gradually round head of enemy's line to N.E. by N.

4.51	Weather fine. Wind light airs. Sea smooth. Visibility 6 miles to windward, 10 to 12 miles to leeward.

4.52	German battle-cruisers turned north.

4.53	*Barhams* coming under intermittent fire of enemy's leading battleships and finding some difficulty in drawing ahead of leading battleships of German High Seas Fleet.

5.00	Battle Fleet approach stations taken up. *Iron Duke's* position 57° 24′ N., 5° 12′ E. Course S.E. by S. Speed 20 knots.

Lion's position 56° 46′ N., 5° 44′ E. Course N.N.W. Speed 25 knots.

" The weather conditions now became unfavourable, our ships being silhouetted against a clear horizon to the westward, while the enemy were for the most part obscured by mist, only showing up clearly at intervals. These conditions prevailed until we had turned their van at about 6 p.m. Between 5 and 6 p.m. the action continued on a northerly course, the range being about 14,000 yards. During this time the enemy received very severe punishment, and one of their battle-cruisers quitted the line in a considerably damaged condition. This came under my personal observation, and was corroborated by *Princess Royal* and *Tiger*. Other ships also showed signs of increasing injury " (Beatty's despatch).

5.00	*Moresby* fired one torpedo, and *Nerissa* fired two torpedoes at enemy battle-cruisers after they had turned north and one hit was claimed on the rear ship of the line.
5.10	*Fearless* reported a German battle-cruiser leaving the line.

JELLICOE.

5.15	Battle Fleet could see flashes and could hear heavy gunfire south or on the starboard bow. Cruisers and destroyers were ordered to take station for action.

Beatty reported enemy battle fleet bearing S.E.

HOOD.

5.30	Hood with *Invincibles* steering S. by E. observed flashes of gunfire to S.W. *Chester* sent to scout. Squadron found visibility much decreasing. On some bearings could see 16,000 yards, on others only 2,000 yards. Then on to dusk visibility ranged from 14,000 to 4,000 yards.

HOOD.

5.40 to 6.10	*Chester* engaged with enemy light cruisers at about 6,000 yards.
	Invincible sighted enemy cruisers to westward and turned to N. 30° W.

Destroyers joined in, and shortly afterwards sighted enemy battle-cruisers. *Acasta* fired torpedo at leading enemy battle-cruiser at 4,500 yards and claimed a hit. *Acasta* was disabled and drifted inside the lines. *Shark* was sunk (see 5.59).

JELLICOE.

5.44	Light cruisers and cruisers ahead of Battle Fleet altered course to S.E. at full speed and opened fire with starboard guns at an enemy not in sight of Battle Fleet but bearing E.S.E. of *Iron Duke*. Flashes also seen to S. and S.S.W., creating doubt as to position of enemy Battle Fleet.

HOOD.

Invincibles relieved *Chester* and fired with port guns at enemy light cruisers at 8,000 to 12,000 yards. British destroyers, etc., attacking. The cruisers fired torpedoes and then turned, and it was observed that two were heavily on fire and one lost two funnels. This lasted until 5.55 (which see for fate of one of the cruisers). Tracks of torpedoes seen close to battle-cruisers.

5.45	*Comus* reported to *Iron Duke* that heavy firing was heard from the south.

JELLICOE.

5.49
Erroneous wireless report received by *Iron Duke* from Second Light Cruiser Squadron (Southampton) that enemy's Battle-cruiser Squadron bore S.W. from their Battle Fleet, which would lead to the supposition that the slower force had passed the faster and become the leaders. It should have been N.E.

JELLICOE.

5.50
Armoured cruisers on right flank of Jellicoe's cruiser line in contact with enemy cruisers. *Defence* and *Warrior* fired on large four-funnelled cruiser which drifted between the lines and was reported as sunk (apparently *Wiesbaden*).

JELLICOE AND BEATTY.

5.50
Iron Duke sighted our battle-cruisers on starboard bow, bearing S.S.W. of *Iron Duke* and standing E.S.E. Visibility 5-6 miles towards enemy. Cruisers on right flank of Jellicoe's cruiser line in contact with enemy cruisers. *Defence* and *Warrior* fired on a large four-funnelled cruiser which drifted between the lines and was believed to be sunk. (The *Defence* and *Warrior* in this fighting had turned to starboard and got between our own and the enemy battle-cruisers and were at close range to the enemy Battle Fleet, at 6.15, when the *Defence* was sunk just after crossing ahead of the *Lion*. The *Warrior* passed down between the lines and was saved from being sunk by the inadvertent turn towards the enemy of 16 points by the *Warspite* with broken down helm which took off the attention of the enemy to the more important unit.)

5.55
Another enemy cruiser was fired on by Hood's Third Battle-cruiser Squadron. This cruiser was disabled and drifted down between the lines. She was fired on by *Colossus* at 6.32 and *Marlborough* at 7.03 at ranges of 12,000 and 9,800 yards respectively. *Marlborough* hit with four salvoes. Cruiser was seen to be sinking fast.

BEATTY AND JELLICOE.

5.56
Beatty's force had been gradually altering course round the head of the enemy line to N.E. by N. and now sighted Grand Fleet. *Lion's* position 57° 4' N., 5° 36' E.
The enemy bearing S.E. hauled off to starboard, Beatty's force conforming to this movement. Grand Fleet from Beatty north 5 miles. Enemy battle-cruisers from Beatty south-east 6 miles.
On sighting Grand Fleet Beatty went full speed, closing enemy to 12,000 yards.

6.00	Enemy battle-cruisers hauling off to starboard. *Iron Duke's* position 57° 11′ N., 5° 39′ E. *Lion*, in sight from *Iron Duke* (Jellicoe's flagship), reported enemy battle-cruisers bearing S.E. *Lion* bearing S.S.W. from *Marlborough* steering east and heavily engaged. It afterwards transpired that the enemy battle-cruisers made a complete turn of 32 points between 6 o'clock and 6.16.
6.02	Grand Fleet altered course to south, so as to take position further west; but almost immediately turned back to original course of S.E. by S. and speed was reduced to 18 knots as it was realised that enemy Battle Fleet must be close at hand. (See 6.16 and 6.33 for further alterations of speed.)
6.03	*Barhams* seen from Grand Fleet to be firing well astern of Beatty.

JELLICOE AND BEATTY.

6.05	*Lion* bearing S.S.E. two miles from *Colossus* (the leading ship of Fifth Division). This would indicate that *Lion* was right ahead of *Marlborough* and at the right distance, allowing for the eight spaces required for the Rosyth Force to be ahead of *Marlborough*.

JELLICOE, BEATTY AND HOOD.

6.06	Jellicoe received Beatty's signal that enemy battle-cruisers bore S.E. (this was the position at 5.56).
	Barham sighted *Marlborough* and believing, like Beatty, that Grand Fleet would deploy to starboard and towards the enemy Evan-Thomas steered to take station with his four *Barhams* ahead of *Marlborough* or Sixth Division, which, with a deployment to starboard, would become the leading division, making a line of eight battleships and four battle-cruisers to attack head of enemy's line, while the other divisions formed astern.
	Enemy battle-cruisers mistaking their scouting cruisers' reports of the arrival of the *Invincibles* for the leading ships of Grand Fleet made a complete turn to starboard to regain closer contact with their Battle Fleet.

JELLICOE AND BEATTY.

6.07	*Defence* and *Warrior* ahead of Battle Fleet in fighting enemy cruisers had led round to starboard, crossing bow of the *Lion*, and causing battle-cruisers to alter course to port and to cease fire while the *Defence* and *Warrior* came under fire of enemy's Battle Fleet. (See plan.)

JELLICOE.

6.08 Destroyers ordered to take up battle positions as in diagram.

Owing to this movement having been deferred until 6.08 p.m., the destroyers were all moving across front at moment of deployment.

As the *signal* for deployment followed 5 minutes later, at 6.13, and alterations of course intervened, the destroyers which occupied the van positions were greatly delayed in gaining their positions. The destroyers did not gain their positions three miles ahead of the van until 7.10 p.m

HOOD AND BEATTY.

6.10 *Invincibles* under Hood sighted Beatty's Fleet and steered to join up. Torpedoes passing close to *Invincibles*. *Lion* reported apparently on fire. This was the ejector to forward submerged torpedo-room in use and supplies a possible explanation of false reports of ships on fire.

JELLICOE.

6.14 Beatty in reply to signal reported enemy battleships bearing S.S.W. " This report," says Jellicoe, " gave me the first information on which I could take effective action for deployment."

Signal hoisted to form single line on the port wing column led by *King George V* (Admiral Jerram). This involved deploying to port and turning up into single line on a course S.E. by E.

JELLICOE AND BEATTY.

6.15 *Barham's* report received that enemy's Battle Fleet bore S.S.E. Assuming visibility to be five miles for both Beatty's and Evan-Thomas's report, this placed leading enemy battleship 30° before *Iron Duke's* starboard beam, 59° before *Marlborough's* starboard beam, " apparently in close proximity."

BEATTY.

6.15
to
7.00 Destroyers attacking German battle-cruisers as they turned south (*Acasta* disabled and drifted down line of our battleships as they came up in single line).

JELLICOE.

6.15 Enemy salvo pitched short of and over the bow of *Hercules* (third ship following *Marlborough* of Sixth Division).

HOOD.

Invincible opened fire on leading enemy battle-cruiser at 8,000 yards and made good shooting. *Inflexible* and *Indomitable* came into action at same range.

JELLICOE AND BEATTY.

6.16 *Lion* 6,000 yards ahead of *Marlborough*.
Battle Fleet deployed to port (the official chart says 6.14). *Defence* blew up. *Warrior*, disabled, drifted out of battle. (She was some time after taken in tow by *Engadine*, but subsequently sank.)

Enemy could now be made out from Grand Fleet to be battle-cruisers leading, destroyers ahead of battleships, then four *Königs*, four or five *Kaisers*, and four *Heligolands*, while beyond that could not be seen. Beatty's despatch said that from 6 o'clock onwards the visibility was in our favour.

The deployment signal was made at 6.13 and the official chart gives the time it was executed as 6.14. Lord Jellicoe reproduces this chart, but in the text and in the deployment diagram gives the time as 6.16.

As the line was deploying to port or nearly 6 miles further eastward, the speed was reduced to 14 knots to allow the Battle-cruiser Squadron to pass ahead of the *King George V.*, the *Lion* having to alter course away from the enemy to do so. (See 6.33 for next alteration of speed.) The reduction of speed, the unexpectedness of the direction of deployment, the large turn of the *Barhams*, and other causes brought about bad bunching of the line at the rear, or nearest the enemy. Some ships were going only 10 knots, and others had engines stopped. No torpedo attack was, however, made on them. This dangerous state of affairs was not relieved until speed could be increased in front to 17 knots and the line straightened itself out at proper intervals between ships.

JELLICOE.

6.17 *Marlborough* and her division opened fire on enemy. *Marlborough* fired at range of 13,000 yards at a battle-ship bearing 20° before the starboard beam.

237

" The fire of *Marlborough* (Captain George P. Ross) was
particularly rapid and effective. This ship commenced
at 6.17 p.m. by firing seven salvoes at a ship of the
Kaiser class, then engaged a cruiser, and again a battleship, and at 6.54 she was hit by a torpedo and took up
a considerable list to starboard, but reopened at 7.03 p.m.
at a cruiser and at 7.12 p.m. fired fourteen rapid salvoes
at a ship of the *König* class, hitting her frequently
until she turned out of the line. The manner in which
this effective fire was kept up in spite of the disadvantages
due to the injury caused by the torpedo was most credit-
able to the ship and a very fine example to the squadron."
(Jellicoe's Despatch.)

JELLICOE AND BEATTY.

6.19   Evan-Thomas who had intended forming division in the
van ahead of Burney (*Marlborough*), realising that Jellicoe
was unexpectedly turning to port, made a large turn to
port so as to form astern of *Marlborough's* division.
Warspite's helm jammed, and she turned 16 points to
starboard or towards the enemy, coming under severe
fire. She had to quit battle and return to the base.
This movement on the part of the fast Fifth Battle
Squadron was necessitated by the time it would have
taken them to gain the van ahead of *King George V.*,
owing to nearly six miles of the front of the fleet that
they would have to cross.

" It is interesting to note that after 6 p.m., although
the visibility became reduced, it was undoubtedly more
favourable to us than to the enemy. At intervals their
ships showed up clearly, enabling us to punish them very
severely and establish a definite superiority over them.
From the report of other ships and my own observation
it was clear that the enemy suffered considerable damage,
battle-cruisers and battleships alike. The head of their
line was crumpled up, leaving battleships as targets
for the majority of our battle-cruisers. Before leaving
us the Fifth Battle Squadron was also engaging battleships. The report of Rear-Admiral Evan-Thomas shows
that excellent results were obtained, and it can be safely
said that his magnificent squadron wrought great
execution."   (Beatty's Despatch.)

JELLICOE.

**6.20
to
6.25**   A three-funnelled cruiser of enemy was seen approaching
from starboard with two T.B.D.'s. *Iron Duke* and others
opened fire on her at 9–10,000 yards range (6.28). She
was heavily hit and passed out of sight to the westward.

At 6.20 *Hercules* opened fire at what was stated to be second enemy battle-cruiser (*Hercules* was third ship in Sixth Division following *Marlborough* and *Revenge*).

HOOD AND BEATTY.

6.21   Third Battle-cruiser Squadron of three *Invincibles* turned, taking station ahead of *Lion* and engaging enemy's leading battle-cruisers.

BEATTY AND HOOD.

6.25   Beatty altered course to E.S.E. in support of Hood's Third Battle-cruiser Squadron, who were only 8,000 yards from enemy's leading ship. Battle Fleet still going 14 knots.

"From the report of Rear-Admiral T. D. W. Napier, M.V.O., the Third Light Cruiser Squadron, which had maintained its station on our starboard bow well ahead of the enemy, at 6.25 p.m. attacked with the torpedo. *Falmouth* and *Yarmouth* both fired torpedoes at the leading enemy battle-cruiser, and it is believed that one torpedo hit, as a heavy under-water explosion was observed. The Third Light Cruiser Squadron then gallantly attacked the heavy ships with gunfire, with impunity to themselves, thereby demonstrating that the fighting efficiency of the enemy had been seriously impaired. Rear-Admiral Napier deserves great credit for his determined and effective attack. *Indomitable* reports that about this time one of the *Derfflinger* class fell out of the enemy's line."   (Beatty's Despatch.)

JELLICOE AND BEATTY.

6.26   *King George V.* (leading) inserted in log that she altered course to port to avoid Battle-cruiser Fleet.

JELLICOE.

6.27   *Benbow* (No. 13 in line of 27 battleships) sighted *Königs* S.S.E.

JELLICOE.

6.29   Three vessels in sight from *Benbow*, range 11,000 yards, a little before starboard beam (15°).

JELLICOE AND BEATTY.

6.30   Three ships of *König* class were sighted by *Iron Duke* (leading ship) bearing S. by W., range 11,000 yards. They were engaged by the Battle Fleet and hits were observed. *Iron Duke* firing at leading *König*, *Benbow* firing at *Lützow*.

Enemy did not reply to our fire, possibly because of poor visibility to eastward. Our visibility about 12,000 yards, but smoke and mist made the gunnery difficult. Correspondingly our position was extremely favourable for a torpedo attack had one been launched.

Battle-cruisers well ahead of Grand Fleet and reduced speed to 18 knots, gradually closing enemy van and firing at leading ship. One German battle-cruiser reported to have left the line at this time.

" The ships of the Second Battle Squadron, under Vice-Admiral Sir Thomas Jerram, were in action with vessels of the *Kaiser* or *König* classes between 6.30 and 7.20 p.m., and fired also at an enemy battle-cruiser which had dropped back apparently severely damaged."

(Jellicoe's Despatch.)

BEATTY AND JELLICOE.

6.33   *Invincible* blew up. Enemy turning. Grand Fleet increased speed from 14 knots, at which it had been proceeding since 6.16, to 17 knots, at which it remained until it left for its base on June 1st. (The battle-cruisers had passed well ahead when this increase was made.)

BEATTY.

6.34   One of *Derfflinger* class falling out of line.

JELLICOE AND BEATTY.

6.35   *Iron Duke* observed our battle-cruisers turning to starboard.

JELLICOE AND BEATTY.

6.36   Enemy abeam of *Iron Duke*.

Lion proceeded full speed and drew ahead. At 6.50 Beatty ordered two remaining *Invincibles* to take station astern, then reduced to 18 knots, closing enemy ships, forcing them to alter course to westward, and so getting between them and their base.

JELLICOE AND BEATTY.

6.38   The line formed with Fifth Battle Squadron (*Barhams*) astern of *Agincourt*, the last ship of Sixth Division.

Enemy bearing 15° before *Iron Duke's* beam.

Lion passed wreck of *Invincible*, and owing to alteration of course passed it again at 6.50. Between 6.55 and 7.05 *Lion* turned through 82 points, so that 6.55 and 7.05 positions were the same.

6.40   Second *König* last seen to turn to starboard about 16 points.

Enemy had so turned to starboard as to pass out of sight. *Iron Duke* noted that enemy was steering almost in the line of its fire, bearing 20° abaft the beam.

At no time were more than three ships of enemy line in sight from *Iron Duke*, and these were probably the head of their line. The British deployment was favourable for both gun and torpedo attack. Wind W.S.W., force 2.

JELLICOE.

6.42   Grand Fleet's course S.E. Visibility 3 to 4 miles.

JELLICOE AND BEATTY.

6.50   Leading battleship, *King George V.*, bore N.N.W. 3° from *Lion*. *Lion* from *Iron Duke* 18° to starboard.

Lion reduced to 18 knots. *Inflexible* and *Indomitable* ordered to prolong the line astern. Visibility 4 miles, and enemy lost sight of from *Lion*.

Order of the battle-cruiser line became : *Lion, Princess Royal, Tiger, New Zealand, Indomitable* and *Inflexible*.

JELLICOE.

6.51   *King George V.* had to alter course to starboard to avoid collision with small craft in the van.

Course of Grand Fleet altered by divisions to S. towards our Battle-cruiser Squadron, and this course was held until 7.05, when a turn of 8 more points towards the enemy was made, but course S. was again resumed at 7.10 (7.07 according to the official chart) because a destroyer movement on the part of the enemy was seen. At 7.21 the whole fleet turned away through 2 points and some minutes later another 2 points (in all 45°).

JELLICOE.

6.54   *Marlborough* hit by a torpedo, but continued in line at 17 knots, firing 14 more salvoes. *Revenge* following hauled out to port and struck what was believed to be a submarine, as oil and wreckage came to the surface. If this is correct, the submarine must have dived under the line after discharging her torpedo. (The Germans state that they had no submarines at the battle.)

241

| 6.59 | H.M. Destroyer *Shark* attacked by two German destroyers. Sunk by a torpedo. |

BEATTY AND JELLICOE.

| 7.00 | Between now and 7.12 Beatty gradually altering course to S.W. by S. to regain touch. |

Beatty signalled that enemy was to westward.

JELLICOE.

| 7.02 | Our ships at rear end of line opened fire. |

Jellicoe signalled *Badger* : " Is wreck one of our ships ? " *Badger* replied : " Yes, the *Invincible*."

Jellicoe, page 358 : " It was assumed at the time that she had been struck by a mine or by a torpedo, and the latter appeared to be the more probable cause of her loss. Subsequent information, however, showed that she was destroyed by gun-fire, causing her magazine to explode."

JELLICOE.

| 7.04 | *Iron Duke* passed wreck of *Invincible*. |
| 7.05 | Three points alteration of course to starboard to close the range. |

JELLICOE.

| 7.10 | Enemy destroyers approaching S. 50° W. from *Iron Duke*. Report of a submarine on port bow. Fleet resumed original course S., in order, says Jellicoe, " to turn on to the submarine and bring the ships in line ahead ready for any required manœuvre." |

An enemy battle-cruiser seen heavily on fire and passed out of sight. Rear of Battle Fleet firing at second of three of *König* (?) class. (*Marlborough* fired 14 salvoes.) On investigations later, this ship was stated to have turned out of the line at 7.16 low in the water and sinking. An officer in *Colossus* said he saw the ship sink at 7.26, and this evidence was confirmed by *Benbow* and ships in second division. (The pre-Dreadnought *Pommern* and the battle-cruiser *Lützow* were the only big ships sunk in the battle. The German accounts state that the *Lützow* was hit by at least fifteen heavy shell in the battle and she was unable to remain in her place in the line. Admiral Hipper by means of a destroyer transferred to the *Moltke*. See 7.16 p.m. The *Pommern* was sunk by a torpedo during the night actions according to the German accounts. *König* was acknowledged by

242

Germans to be hit by 25 shell in the battle and much down by bow. She was completely repaired and in the Fleet by August 12, and proceeded with the rest of the Fleet into the North Sea on Aug. 19, 1916.)

JELLICOE.

7.12   Enemy battle-cruisers emerged from mist 10,000 yards on starboard beam of *Colossus*. *Colossus*, *Neptune*, *Collingwood*, and *Revenge* all firing at and hitting them. (All these ships belonged to the rear two divisions.)

These enemy battle-cruisers must have been so damaged as to have dropped down the line, and thus come under fire on the beam of Grand Fleet's rear divisions. Visibility much improved as sun descended below clouds.

BEATTY.

7.14   Beatty regained touch with High Seas Fleet, sighting two battle-cruisers and two battleships at 15,000 yards.

JELLICOE.

Fourth Light Cruiser Squadron and Fourth and Eleventh Destroyer Flotillas reached stations in the van. Lord Jellicoe says: " they were in a very favourable position to counter the second destroyer attack which took place at 7.25 p.m."

JELLICOE.

7.15   *Iron Duke* firing 74° to starboard at a battleship 15,000 yards range, and at 7.20 at a battle-cruiser of *Lützow* type abaft the beam. *Colossus* also fired 5 salvoes at 10,000 and 8,000 yards at *Lützow* or *Derfflinger* from 7.12 to 7.20 (see 6.34). *St. Vincent* firing until 7.26, ranges 10,000 and 9,500 yards.

Eleven enemy destroyers, supported by a cruiser, attacked from westward. Made heavy smoke screen to escape after firing torpedoes. Battle Fleet was turned 4 points in all to port at and after 7.21 when destroyers turned to fire. Rear of Fleet turned 8 points to avoid torpedoes. Eleven torpedoes were seen in or near the track of the ships in rear of the line.

Destroyers' smoke drifted to leeward over our line, the wind being from W.N.W. Bearing of destroyers attacking, when sighted, was S. 50° W. (30° before beam) from *Iron Duke*. Range 10,000 to 8,000 yards.

There was no further fighting as regards our twenty-seven battleships, though touch was regained by Battle Fleet with the enemy for a few minutes (see 7.59). As both Fleets had turned away from each other they had opened the range considerably, and when all danger of torpedoes was over speed was still kept at 17 knots instead of an endeavour being made to recover the ground.

German Battle-cruisers.

7.16 German Admiral Hipper's flag about this time flying in *Moltke*, having been transferred from the disabled *Lützow*.

BEATTY AND JELLICOE.

7.17 Mist lifted. Beatty's battle-cruisers firing at enemy, and increased speed to 22 knots. (Battle-cruisers were now on starboard bow of Grand Fleet, four to five miles ahead of the van, increasing this distance to eight miles.)

Leading battleship, *King George V.*, fired a salvo, but target afterwards obscured by smoke.

Enemy Battle Fleet.

7.23 Enemy Battle Fleet after the launching of destroyer attack (7.15 and on) made smoke screens and edged away, turning at least 8 points, so that their sterns were towards our line. A flotilla of destroyers also passed through their line making smoke screen.

Captain of the *Malaya* reported: " This was the last of the enemy seen in daylight, owing to the Battle Fleet having turned away." The other seven ships from the rear of the line generally reported that the enemy making artificial smoke turned 8 points, one ship said " 8 or 10 points." *Revenge* reported " a flotilla of destroyers passed through the line, and made a most efficient smoke screen. At this period the enemy's fleet turned 8 points to starboard and rapidly drew out of sight."

JELLICOE.

7.25 *King George V.* had to alter course to starboard to avert collision with light craft in the van. *Duke of Edinburgh* much in the way and making a lot of smoke.

BEATTY.

7.26 Battle-cruisers firing at enemy line, range about 14,000 yards and decreasing to 8,000 yards. Enemy making smoke screens. Firing continued by battle-cruisers until 7.40 and was again resumed at 8.22. Several torpedoes were fired by the destroyers at the battle-cruisers, but the attack was beaten off and the torpedoes easily avoided as they crossed the line.

BEATTY.

7.32 Course S.W., speed 18 knots. Leading enemy battleship bearing N.W. by W.

JELLICOE.

7.33 Grand Fleet brought back to course S. by W. or one point westward of former course, that is, away from enemy, who had been steadily going well to starboard or to westward.

JELLICOE AND BEATTY.

7.40 "At about 7.40," says Lord Jellicoe, "I received a report from Sir David Beatty stating that the enemy bore N.W. by W. from the *Lion*, distant 10 to 11 miles, and that the *Lion's* course was S.W. Although the battle-cruisers were not in sight from the *Iron Duke*, I assumed the *Lion* to be 5 or 6 miles ahead of the van of the Battle Fleet, but it appeared later from a report received in reply to directions signalled by me at 8.10 p.m. to the *King George V.* to follow the battle-cruisers, that they were not in sight from that ship either. At this time the enemy's Battle Fleet seems to have become divided, for whilst Sir David Beatty reported the presence of battleships N.W. by W. from the *Lion*, other enemy battleships were observed to the westward (that is, on the starboard bow of the *Iron Duke*), and the course of the Fleet was at once altered 'by divisions' to W. in order to close the enemy. This alteration was made at 7.59 p.m."

JELLICOE.

7.41 Battle Fleet turned to S.W. to form single line ahead again to endeavour to regain touch with enemy, some of whose ships were sighted for a few minutes to westward at 7.59.

First Flotilla proceeded to attack enemy Battle Fleet, but was recalled.

BEATTY.

7.45 Beatty lost sight of enemy under cloud of grey smoke made by destroyers.

JELLICOE.

7.46   Visibility from Grand Fleet 8 miles.

BEATTY.

7.58   Beatty ordered Third and First Light Cruiser Squadrons who were ahead to sweep to the westward and locate head of enemy's line, and at 8.20 he altered course to W.

JELLICOE.

7.59
to
8.22

Grand Fleet's course altered to W. on cruisers sighting enemy 7.59. Evident that enemy Fleet was divided as enemy battleships were reported by the cruisers at 7.59 N.W. of *Iron Duke*. Grand Fleet's course was W. but there was no increase from 17 to 20 knots, and the ships sighted "turned away and touch could not be regained." Our small craft got so close that the cruiser *Calliope* of the Fourth Cruiser Squadron fired a torpedo at 6,500 yards range and an explosion took place. Lord Jellicoe omits to state that he once again turned back at 8.22 to S.W. because of the torpedo attack which the Fourth Cruiser Squadron moved out to repel at 8.18.

JELLICOE AND BEATTY.

8.00   Battle-cruisers were heard firing from a position about 6 miles ahead to W.

Engadine took *Warrior* in tow (abandoned 7.45 a.m., June 1st, the crew being taken off).

JELLICOE.

8.03   Enemy's battleships bearing N.W. by W. from *Orion*.

JELLICOE.

8.04   Line of ships bearing 45° to starboard from *Iron Duke*.

BEATTY.

8.20   Beatty altered course to W. and shortly after engaged enemy ships at range of about 10,000 yards (two enemy battle-cruisers and some battleships).

JELLICOE.

8.21   Twelfth Flotilla and Fourth Cruiser Squadron engaging enemy destroyers on starboard bow.

JELLICOE.

8.22 Enemy opened fire on light cruisers. Battle Fleet altered course to S.W. to avoid a destroyer attack. Fourth Light Cruiser Squadron and Flotillas engaging enemy destroyers. *Calliope* fired torpedo at enemy battleship at 6,500 yards range at about 8.30 (explosion at 8.38).

BEATTY.

Battle-cruisers engaging enemy ships at 10,000 yards until 8.28 p.m., when they turned away.

BEATTY.

8.26 *Indomitable* being straddled but not hit. *Inflexible* 6,000 yards from enemy battleships. *Seydlitz* appeared to be heavily damaged and turned away from fire of battle-cruisers and her fire lessened. One enemy battleship on fire.

BEATTY.

8.30 Beatty again sighted two enemy battle-cruisers and engaged them. Enemy's battleships then came into sight and opened fire, forcing our battle-cruisers to haul off to port. *Minotaur* in sight on port quarter reported no support from Grand Fleet, so in accordance with orders Beatty altered course to S. at 17 knots. Enemy last seen by *Falmouth* at 8.38. (Visibility of grey ships at 8.45 stated to be 8,000 yards: *Shannon's* report.)

JELLICOE.

8.33 Enemy's light cruiser bearing 50° to starboard of *Iron Duke*, turning away from us.

BEATTY.

8.38 *Falmouth*, last ship of Battle-cruiser Squadron in touch with enemy and enemy ships then in sight from her, turned 8 points away. (Some accounts place the time some minutes later for losing sight of enemy ships, but 8.38 is the time given by Lord Jellicoe and Beatty.)

JELLICOE.

8.40 Beatty's despatch says: "at 8.40 p.m. all our battle-cruisers felt a heavy shock as if struck by a mine or torpedo." *Calliope* had fired a torpedo at about 8.30, and this may have hit. Jellicoe's despatch stated: "an explosion on board a ship of the *Kaiser* class was seen, however, at 8.38 p.m."

8.45 Visibility of grey ships 10,000 yards (*Shannon's* report).

9.00   *Warspite* reported damages had reduced speed to 16 knots. Ordered to Rosyth. Ship, steered from engine room, arrived at Rosyth at 3 p.m., June 1st.

Course of Grand Fleet S. to avoid night action and mine area, and to place Fleet so as to intercept enemy's return by the Ems Channel in the morning. Maintaining this course at 17 knots it would still be open to the Fleet, by altering course sufficiently early, to intercept his return by the more likely route, the Horn Reef Channel, as he could not reach there before 3.30 to 4.30 the next morning.

9.05   *Caroline* fired two torpedoes at centre ship of three ships believed to be *Deutschland* class at 7,600 yards.

9.09   Sound of firing heard from *Iron Duke* on starboard bow.

Battle-cruisers in sight from Grand Fleet.

9.10   *Royalist* fired a torpedo at centre of three ships believed to be *Nassau* class.

JELLICOE.

9.15   Star shell fired on beam of Iron Duke.

JELLICOE AND BEATTY.

9.15   The Battle Fleet having been turned south and formed in divisions one mile apart, the destroyers were ordered to take up positions five miles astern of Battle Fleet in order west to east: Eleventh, Fourth, Twelfth, Ninth, Tenth and Thirteenth Flotillas, the Eleventh Flotilla being slightly to the westward of the right-hand column's track.

Second Light Cruiser Squadron, which came into action with enemy cruisers, was astern, following in the wake of the middle of the Fleet, and the Fourth Light Cruiser Squadron was ahead of the Battle Fleet.

It will be found that the most westerly of the rear-guard came into action with enemy forces first and then the others, but the Ninth, Tenth and Thirteenth Flotillas were taken beyond the enemy's S.E. course by steaming S. at 17 knots, which, it should be remembered, was the unvarying speed for the whole daylight action and the night. The battle-cruisers throughout the day varied their speed to suit the emergency.

9.32 *Abdiel* sent to lay mine-field in wide zigzags from a position 15 miles S.W. by S. of the Vyl Light vessel in a south direction, ten mines to the mile, so as to make as dangerous as possible the channel by S. of the Horn Reef.

A submarine stationed near there reported hearing eleven under-water explosions between 2.15 a.m. and 5.30 a.m. on June 1st, but some of these might have been the result of sweeping. Estimated time of heavy ships passing over this minefield being 5.0 a.m.

10.00 *Iron Duke's* position 56° 22′ N., 5° 47′ E. Course S., 17 knots.

JELLICOE (*Torpedo Flotillas*).

10.04 *Castor* and Eleventh Flotilla (this flotilla was the furthest west) sighted three enemy cruisers. *Castor* attacked with guns and torpedoes ; *Marne* with torpedoes. Detonation occurred.

JELLICOE (*Light Cruisers*).

10.20 *Southampton* and *Dublin* of Second Light Cruiser Squadron engaged a cruiser and four light cruisers of German Fourth Scouting Group. Lat. 56° 10′ N. and long. 6° 11′ E. Course S.S.E., but when beaten off appeared to retire to westward. German light cruiser *Frauenlob* was supposed to have been sunk in this action. Engagement lasted 15 minutes.

JELLICOE (*Torpedo Flotillas*).

10.40 *Broke* observed large explosion S. by E. (*Broke* then astern of *Tipperary*).

11.00 *Active* saw firing 1 mile astern at four-funnelled ship (enemy probably firing at own ship).

This vessel had previously shown coloured recognition signals. Ship was hit repeatedly, and burst into flames. Another alternative suggested by Lord Jellicoe is that it was our own cruiser *Black Prince*, which had got detached in the daylight action. The enemy claim to have sunk a vessel by gun-fire about this time.

Spitfire with Fourth Flotilla attacked and claimed to have sunk with torpedoes a four-funnelled cruiser, and shortly afterwards *Spitfire* rammed and carried away 20 feet of side plating of an enemy three-funnelled cruiser.

11.15 *Active* bumped something heavily and tore off 15 feet of starboard bilge keel. Was it a submarine ?

11.30 *Colossus* passed over submerged vessel and slightly damaged starboard propeller blades.

JELLICOE (*Torpedo Flotillas*).

Tipperary and Fourth Flotilla attacked enemy cruisers steering S.E. Enemy opened fire. *Tipperary* disabled (sank 1.45 a.m.).

Sparrowhawk rammed by *Broke* on steering-gear being disabled. The *Sparrowhawk* was abandoned a few hours later.

This attack on enemy cruisers and light cruisers could be seen from the *Malaya* in the rear of the Grand Fleet, so that in the light of an explosion those on board could see the large German ship, which was hit by a torpedo from *Spitfire*. The latter also collided with a German light cruiser, taking off about 29 feet of her skin plating. The remainder of flotilla altered course to E. and then S.E., and at midnight came in contact with German Second Battle Squadron.

11.35 *Birmingham* reported enemy battle-cruisers steering S. in lat. 56°46′ N., 5°46′ E. If this was the case they must have turned from where Beatty fought two of them last at 8.30 and steered for this point 70 miles N. of Horn Reef Light vessel, or they were two remaining battle-cruisers which had dropped out of the fight. In either case their route was for the Horn Reef Channel.

12.00 *Fearless*, then astern of *Agincourt*, saw German battleship pass down starboard side. She and other battleships were attacked by our Fourth Flotilla.

The *Pommern* is believed to have been sunk, and we lost the destroyer *Fortune*. Gun-fire forced flotilla to retire to northward.

June 1st.   JELLICOE (*Torpedo Flotillas*).

12.10 a.m. Fourth Flotilla again in action with German battleships. We lost the destroyer *Ardent*.

12.15 A German ship, supposed *Wittlesbach* class, passed at high speed, rammed and sank the *Turbulent*, and with searchlights on damaged *Petard* by gun-fire. These destroyers belonged to the Thirteenth Flotilla which had got scattered, and at first they mistook the German ship for one of our own.

JELLICOE (*Torpedo Flotillas*).

12.45   *Malaya* saw a torpedo attack some way astern, and then a brilliant flare lit up the sky.

1.15   *Broke* opened fire on enemy destroyers.

1.45   Twelfth Flotilla from various causes was to the north-eastward of its proper position by some miles, and this fortunate accident enabled it to sight an enemy battle squadron steering S.E. and the flotilla thereupon manœuvred for position, steaming 25 knots.

2.00   Twelfth Flotilla attacked the line of six battleships from ahead. It was evident that German Fleet was returning astern of our battle fleet by the Horn Reef Channel.

     In the attack the destroyers steered N.W. or the opposite course to the enemy, and fired torpedoes at about 3,000 yards range at second and third ships. The third battleship was torpedoed, the explosion being so violent and with so much flame as to suggest that the magazine had exploded. Destroyers were forced by gun-fire to retire to N.

JELLICOE (*Torpedo Flotillas*).

2.25   *Maenad*, of Twelfth Flotilla, which had got separated in the attack at 2 o'clock, fired two torpedoes at the fourth battleship at a range of 4,000–5,000 yards and one hit. Flame of explosion reached to masthead of ship.

JELLICOE.

2.30   *Marlborough* reported bulkheads would not stand greater speed than 12 knots. Ordered to proceed to harbour, keeping one ship as escort if necessary. (*Fearless* used.) Burney transferred his flag to *Revenge*.

JELLICOE (*Torpedo Flotillas*). *The Last Shot.*

2.35   *Moresby*, of the Thirteenth Flotilla, saw four *Deutschland* class bearing W., 4,000 yards, and fired one torpedo. An explosion was heard.

2.40   Dawn breaking.

JELLICOE.

2.47   The Grand Fleet, being now to the south-westward of the Horn Reef course, was altered to N. to collect the fleet and destroyers. Visibility 3 miles.

     Fleet formed single line.

     The Fleet had steamed 97 miles to the southward since the daylight action ended at 8.80 p.m.

JELLICOE.

2.52   Weather fine. Wind force, 3 from S.S.W. Sea smooth. Visibility 3 miles.

Twenty battleships in line, one destroyer and three cruisers.

3.00   *Sparrowhawk*, disabled in lat. 55°54′ N., long. 5°59′ E., saw a German cruiser (three funnels) steering slowly N., and two miles to the E. she turned slowly over and sank bows first. *Sparrowhawk* was subsequently sunk after her crew had been taken off.

3.21   Sound of distant firing from heavy guns, apparently from port quarter, no flashes seen.

3.30   Light cruiser *Champion* was attacked by four destroyers. Only two torpedoes seen, and these were avoided by use of helm.

3.33   Fifth Battle Squadron (three ships) rejoined.

3.35   Sound of distant firing, no flashes seen. Third Light Cruiser Squadron reported engaging a Zeppelin to westward of Battle Fleet.

JELLICOE AND BEATTY.

3.36   Battle-cruisers ordered to look out ahead for *Lützow*, a damaged enemy battle-cruiser, probably with large number of destroyers.

3.40   Sound of firing continues, apparently from port quarter.

JELLICOE and VON SCHEER.

3.44   Four more battleships joined.

Course altered to W., as it was thought that the Zeppelin might indicate the presence of the High Sea Fleet.

This is the estimated time of High Sea Fleet passing Horn Reef Light vessel abeam.

Zeppelin.

3.50   Zeppelin in sight from Grand Fleet. Zeppelin disappeared to eastwards. She was sighted several times later. Course altered back to N.

4.10   Grand Fleet formed in divisions in line ahead to reduce danger of submarine attack and widen the front.

4.25   *Dublin* reported by wireless that she had sighted an enemy cruiser and two destroyers.

At 5.15 a.m. Battle-cruiser Fleet was ordered to search for the cruiser which was presumed to be in a damaged condition. *Dublin* was sighted at 7.55 a.m. and reported having lost sight of in a fog in 55°28′ N., 6°32′ E. of cruiser and destroyers, and the cruiser was not damaged but steaming fast.

4.31   Leading ships ordered to look out for *Lützow* and damaged light cruiser.

4.36   Firing ahead, distant sound only.

4.44   *Barham* reported our Battle-cruiser Fleet bearing N.N.W..

        Iron Duke, 55°29′ N. 6°2′ E.

        Destroyers' position, 55°48′ N., 6°22′ E., rejoining.

        Battle-cruisers, 55°45′ N., 6°16′ E., rejoining, steering S.E. at 18 knots and at 6.15 course altered to S.

4.57   Fourth Light Cruiser Squadron on port bow, 5 vessels.

4.59   Three destroyers with Fourth Light Cruiser Squadron.

5.01   Five or six battle-cruisers, 8 of Second Light Cruiser Squadron on port bow, rejoining in accordance with signalled orders.

5.15   Battle-cruisers rejoined.

        Battle-cruiser Squadron sent to search for enemy cruiser reported by *Dublin*

5.25   Three light cruisers *Southampton* class rejoined.

5.40   The Vice-Admiral Battle-cruiser Fleet closed the Commander-in-Chief, and was directed to sweep to the northward and eastward, whilst the Commander-in-Chief swept with the Battle Fleet first to the southward and eastward and then northward.

5.43   Apparently light cruisers' smoke 4 points on starboard bow.

6.00   Battle Fleet altered course to S.E., 17 knots, in search of our destroyers.

6.51   Visibility 4 miles.

7.00   Four destroyers of Harwich Flotilla ordered to screen *Marlborough*.

        (8.0 a.m., June 2nd, *Marlborough* arrived in Humber screened by *Fearless* and eight destroyers from Harwich.)

7.05	Sun shining.
7.15	Mine off starboard bow. Course altered to N.
7.25	Trawler off starboard bow. Ships ordered to keep a sharp look-out for damaged enemy cruiser and light cruiser.
7.55	Two cruisers joined up.
8.05	*Sparrowhawk* was sunk by order, as *Marksman* was unable to tow her into port.
8.15	*Iron Duke* 55°54′ N., 6°10′ E. Course N., 17 knots.
8.40	Passed quantity of wreckage and oil from *Ardent*.
	(Wreckage and dead German sailors and drifting mines passed during forenoon. There were also reports of submarines.)
8.50	Course S.W.
9.00	Commander-in-Chief ordered Vice-Admiral commanding Battle-cruiser Fleet, who was to eastward of the Battle Fleet, on a northerly course, to sweep as far as lat. 57°30′ N., long. 5°45′ E.
9.10	Destroyers joined up. Visibility 4 miles.
	Except for the *Dublin's* report at 4.25 a.m. no enemy vessels were sighted by the fleet during daylight on June 1st.
	The cruisers and destroyers gradually joined up, but owing to the low visibility and absence of sun observations it was not easy. The ships' reckonings after the action were not accurate.
10.31	Fifth Battle Squadron joined up with the remainder of the Battle Fleet.
1.15 p.m.	The Battle Fleet having swept out the area S. of the scene of action, proceeded N.W. for Scapa, the Battle-cruiser Fleet and *Valiant* proceeding to Rosyth.

The times given are the times of the actual movements as nearly as can be ascertained, and it must be understood that the information would, in some cases, be received in the *Iron Duke* later because of the time it takes for the signals to get through.

Note

The following is the description given by Grand Admiral von Tirpitz in the Sunday Times, Sept. 14, 1919, of von Scheer's position from 6.30 to 7.30 p.m. on May 31, 1916:—

Not only would our ships have had to deploy under the fire of the whole enemy fleet in order to gain a good tactical position, but the light was such that the German ships were silhouetted against the evening sky in the west, thus presenting, in the occasional moments of good visibility, admirable objects for artillery observation; while, on the other hand, the haze to the east so obscured the hulls of the British ships that their position was hardly to be discerned save by the flashes of their guns.

Admiral Scheer escaped from a position which had become dangerous by turning his fleet together, a manoeuvre which few fleets in the world would have succeeded in carrying out under a rain of fire. He was supported in this manoeuvre by two of our torpedo-boat flotillas under Captain Heinrich, who, recognising the dangerous position of our fleet, attacked the main body of the British fleet, and drew its whole fire upon himself.

Subsequent to the completion of this book in August, 1919, the author read the extracts published from Ludendorf's memoirs with reference to the fear felt for the Russian Armies by the German General Staff in 1916, and the perilous position for Germany which Brusiloff's offensive nearly brought about after the Battle of Jutland. These revelations he regards as a striking confirmation of his own views as to what might have been achieved had Jutland been fought to a decisive end, and the Baltic thereby opened up for supplies to pass to Russia while the German Baltic coasts were threatened. It is not too much to say that Bolshevism is the legacy of Jutland.

LEONAUR

ALSO FROM LEONAUR
AVAILABLE IN SOFTCOVER OR HARDCOVER WITH DUST JACKET

THE FALL OF THE MOGHUL EMPIRE OF HINDUSTAN *by H. G. Keene*—
By the beginning of the nineteenth century, as British and Indian armies under Lake
and Wellesley dominated the scene, a little over half a century of conflict brought the
Moghul Empire to its knees.

LADY SALE'S AFGHANISTAN *by Florentia Sale*—An Indomitable Victorian
Lady's Account of the Retreat from Kabul During the First Afghan War.

THE CAMPAIGN OF MAGENTA AND SOLFERINO 1859 *by Harold Car-
michael Wylly*—The Decisive Conflict for the Unification of Italy.

FRENCH'S CAVALRY CAMPAIGN *by J. G. Maydon*—A Special Correspo-
nent's View of British Army Mounted Troops During the Boer War.

CAVALRY AT WATERLOO *by Sir Evelyn Wood*—British Mounted Troops
During the Campaign of 1815.

THE SUBALTERN *by George Robert Gleig*—The Experiences of an Officer of
the 85th Light Infantry During the Peninsular War.

NAPOLEON AT BAY, 1814 *by F. Loraine Petre*—The Campaigns to the Fall of
the First Empire.

NAPOLEON AND THE CAMPAIGN OF 1806 *by Colonel Vachée*—The Napoleonic Method of Organisation and Command to the Battles of Jena & Auerstädt.

THE COMPLETE ADVENTURES IN THE CONNAUGHT RANGERS *by
William Grattan*—The 88th Regiment during the Napoleonic Wars by a Serving
Officer.

BUGLER AND OFFICER OF THE RIFLES *by William Green & Harry
Smith*—With the 95th (Rifles) during the Peninsular & Waterloo Campaigns of the
Napoleonic Wars.

NAPOLEONIC WAR STORIES *by Sir Arthur Quiller-Couch*—Tales of soldiers,
spies, battles & sieges from the Peninsular & Waterloo campaingns.

CAPTAIN OF THE 95TH (RIFLES) *by Jonathan Leach*—An officer of Wellington's sharpshooters during the Peninsular, South of France and Waterloo campaigns of the Napoleonic wars.

RIFLEMAN COSTELLO *by Edward Costello*—The adventures of a soldier of
the 95th (Rifles) in the Peninsular & Waterloo Campaigns of the Napoleonic wars.

www.ingramcontent.com/pod-product-compliance
Lightning Source LLC
Chambersburg PA
CBHW032039080426
42733CB00006B/139